First World War
and Army of Occupation
War Diary
France, Belgium and Germany

3 DIVISION
Headquarters, Branches and Services
Commander Royal Engineers
4 August 1914 - 28 October 1919

WO95/1397

The Naval & Military Press Ltd
www.nmarchive.com
Published in association with The National Archives

Published by

The Naval & Military Press Ltd

Unit 10 Ridgewood Industrial Park,

Uckfield, East Sussex,

TN22 5QE England

Tel: +44 (0) 1825 749494

www.naval-military-press.com

www.nmarchive.com

This diary has been reprinted in facsimile from the original. Any imperfections are inevitably reproduced and the quality may fall short of modern type and cartographic standards.

© Crown Copyright
Images reproduced by permission of The National Archives, London, England, 2015.

Contents

Document type	Place/Title	Date From	Date To
Heading	3rd Div. R.E. War Diary By O.C. Aug.-Dec. 1914		
Heading	C.R.E. 3rd Division August & September 1914		
Heading	3rd Divisional Engineers. C.R.E. 3rd Division August & September 1914		
Miscellaneous	A.G. The Base Herwith War Diary of C.R.E. III Division upto 30-9-14	01/10/1914	01/10/1914
War Diary		04/08/1914	30/09/1914
Miscellaneous	9th Brigade "A"	07/09/1914	07/09/1914
Heading	3rd 5th Divisional RE Hd. Qrs. Vol III 1-31-10-14		
War Diary		01/10/1914	31/10/1914
Heading	Hd. Qrs. RE 3rd Division Vol IV 1-30-11-14		
War Diary		01/11/1914	10/11/1914
War Diary	Appendix "A"	11/11/1914	20/11/1914
War Diary	Appendix "B"	21/11/1914	21/11/1914
War Diary	Appendix C	22/11/1914	23/11/1914
War Diary	Bricks	24/11/1914	24/11/1914
War Diary	Composite Company	25/11/1914	29/11/1914
War Diary	Appendix "D"	29/11/1914	30/11/1914
Miscellaneous	Additional List of Appendix	05/12/1914	05/12/1914
Diagram etc	Appendix "A"		
Miscellaneous	Appendix B	21/11/1914	21/11/1914
Miscellaneous	A Form Messages And Signals Appendix C	24/11/1914	24/11/1914
Miscellaneous	Appendix "D"	30/11/1914	30/11/1914
Miscellaneous	Appendix "E"	21/11/1914	21/11/1914
Miscellaneous	Appendix "F"	21/11/1914	21/11/1914
Miscellaneous	Appendix "G"	21/11/1914	21/11/1914
Miscellaneous	Appendix "H"	22/11/1914	22/11/1914
Miscellaneous	Appendix "I"	22/11/1914	22/11/1914
Miscellaneous	Appendix "J"	28/11/1914	28/11/1914
Miscellaneous	Appendix "K"	19/11/1914	19/11/1914
Miscellaneous	Appendix "L"	16/11/1914	16/11/1914
Miscellaneous	Appendix "M"	18/11/1914	18/11/1914
Miscellaneous	Appendix "N"	19/11/1914	19/11/1914
Heading	Hd. Qrs. RE 3rd Division Vol V 1-31.12.14		
War Diary		01/12/1914	02/12/1914
War Diary	Appendix "H"	03/12/1914	07/12/1914
War Diary	Appendix "B"	08/12/1914	14/12/1914
War Diary	Appendix "D"	14/12/1914	31/12/1914
Miscellaneous	Appendix A to J	06/01/1915	06/01/1915
Miscellaneous	C.E. II Corps. Appendix "A"	07/12/1914	07/12/1914
Miscellaneous	3rd Division with reference to I C 918 of 12th Dec. Appendix "B"	12/12/1914	12/12/1914
Miscellaneous	III Division with reference to your E 198 Appendix "C"	15/12/1914	15/12/1914
Miscellaneous	C E II Corps. Appendix "D"	15/12/1914	15/12/1914
Miscellaneous	Appendix "E"	24/12/1914	24/12/1914
Miscellaneous	III Division Appendix "F"	25/12/1914	25/12/1914
Miscellaneous	III Division Appendix "G"	27/12/1914	27/12/1914
Miscellaneous	Appendix "H" III Division	07/12/1914	07/12/1914
Miscellaneous	Appendix "J"	30/12/1914	30/12/1914
Heading	3rd Div. R.E. H.Q. War Diary Jan-Dec 1915		

Heading	3rd Division Command. 7.9.14 Composite Coy. R.E. 3rd Division Vol I Jan. 12 1915		
Miscellaneous	Composite Company Royal Engineers 8th Brigade 3rd Division Sept. 7th 1914		
War Diary		07/09/1914	21/09/1914
War Diary	Reinforcement 2 Drivers 1 riding horse 4 draught horses	21/09/1914	07/12/1914
War Diary	Reinforcement 15 Sappers	08/12/1914	16/12/1914
War Diary	Westoutre	16/12/1914	12/01/1915
Heading	Hd. Qrs. RE 3rd Division Vol VI 1-31-1-15		
War Diary		01/01/1915	03/01/1915
War Diary	Appendix "A"	03/01/1915	08/01/1915
War Diary	Appendix "C"	09/01/1915	14/01/1915
War Diary	Appendix "F"	14/01/1915	15/01/1915
War Diary	Appendix "G"	16/01/1915	17/01/1915
War Diary	Appendix "H" Appendix "I"	18/01/1915	31/01/1915
Miscellaneous	III Division Appendix "A"	03/01/1915	03/01/1915
Miscellaneous	III Division Appendix "B"	05/01/1915	05/01/1915
Miscellaneous	A Form Messages And Signals		
Miscellaneous	CE II Corps Appendix "D"		
Miscellaneous	Divisional Bridging Train Proposed Establishment	10/01/1915	10/01/1915
Miscellaneous	C E II Corps. Mechanical Fuze Lighter Appendix "E"	12/01/1915	12/01/1915
Miscellaneous	Appendix "F"	13/01/1915	13/01/1915
Miscellaneous	Draft For Routine Orders Appendix "G"	14/01/1915	14/01/1915
Miscellaneous	Appendix "H"	19/01/1915	19/01/1915
Miscellaneous	Report on 14 in (Oxy acalylene) Portable field Searchlight. Appendix I	23/00/1915	23/01/1915
Miscellaneous	Appendix "J"	21/01/1915	21/01/1915
Miscellaneous	III Division Report on Grenade Double Cylinder Appendix "K"	23/01/1915	23/01/1915
Miscellaneous	Appendix "L"	30/01/1915	30/01/1915
Miscellaneous	Appendix "M"	31/01/1915	31/01/1915
Heading	Hd. Qrs. RE 3rd Division Vol VII 1-28-2-15		
War Diary		01/02/1915	02/02/1915
War Diary	Appendix "A"	02/02/1915	11/02/1915
War Diary	Appendix "C"	12/02/1915	28/02/1915
Miscellaneous	Appendix War Diary February 1915		
Miscellaneous	Appendix A	02/02/1915	02/02/1915
Miscellaneous	Appendix B	04/02/1915	04/02/1915
Miscellaneous	Report on Boricy Plant Unsatisfactory		
Miscellaneous	C.E. II Corps Appendix C	13/03/1915	13/03/1915
Heading	Hd. Qrs. RE 3rd Division Vol VIII 1-31.3.15		
War Diary		01/03/1915	08/03/1915
War Diary	Appendix "A"	09/03/1915	11/03/1915
War Diary	Appendix "B"	12/03/1915	31/03/1915
Miscellaneous	Appendix A	10/03/1915	10/03/1915
Miscellaneous	Appendix B		
Heading	Hd Qrs. RE 3rd Division Vol IX 1-30.04.15		
War Diary		01/04/1915	30/04/1915
Miscellaneous	Appendix A	15/04/1915	15/04/1915
Miscellaneous	Appendix "B"	16/04/1915	16/04/1915
Miscellaneous	Appendix "C"	28/03/1915	28/03/1915
Miscellaneous	Appendix "D"	20/04/1915	20/04/1915
Miscellaneous	Recommendations	20/04/1915	20/04/1915
Heading	Hd. Qrs. RE 3rd Division Vol IX 1-31.5.15		
War Diary		01/05/1915	31/05/1915
Miscellaneous	3rd Division Appendix A	04/05/1915	04/05/1915

Type	Description	Start	End
Heading	3rd Division Hd Qrs. RE 3rd Division Vol XI 1-30.6.15		
War Diary		01/06/1915	30/06/1915
Miscellaneous	3rd Division A	13/06/1915	13/06/1915
Miscellaneous	Operation Order by C.R.E. 3rd Division		
Miscellaneous	III Division C	19/06/1915	19/06/1915
Miscellaneous	3rd Division D	22/06/1915	22/06/1915
Heading	3rd Division Hd. Qrs. RE 3rd Division Vol XIL July 15		
War Diary		01/07/1915	31/07/1915
Miscellaneous	3rd Division Appendix A	03/07/1915	03/07/1915
Miscellaneous	3rd Division Appendix B	07/07/1915	07/07/1915
Operation(al) Order(s)	3rd Division Operation Order No. 19	18/07/1915	18/07/1915
Diagram etc	Tracing From Aeroplane Photograph Shewing German Trenches		
Miscellaneous	3rd Division Missing Operation Round Hooge	23/07/1915	23/07/1915
Miscellaneous	3rd Division Appendix D	23/07/1915	23/07/1915
Miscellaneous	3rd Division Appendix E	28/07/1915	28/07/1915
Miscellaneous	Operation Order by C R E Division Appendix F	18/07/1915	18/07/1915
Heading	Hd. Qrs. R.E. 3rd Division Vol XIII August 15		
War Diary		01/08/1915	31/08/1915
Miscellaneous	3rd Division Appendix A	01/08/1915	01/08/1915
Miscellaneous	App. B 3rd Division	04/08/1915	04/08/1915
Miscellaneous	3rd Division. App. C	14/08/1915	14/08/1915
Heading	Hd. Qrs. R.E. 3rd Division Vol XIV Sept. 15		
War Diary		01/09/1915	30/09/1915
Miscellaneous	3rd Division Appendix A	07/09/1915	07/09/1915
Miscellaneous	3rd Division Appendix B	07/09/1915	07/09/1915
Miscellaneous	Notes on preparation of Etable standings Appendix C		
Miscellaneous	3rd Division Appendix D	19/09/1915	19/09/1915
Miscellaneous	C.R.E. 3rd Division Draft Operation Order Appendix E	22/09/1915	22/09/1915
Miscellaneous	Operation Order by C.R.E. 3rd Division Appendix F	23/09/1915	23/09/1915
Miscellaneous	3rd Division Appendix G	28/09/1915	28/09/1915
Miscellaneous	Appendix H 3rd Division	28/09/1915	28/09/1915
Miscellaneous	Report on operations on 25-9-15 Appendix I	29/09/1915	29/09/1915
Heading	H.Q. R.E. 3rd Divn. Oct. 15 Vol XV		
War Diary		01/10/1915	31/10/1915
Miscellaneous	5th Corps Appendix "A"	01/10/1915	01/10/1915
Diagram etc	Dug Out Frames For 5 Men Dugout		
Heading	H.Q. 3rd Div. Nov. 15 Vol XVI		
War Diary	H.Q, R.E. 3rd Div. 3rd div. Vol. II.	01/11/1915	30/11/1915
Miscellaneous	Tactical O.C. 172 R.E.	28/11/1915	28/11/1915
Miscellaneous	3rd Div.	01/12/1915	01/12/1915
Heading	H.Q. R.E. 3rd Div. Dec. 15 Vol XVII		
War Diary		01/12/1915	31/12/1915
Miscellaneous	3rd Division By Lt. Col. C.S. Wilson R.E. Appendix I	07/12/1915	07/12/1915
Heading	3rd Division Commanding Roy. Engr. Aug. 1914-Oct. 1919		
Heading	3rd Division War Diaries C.R.E. January To December 1916		
Heading	3rd Divisional Engineers. C.R.E. 3rd Division January 1916		
War Diary	Reninghelst	01/01/1916	31/01/1916
Miscellaneous	3rd Division Appendix I	01/01/1916	01/01/1916
Miscellaneous	3rd Division Appendix II	01/01/1916	01/01/1916
Miscellaneous	3rd Division Appendix III	01/01/1916	01/01/1916
Miscellaneous	3rd Division Appendix IV	05/01/1916	05/01/1916
Miscellaneous	Appendix V 3rd Division	03/01/1916	03/01/1916

Miscellaneous	G	02/02/1916	02/02/1916
Miscellaneous	V Corps	31/01/1916	31/01/1916
Miscellaneous	3rd Division	31/01/1916	31/01/1916
Miscellaneous	C.E., V Corps	29/01/1916	29/01/1916
Miscellaneous	C.R.E. 3rd Division	30/01/1916	30/01/1916
Heading	3rd Divisional Engineers. C.R.E. 3rd Division February 1916		
Heading	War Diary of H.Q. R.E. 3rd Division From 1-2-16 To 29-2-16 Vol XIX		
War Diary	Reninghelst	01/02/1916	08/02/1916
War Diary	Nordausque	09/02/1916	29/02/1916
Heading	3rd Divisional Engineers C.R.E. 3rd Division March 1916		
War Diary	Nordausque	01/03/1916	06/03/1916
War Diary	Reninghelst	07/03/1916	31/03/1916
Heading	3rd Divisional Engineers. C.R.E. 3rd Division April 1916		
War Diary	Reninghelst	01/04/1916	05/04/1916
War Diary	Fletre	06/04/1916	30/04/1916
War Diary	Add	26/04/1916	28/04/1916
Heading	3rd Divisional Engineers. C.R.E. 3rd Division May 1916		
War Diary	Westoutre	01/05/1916	27/05/1916
War Diary	Fletre	28/05/1916	31/05/1916
War Diary	Add	29/00/1916	29/00/1916
Heading	3rd Divisional Engineers. C.R.E. 3rd Division. June 1916		
War Diary	Fletre	01/06/1916	18/06/1916
War Diary	Wemaers Cappel	19/06/1916	19/06/1916
War Diary	Samank	20/06/1916	20/06/1916
War Diary	Tilques	21/06/1916	30/06/1916
Heading	3rd Divisional Engineers. C.R.E. 3rd Division July 1916		
War Diary	Tilques	01/07/1916	02/07/1916
War Diary	Le Meillard	03/07/1916	03/07/1916
War Diary	Olincourt	04/07/1916	04/07/1916
War Diary	Corbie	05/07/1916	08/07/1916
War Diary	Bray	09/07/1916	19/07/1916
War Diary	A 20 d 7-7 (Sheet 62 c)	20/07/1916	20/07/1916
War Diary	A 20 d 7.7	22/07/1916	25/07/1916
War Diary	Bray	26/07/1916	27/07/1916
War Diary	Treux	28/07/1916	31/07/1916
Heading	3rd Divisional Engineers. C.R.E. 3rd Division August 1916		
War Diary	Treux	01/08/1916	12/08/1916
War Diary	Forked Tree	13/08/1916	15/08/1916
Miscellaneous			
War Diary	Bernaville	25/08/1916	25/08/1916
War Diary	Frohen-Le-Grand	26/08/1916	26/08/1916
War Diary	Flers	27/08/1916	27/08/1916
War Diary	Monchy-Cayeux	28/08/1916	28/08/1916
War Diary	Noeux Les Mines	29/08/1916	31/08/1916
Heading	3rd Divisional Engineers. C.R.E. 3rd Division September 1916		
War Diary	Noeux-Les-Mines	01/09/1916	22/09/1916
War Diary	Bomy	23/09/1916	30/09/1916

Heading	3rd Divisional Engineers. C.R.E. 3rd Division October 1916		
War Diary	Bomy	01/10/1916	05/10/1916
War Diary	Monchy Cayeux	06/10/1916	07/10/1916
War Diary	Bertrancourt	08/10/1916	18/10/1916
War Diary	Bus	19/10/1916	31/10/1916
Heading	3rd Divisional Engineers. C.R.E. 3rd Division November 1916		
War Diary	Bus-Les-Artois	01/11/1916	30/11/1916
Heading	3rd Divisional Engineers. C.R.E. 3rd Division December 1916		
War Diary	Bus-Les-Artois	01/12/1916	31/12/1916
Heading	3rd Division War Diaries C.R.E., January To December 1917		
War Diary	Bus-Les-Artois	01/01/1917	09/01/1917
War Diary	Canaples	10/01/1917	28/01/1917
War Diary	Flers	29/01/1917	30/01/1917
War Diary	Villers-Chatel	31/01/1917	07/02/1917
War Diary	Lignereuil	08/02/1917	10/02/1917
War Diary	Warlus	11/02/1917	28/02/1917
Miscellaneous	Report on R.E. Preparations during February, March & April for Offensive Operations on 9th April 1917 Appendix "A"		
War Diary	Warlus	01/03/1917	31/03/1917
War Diary	Arras	10/04/1917	14/04/1917
War Diary	Warlus	15/04/1917	20/04/1917
War Diary	Arras	07/04/1917	09/04/1917
War Diary	Warlus	21/04/1917	23/04/1917
War Diary	Arras	24/04/1917	25/04/1917
War Diary	Advanced Divl. H.Q.	26/04/1917	14/05/1917
War Diary	Warlus	15/05/1917	18/05/1917
War Diary	Lignereuil	19/05/1917	01/06/1917
War Diary	Arras	02/06/1917	19/06/1917
War Diary	Le Cauroy	20/06/1917	30/06/1917
Miscellaneous	Relief of 3rd Divl. Engineers by 12th Divl. Engineers.	15/06/1917	15/06/1917
Heading	War Diary for month ending 31st July 1917 Headquarters R.E. 3rd Division Vol 36		
War Diary	Liencourt	01/07/1917	01/07/1917
War Diary	I. 34a 3.5	02/07/1917	31/07/1917
War Diary	I 34.a. 3.7	01/08/1917	31/08/1917
War Diary	I 34a 3.7 (Sheet 57c)	01/09/1917	16/09/1917
War Diary	Watou	17/09/1917	21/09/1917
War Diary	Poperinghe	22/09/1917	23/09/1917
War Diary	Ramparts Ypres	24/09/1917	30/09/1917
War Diary	Ypres	01/10/1917	01/10/1917
War Diary	Winnezeele	02/10/1917	04/10/1917
War Diary	Renescure	05/10/1917	05/10/1917
War Diary	Haplincourt	06/10/1917	11/10/1917
War Diary	Monument H 15 C.	12/10/1917	31/10/1917
War Diary	Monument Commemoratif H 15 C	01/11/1917	30/11/1917
War Diary	Monument Commemoratif Bapaume	01/12/1917	13/12/1917
War Diary	Behagnies	14/12/1917	31/12/1917
Heading	3rd Division War Diaries R.E. H.Q. Jan. 1918-Oct. 1919		
War Diary	Behagnies	01/01/1918	06/01/1918
War Diary	Gomiecourt	07/01/1918	28/01/1918

War Diary	Boisleux-au-Mont	29/01/1918	28/02/1918
Heading	3rd Divisional Engineers. C.R.E. 3rd Division March 1918		
War Diary	Boisleux au-Mont	01/03/1918	22/03/1918
War Diary	Bretencourt	23/03/1918	29/03/1918
War Diary	Lucheux	30/03/1918	31/03/1918
Heading	War Diary C.R.E. 3rd Division April 1918		
War Diary	Bruay	01/04/1918	02/04/1918
War Diary	Labeuvriere	03/04/1918	05/04/1918
War Diary	Fouquieres	06/04/1918	08/04/1918
War Diary	Labeuvriere	09/04/1918	10/04/1918
War Diary	Oblinghem	11/04/1918	12/04/1918
War Diary	Labeuvriere	13/04/1918	07/08/1918
War Diary	Auchel	08/08/1918	13/08/1918
War Diary	Bavincourt	14/08/1918	20/08/1918
War Diary	Pommier	21/08/1918	31/08/1918
War Diary	Hamlincourt	01/09/1918	03/09/1918
War Diary	Ransart	04/09/1918	05/09/1918
War Diary	Humbercamp	06/09/1918	10/09/1918
War Diary	Triangle Copse Nr Gomiecourt	11/09/1918	14/09/1918
War Diary	Sunken Road Marchies-Beugny	15/09/1918	30/09/1918
War Diary	Flesquieres	01/10/1918	08/10/1918
War Diary	Hermies	09/10/1918	12/10/1918
War Diary	Flesquieres	13/10/1918	19/10/1918
War Diary	Cattenieres	20/10/1918	21/10/1918
War Diary	Sipythona Quievy	22/10/1918	22/10/1918
War Diary	Solesmes	23/10/1918	30/10/1918
War Diary	Quievy	31/10/1918	31/10/1918
Operation(al) Order(s)	3rd R.E. Operation Order No. 95	22/10/1918	22/10/1918
War Diary	Quievy	01/11/1918	05/11/1918
War Diary	Ruesnes	06/11/1918	08/11/1918
War Diary	Frasnoy	09/11/1918	17/11/1918
War Diary	Sous-Le-Bois	18/11/1918	19/11/1918
War Diary	Cousolre	20/11/1918	23/11/1918
War Diary	Thuin	24/11/1918	24/11/1918
War Diary	Loverval	25/11/1918	27/11/1918
War Diary	Bioul	28/11/1918	29/11/1918
War Diary	Emptinne	30/11/1918	04/12/1918
War Diary	Grandham	05/12/1918	07/12/1918
War Diary	Salmchateau	08/12/1918	13/12/1918
War Diary	Losheim	14/12/1918	15/12/1918
War Diary	Euskirchen	16/12/1918	18/12/1918
War Diary	Duren	19/12/1918	31/12/1918
Miscellaneous	Report on Engineer work of 3rd Divnl. R.E. July-Dec 1918 (Rec: from R.E. Library 5th Dec 1934)		
Miscellaneous	Report on Engineer work of 3rd Divisional R.E. period July to December 1918	02/01/1919	02/01/1919
Miscellaneous	The following figures show some of the work, exclusive of roads and water supply, carried out by 3rd Divisional R.E. during the period 21/8/18 to 11/11/18		
War Diary	Duren	01/01/1919	22/01/1919
War Diary	Duren	06/02/1919	28/02/1919
War Diary	Cologne	01/03/1919	31/03/1919
Heading	Headquarters Royal Engineer Northern Division War Diary- Month of April 19		
War Diary	Cologne LRS	01/04/1919	22/04/1919

Heading	War Diary For Month of May 1919 C.R.E. North. Div.		
War Diary	Cologne LRS	05/05/1919	30/06/1919
Operation(al) Order(s)	Royal Engineers Northern Division Operation Order No. 1	17/06/1919	17/06/1919
Miscellaneous	Royal Engineers Northern Division Operation Order No. Appendix "A"	17/06/1919	17/06/1919
Miscellaneous	Requisitions During The Advance Appendix B	30/05/1919	30/05/1919
Miscellaneous	Locations of D.H.Q. and Field Company R.E. Appendix "C"		
Miscellaneous	Appendix "D"	17/06/1919	17/06/1919
Operation(al) Order(s)	R.E. Operation Order No.1 App 2	17/06/1919	17/06/1919
War Diary	Cologne	02/07/1919	18/08/1919
War Diary	Cologne	26/08/1919	28/10/1919

Index..........................

SUBJECT.

3RD DIV

No.	Contents.	Date.
	R.E. War Diary by O.C. Aug – Dec. 1914	

C.R.E.
3rd Division.
August & September
1914.

3rd Divisional Engineers.

C. R. E.

3rd Division

AUGUST & SEPTEMBER 1914

A.G. The Base

Herewith War Diary
of C R E III Division
up to 30-9-14

1-10-14

J P Wallis
Cpt M
Adj Div Engrs
for C R E III Div

Aug + Sept 1914

1

August 4th Order to mobilize received at 6.0 p.m.
5th 1st day of mobilization which pursued the normal course, some trouble was experienced about the horses, the first batch were very bad & half had to be cast being dead lame, mange or foot & suffering from strangles. the later horses were good, & finally, the units were well horsed.
7th All units complete by 5.30 p.m.
   Railway time table postponed
16th Entrained at AMESBURY 3.0. a.m.
   arrived SOUTHAMPTON 6.30 a.m.
   embarked on ITALIAN PRINCE & sailed at noon
17th arrived ROUEN 1.0 p.m. disembarked 2.30 a.m.
   went into rest camp — no casualties
18th Entrained at ROUEN 4.0 a.m.
   arrived LANDRECIES 6.30 p.m. detrained & billeted no casualties
20th marched to AUNOYE. all units concentrated. Work done on improving roads & water supply.
21st To GOGNIES. Units at work on outpost line
22nd to HOURGNIES. 56 late 8th Bgd & 57th late 9th struck on outpost line & reconnaissance of Canal
23rd 6.0 a.m. orders received to prepare all bridges over the Canal for demolition, sent to by 4 Signal service & CRE personally went out, orders given that no bridge was to be demolished without an order from the Divisional Staff. The Coys were scattered on outpost works, and

2

From a little time to collect, with the result that the GERMANS attacked and the battle of MONS began, on the right the posts at the bridges were rushed before the work was finished, only one section of 56 Co getting down which was practically wiped out, the officer Lt HOLT was missing, said to be killed — On the left there was more time & the five bridges were prepared but only 3 charges were fired as leads & exploders were lacking, 2 sections of the Coy having been ordered elsewhere, the Adjutant was sent out to see the demolitions carried out 3 bridges were blown successfully but Lt DAY was killed & Captain WRIGHT wounded trying to connect up to destroy the others, all the parties showed great coolness & gallantry — There seems to be no reason why the order for demolition should not have been given at once on 22nd when all the bridges could have been destroyed that night, as very superior forces were known to be advancing on us, preparing bridges for demolition takes time, which we were not given and consequently there was failure —

In the afternoon the CRE arranged for civil labour to assist in entrenching a 2nd line from FLAMIERES to NOUVELLE and 57 Co was hard at work to assist, and worked well under their front still fire —

24th During the night 56 biv'd in 57 at NOUVELLES & 57 was moved to FLAMMERIES where they assisted in putting the village in a state of defence. The position was heavily attacked in the early morning, but the CRE was called back to Genl HQ & in confy with the CE & GOC RA sent over a position proposing for the Division on the line BAVAY VALENNCIENNES. The division however retired 30 by 35 miles.

25. Retirement continued to the LE CATEAU position.

26. 56 moved to CAUDRY. 57 less section to TROISVILLES, 1 section 57 to OUDAINCOURT to help entrench the attack of heard at dawn & the Coys worked under fire during good work, 56 was so involved in CAUDRY that when work was handed on that side section had the withdrawn from 57 at this battle of LE CATEAU as well as at MONS the count of sixteen marching inhale by only having 2 thirds hrs to the Division was being considerable and the men were worn out by it they however marched see, well & withessly, & suffered some loss, in CAUDRY the 56 had to be used as infantry & did very well. The retirement was ordered in the afternoon, & companies got away in good order, 56 however had some wagons disabled by shell fire in CAUDRY.

27.28. Retreat continued with little rest, during the night part of the division including 56 Co took a wrong road & got separated.

29. HAM Bridges over canal 2 ended the demolition. One was successfully destroyed as soon as ready, the other was prepared & kept open for the cavalry, one Hussar[?] & also some FRENCH officer the pursuit was found to have slackened & the CRE representing this to the G.O.C. Division, the destruction of the 2nd bridge was left to his discretion, he finally decided to draw the charges & leave the bridge, which was as well as shortly afterwards a French cavalry brigade was met advancing to cross it.

29ᵗʰ arrived at CUTS & stopped[?] [of] division beyond 2 bridges over the river were successfully destroyed, a party of Uhlans tried to interfere at one bridge but the demolition party under Capt HENDERSON drove them off with a loss of 2 men & in after[?] a supply[?] of the 5ᵗʰ division they had taken prisoner

Sept 3ᵈ Retreat continued to MEAUX where 3 bridges & a weir[?] [both?] types were destroyed at night, just [before?] in the division was short. This ran all units completely out of explosives, though during this the CRE hs[?] obtained there and at LYONS by 500 lbs of dynamite obtained on requisition. The exp[?] need of a reserve of explosives became evident, a reserve base was very shortly brought into...

a wagon load of desern 9 + plenin in the R E
shines from part of the Divisional Ammunition Column —
The CRE prepared a scheme for forming a 3rd Co from
the 9 + only 2 which was put in force later, + approved
by the G.O.C

Sept 5th. Retreat continued to CHATRES where it ceased,
+ during the night a body load of explosives was
received + the loss of the ups —
During this long and trying retreat it was very
satisfactory to notice that the Coys maintained
their discipline and had not a single straggler
or man missing since the retirement was ordered
during the battle of LE CATEAU —

  6   The Division advanced.
  7.   Reorganization of Divisional Engineers laid down vide
        appendix A — a 3rd Co called "Composite Co" formed
        by taking one section each from 5 6 & 57 + a coy wagons
        from technical, contact etc — Coys of HQ to Bryes.
        56 to 7th Bde, Bryes, Coy to 8th, 57 to 9th
        bryes, wagons beyond with an N.C.O. + attached to
        Divisional Train.

  8th   continued advance.
  9th   action at ORBY — conned good site of Coys Co
         was shelled by a shrapnel whilst there, however +
         had 5 casualties
 10th   pontoon were got up had bridge over the MARNE
         was fired which + the bridge crossed action
         at BEZU

11 Culm at CHEZY.
12. Action at BRAINE + around there
13 Advance from BRAINE + reconnaissance of River AISNE
    with bridges at VAILLY destroyed.
    During the night 13 & 14 all Coys were constructing a footing
    over the broken road bridge passed over 2 Coys of
    infantry + a footbridge over the broken Railway bridge a 3rd,
    during the night a pontoon bridge was constructed at VAILLY
    as the supply that was not enough trestles were there
    to supplement it. The bridge was ready at dawn when
    a Brigade of cavalry + the 5th Cavalry Brigade crossed.
14 A very heavy shell fire was opened on the bridge about 6.30
    a.m. & kept up until 4 p.m. but it was not damaged
    the Coys suffered somewhat severely especially in horses
    in the bivouac which was badly knocked about +
    set on fire in several places. The 5th Cavalry
    Brigade retired with some loss over the bridge several
    officers & men of the Coys assisting women on horses
    fire in removing dead horses out of the way etc
    The adjutant Captain T. WRIGHT was badly hit by
    a shell + died of his wounds during the night
15. Coys employed in making passages of logs of trees +
    42 to R.E. reported for work on said bridges + were
    posted at BRAINE. Work on bridges over & night
    under fire.
16. Various duties going on Corps & 5th unit were attached
    to D & 19th Brigades & assist in the trenches. 56
    looking after bridges + entirely bivouacs on right bank.

17 — 42ⁿᵈ Co repairing bridge at COURCELLES try sho
   & not finished —

18   42ⁿᵈ Co finish COURCELLES Bridge

19. 2 Cos Infty to help making fascines for heavy
     pontoon bridge. 42 Co to BRENELLE for
     entrenching — 4 pontoons from bridge train
     sent to 5th Division —

20. No change except no Infantry on fascines
     + 2 Cos Infantry entrenching rear position —
     One of the pontoons was nearly sunk by shell fire
     but was bailed out & repaired just in time
     under a heavy shell fire ———

21. Work on rear position stopped — 42ⁿᵈ Co put on
     to making fascines. River rose 3ft pontoon bridge
     adjusted under fire — Foot bridge over railway bridge
     which was under water, screwed at a higher level —
     COURCELLES bridge completed. Capt Welles
                              joined as adjutant

22ⁿᵈ No change.

23ʳᵈ 12ᵗʰ Fld Coy 6ᵗʰ Division relieved the
     57ᵗʰ & Composite Companies. The latter
     Companies withdrew to CHASSEMY to
     rest.

24ᵗʰ 56 Coy preparing approaches for heavy bridge
       at VAILLY
     57ᵗʰ Coy Resting
     Composite Coy repairing road CHASSEMY
       to VAILLY.
     42ⁿᵈ Coy preparing emplacements for

siege battery & repairing road from BRAINE to BRENELLE.

25th Pontoon bridge broken by ammn. wagon. Repairs put in hand with aid of 12th F.W. Coy pontoon & superstructure. Completion slightly delayed by shell fire.
57th Coy. moved to BRENELLE to carry out defences. 42nd Coy also on this work.

26th Companies working as yesterday.

27th 57th Coy working on defence position
42nd Coy working on bridge between COURCELLES and LIME constructing new one by the previous one for heavy traffic.
56th & Composite Coys again forced to move by shell fire. Both companies working by night on approaches for heavy pontoon bridge across the river AISNE.

28th Site selected for alternative bridge to pontoon bridge at VAILLY.
Sapping started to-night from trenches near ROUGE MAISON.

29th COURCELLES bridge finished
57th Coy working at night on alternative site for pontoon bridge
At night 42nd Coy work on new position for 6" Howitzer Battery

30th 57th Coy working on new pontoon bridge
Saps of 12th Coy near ROUGE MAISON out to 51 & 10 ft respectively

1.10.14

No.	Date	Time	Place 9ᵗʰ Brigade "A"
TO			Place

The Divisional Engineers will in future be organized as 3 companies and a bridging train. The third company will be known as the COMPOSITE Field Co. and will be formed by taking one section from each of the 56ᵗʰ & 57ᵗʰ Cos under the command of Captain HENDERSON R.E.

The bridging wagons of the 56ᵗʰ & 57ᵗʰ Cos will be brigaded under an N.C.O. and attached to the Divisional Train.

The 3 field companies will be affiliated to Infantry Brigades in the same manner as brigades of Field Artillery as follows:—

56ᵗʰ Fd Co. to 7ᵗʰ Infantry Brigade
Composite Fd Co. to 8ᵗʰ do do
57ᵗʰ Fd Co. to 9ᵗʰ do do

This organization will take place from today the necessary moves being arranged as early as

From

54

possible 1 section 56ᵗʰ Fd Co from 7ᵗʰ Brigade area to join 8ᵗʰ Brigade and Capt. HENDERSON and one section 57ᵗʰ Co from 9ᵗʰ Brigade area to join 8ᵗʰ Brigade

Sgd C J Wilson
Lt Col
A.D. R.E.
III Division

7ᵗʰ Sept 14

agy

121/1751

121/1751

3rd : 5th Divisional R.E. H'd Qrs.

Vol III 1 — 31.10.14

War Diary. R.E. Headquarters, Oct. 1914
III Division

1st Oct. Alternative pontoon bridge reported complete by 57th Coy at 2.30 AM. 1 trestle + 7 pontoons of 1st Bridging train used. Approaches to heavy bridge practically complete. Composite Coy moved to OULCHY LE CHATEAU.

2nd Oct. Headquarters moved to ARCY
56 Coy ——— SERVENAY
57 Coy ——— CRAMAILLE
Composite Coy ——— TROESNES
Bridging equipment for both Coys with 56 Coy.
Equipment for bridging taken over from 1st Bridging train (except waggons + horses) at BRAINE. Two pontoons etc left in bridge at VAILLY. Forage cart, 2 horses + A.C. down handed over by III Div H.Q.

3rd Oct. All companies with their brigades.
Hd. Qrs. with Div. H.Q. at LA FERTÉ -MILON.

4th Oct. Coys with their brigades.
H.Qrs. with Div H.Q. at CREPY.

5th Oct. Entrained with H.Qrs.

6th Oct. Detrained + marched to ABBEVILLE

7th Oct. II Div. gradually concentrating. Field Coys arriving in sections at different stations + marching to their respective brigade areas

11

Oct 8.   Marched from ABBEVILLE at 11.30 p.m.
  "   Arrived LA BROYE
Oct 9.   Arrived HUBY ST LEU
Oct 10   Arrived PERNES. All bridging
         equipment sent to II Division
         Ammunition column to march with it
         until further orders
— 11   Arrived HINGES
— 12   Arrived ZELOBES. Action against
         enemy mostly cavalry during day
— 13   Advanced to LACOUTURE, action
         continued.
— 14   At LACOUTURE, advance slow
— 15   At LACOUTURE, Coys employed
         in making light bridges for crossing
         dykes. Bridges made of ladders & planks.
— 16   At LACOUTURE. Advance progressing
         more rapidly. Lt BOULNOIS (RE) went to hospital
— 17   Advanced to NEUVE CHAPELLE.
— 18   Pontoon & trestle wagons of 56 & 57
         Coys brought up from Div Amm Col
         at LOCON to NEUVE CHAPELLE
         Reinforcements arrived 24 N.C.O.s & men
         for 56 Coy + 26 N.C.O.s & men for 57 Coy.
         Lieut C.F. NATION sent to hospital.
— 19   NEUVE CHAPELLE. Line for second
         line of defence selected.
— 20   NEUVE CHAPELLE. 400 civilians

Oct 20 employed in digging trenches in
rear positions. Coys employed in
entrenching firing line at night.
Pontoons &c sent back to Div Amm
train at LOCON. 12 heavy draught
horses received, put with bridging
sections & 5 pairs from bridging
sections distributed to Coys. Heavy attack.

" 21ˢᵗ NEUVE CHAPELLE. 400 civilians
again employed entrenching. Coys
night digging in forward positions.
Wagons back at LACOUTRE during
daytime.

" 22ⁿᵈ NEUVE CHAPELLE. 400 civilians (approx)
entrenching back position. Civilians turned
out again at 8.30 P.M. & continued entrenching.
20 miles of barbed wire received.

" 23ʳᵈ Civilians finished digging at 3.0 A.M. & were
paid off. Coys working on rear position
which was occupied by Div at dawn
Hd qrs at LACOUTURE.

" 24ᵗʰ Back position occupied by Div.
Coys working on trenches

" 25ᵗʰ H. qrs still at LACOUTRE
Coys working at night in firing line on
improving trenches & putting up wire
entanglements.

" 26 Arrangements made with French authorities
in BETHUNE to send out 400 civilians

Oct 26 (Cont) to work on new back positions.
Only 143 appeared, no more could be obtained in BETHUNE. 2/Lt MARTIN wounded. +3000 sandbags.

— 27th 50 miles of barbed wire received from Amm railhead & distributed to coys & Brigades. Civilians (143) taken out to line of back positions and taken charge of by Field Coys in LAHORE Div. III Div driven out of trenches by NEUVE CHAPELLE, but held on just W of that place. Lt DAWSON & 2nd Lt DENING joined Company.

— 28th Not advisable to send civilians to back line so they were employed under CRE III Div in entrenching for bridgehead to VIEILLE CHAPELLE bridges.
56 Coy sent up behind counter attack on NEUVE CHAPELLE to destroy houses, found itself in the firing line and had to remain there until relieved during the night. 1 section of 57 Coy sent to work for 7 Bde on right of positions.
Pontoon train sent back with Div Amm Col to EPINETTE.
56 Coy 1 Sergt, 1 Corpl, 1 L/Cpl + 1 sapper wounded.

— 29th Companies (57 Coy) working at night in the firing line. 3 Indian bns relieved 7 Brigade. Civilians working on bridgeheads

Oct 30th 56 Coy sent to MERRIS with 7 Brigade. Pontoon bridge S of VIEILLE CHAPELLE removed by 56 Coy & pontoons returned to Amm Column. 57 Coy moved to SAILLY and placed at disposal of LAHORE Div.

Oct 31st HQrs moved to METEREN. Coy remaining with 8 Bde. 56 Coy at MERRIS.

AG
AG.7.
& D.F.W

121/2649

H.d Qrs R.E. 3rd Division.

Vol IV. 1-30.11.14

War Diary

R.E. Headquarters, III Division

November 1914

Nov 1st 56 Coy with 7 Bde moved to billets near LOCRE
Compo Coy still with 8th Bde with LAHORE Division
57 Coy under LAHORE Division
Headquarters at METEREN

Nov 2nd No change

Nov 3rd No change

Nov 4th 56 employed with 7th Bde on making rear positions

Nov 5th Visited 57 Coy at SAILLY. Still engaged by C.R.E. LAHORE DIVISION. Coy working on rear positions. Sometimes by day, sometimes by night. Capt. MOUNT has joined Coy.

Nov 6th Moved to DICKEBUSCH. Full of French troops, no room. 56 moved near LOCRE

Nov 7th Moved to farm 1½ miles from DICKEBUSCH. 56 to adjacent farm. Joined III Div Hd Qrs leaving wagons behind. Hd Qrs near YPRES. 56, 17 & 59 moved up to work with 7, 9, & 15 Infantry Bdes, now in III Div. area. 17 & 59 Coy under C.R.E III Div.

16

Nov. 7th   All coys out working on front line
—   8th   Coys working with their brigades. Trenches
            & wire entanglements by night.
            R E Div Hd qrs moved to YPRES but vehicles
            & drivers & M.S. stationary left at LA
            CLYTTE with 2nd Echelon
—   9th   Coys working as before. 2nd Echelon moved to POPERINGHE
— 10th   Hand grenades wanted but there were
            none with Div Amm Col. Coys working as
            before
— 11th   Hand grenades made of old jam pots
            filled with scrap iron, packed in mud with
            flaked wet guncotton, 2 ig primers, a
            detonator & 1¾" time fuse to burn 5 seconds.
            Shortage of barbed & plain wire & sandbags.
            Some brought up in car, rest sent up later
            in R E Hd qrs G S wagon. All three coys
            turned out as general reserve owing
            to break in line of 1st Div on our left.
            Eventually not required. 17 coy lent to 1st Div
            59 for night. All coys at work on
            back line. 2nd Lt LEVENTHORPE slightly wounded.

Addendum 'A'

— 12th   Coys working on new line. 59 coy had very
            difficult piece of line to put in state of defence
            owing in one place to stable buildings in
            front of chateau & also some farm
            buildings more to the right
— 13th   56 coy 8 men wounded. 59 1 N C O wounded
            by shell fire.

17

Nov. 13ᵗʰ. Coys working at night as usual. Trenches & paths in woods especially in very bad state. Many trees knocked down by shell fire making communication difficult by night.

— 14ᵗʰ Enormous shell hole in YRES-MENIN road filled in by 1 section of 17ᵗʰ Coy. Brushwood put at bottom & the hole then filled with bricks & stones. Coys working with their Bdes except 1 section of 56ᵗʰ Coy worked with 59ᵗʰ Coy line. Germans got into stable by Chateau in 9ᵗʰ Bde line between the posts 59ᵗʰ Coy 1 man killed, 1 wounded.

— 15ᵗʰ Germans driven out of stable at dawn with aid of field gun. Night work as usual, Especially on communication trenches & drainage.

— 16ᵗʰ Pattern's french coy out for night work. Heavy shelling. Lieut. BEBB, slightly wounded & 1 man killed, both 59ᵗʰ Coy.

— 17ᵗʰ 1ˢᵗ section 59ᵗʰ working in roads which were in a very bad state. 1ˢᵗ Cavalry Bde who had taken over 9ᵗʰ Bde line used some of the home made hand grenades with -out very much success apparently.

— 18ᵗʰ Coys working on their respective lines. 1 section 17ᵗʰ Coy sent to assist 59ᵗʰ Coy to prepare back line.

18

Nov. 19ᵗʰ Shortage of sandbags & wire. Some form
of R.E. park or Depot near front line
urgently required. Sandbags were eventually
obtained from Field Coys of 1ˢᵗ Divⁿ
& got up in time for night work. A further
supply of sandbags arrived about 11.0 P.M.
A large number of sacks were also
obtained from neighbourhood of
POPERINGHE. Stables rendered
untenable by shell fire & partly demolished.

— 20ᵗʰ 59' Coy out at work round Chateau &
stables at night. Had been assisted by
the other coys during daylight in
preparing another position behind
Chateau & stables. 56' Coy marched
to WESTOUTRE & 17' Coy to LOCRE.

— 21ˢᵗ 59' Coy marched to LOCRE & H.Qrs
to MONT NOIR, the line having been
taken over by the French.
N° 1 Coy Royal Monmouths. S.R. R.E.
(Fatters Coy) placed under C.R.E. for
road repair work in III Divⁿ area.
17' & 59' Coy joined their Divⁿ.

Appendix B

— 22ⁿᵈ Comps & 59' Coy ordered back to III
Divⁿ area. All three coys now billeted
close to MONT NOIR.

Appendix C

— 23ʳᵈ 56' Coy. 2 sections on road WESTOUTRE —
LOCRE making 50ˣ sidings, with logs
cut from beechwood. 1 sect. 57' also on this

+1 sect Combrs

1 section 57': instructing Infantry in charcoal burning & throwing hand grenades.
1 Sec Combrs coy commenced hutting at SCHERPENBERG for unknown Bde.

24' Nov. Planking & timber brought up to SCHEPPENBERG where an R E Depot is being formed. Planking & timber for trenches, dug outs & hutting. Combrs coy on hutting, other two coys on road repairs, instructing infantry in charcoal making & grenade throwing. Monmouth Terr. coy using their lorries to bring up bricks for road repairs.

Bricks — Bricks not very much use as they are too soft but there is no other material obtainable. Cardurroying down where possible.

25' Nov. Combrs coy and 1 section each of 56' & 57' coys on hutting assisted by Infantry
Composite? working party. Remainder on charcoal
Company? burning & hand grenade throwing with infantry. 42nd coy R E placed under C R E III Div for work on 2nd line of trenches.

26' Nov. 20 miles barbed wire, 100 picks, 100 shovels 100 bill hooks & 100 hand axes brought up from Amers Railhead and left at R.E. Depot at SCHERPENBERG Work on hutting dug outs and wood

20

Continued. Capt Moreton of Monmouth
siege Coy joined 57' Coy as a temporary
measure, 57' Coy only having two officers.
Combd Coy carrying out experiments
trying to devise a balista or ancient
form of catapult with the idea
of using it in the trenches. Coys also
making a supply of jam-pot hand
-grenades. Working party from ARTISTS

Nov 27' Corps assisting 42" Coy in addition to about 170 civilians
57' Coy went up to trenches with 9" Bde.
Owing to reliefs taking place little work
could be done. Lieut PARKE (57' Coy) wounded
Combd + 56' Coys employed on hutting.
42" Coy employed on rear position
N°1 MONMOUTH siege Coy employed on roads.
Working parties as yesterday with 56" Coy

Nov. 28" Companies employed as yesterday.
Only civilians (about 170) working under 42' Coy

Nov. 29' Companies employed as yesterday.
Working parties of Infantry employed with
MONMOUTH R.E. i.e. 150 on WESTOUTRE
- LOCRE road and 50 on WESTOUTRE
BERTHEN road from 8' Bde.

Nov. 30" 57 Coy returned to their billets near MONT
NOIR after work on trenches in the early
Appendix morning.
D 500 loophole plates arrived

21

Nov 30th. 56 Coy proceeded to take up forward billet vacated by 57 Coy on the 7th Bde relieving 9 Bde. Capt L.J.N. NEVILLE joined the 1st Army.
Compo Coy and 57 Coy employed on hutting at SCHERPENBURG.
12 huts of straw & brushwood complete or very nearly so. The moon for the last few days being nearly full has greatly added to the difficulties of night work.
Twelve carpenters asked for to save time and labour in thatching

Appendix 'A' Sketch of Hand Grenade
  "   "B"   Report on work of 17 & 59 Coys R.E.
  "   "C"   "   "   "   of 57 Coy for H. B'de
  "   "D"   Memorandum on Loop hole Plates
  "   "E"   "   on Rabbit netting over trenches
  "   "F"   "   " breaking up frozen ground
  "   "G"   Letter re supply of Boots Canada
  "   "H"   Memorandum on roofs of dugouts etc
  "   "I"   "   " Supporting Posts
  "   "J"   "   " impervious mat[eri]als

                                    [signature]
                                    Lt Col RE
4-12-14   C.R.E. III Division

Additional list of Appendices

Appendix K   Letter re formation of R E S Lines Park

— " —   L   Memorandum on Japanese trench mortars

— " —   M   Report on work done by Coys during October

— " —   N   Letter to Adsmans re formation of depot locally of R.S Stores

5-12-16

J. M. Ellis
Capt M
Adj III Div¹ Engineers

Appendix 'A'   75

Pattern of improvised hand grenade
made by Field Coys of III Division

                              Time fuze 1⅞" long to burn 5"
        Wire
    binding to keep lid in place
        hole in tin →   ← Lead
                                                        Scraps iron, nails etc
                                                        packed in mud.

    No 8 detonator   2. 1oz g.c.
                                                        primers
                                                        packed in
                                                        flaked wet
                                                        guncotton and
                                                        scrap iron, nails etc

    hole in tin →

                    Case of grenade
            made of ordinary 1lb ration jam tin

            Sketch of improvised Hand grenade
        as made by Field Coys R.E. of III Division
                    (not to Scale).

    11-11-16
                                                G.F.W.
                                                Capt. R.E.

Appendix "B"
1.

Copy of report forwarded by C.R.E. on the work done by the 17' & 59' Field Coys while attached to III Division

To III Division

I have the honour to bring to your notice with a view to its being reported to the 5' Division, the very good work that has been done during the operations round YPRES from 6' to 20' November by the 17' Fld Coy R.E. under Major C.W. SINGER & the 59' Fld Coy R.E. under Major G. WALKER. The work has been trying & arduous & in close proximity to the enemy, & all the officers & men have worked exceedingly hard & well — The work done by the 59' Coy has been especially trying, & I regret they had a fair number of casualties. The men & officers have worked with the greatest coolness & have done particularly good work especially in retrenching the second line which had to be taken up after enemy's attack on the 11th. The following officers & N.C.O's have done particularly good work:—

    Lieut C.E.R. POTTINGER   17' Coy R.E.
Captain WILLIAM HENRY JOHNSTON
Lieut ROBERT BRADFORD FLINT
  Nº 12075   Corpl F BARRY
  Nº 17244   —   J JAMES
  Nº 7786   —   S WRIGHT
  Nº 9321   Le Corp. H WHITING
  Nº 23972   "   A.L. GONIAN
  Nº 23091   Sapper H STARES.

I beg to recommend that Major GEORGE-WALKER

Appendix "B"
2.

59' Coy R.E. may be recommended for a brevet, he has been untiring in carrying out the necessary & urgent work under very trying conditions & by his energy & coolness has set a fine example to his men and accomplished work which has been of material assistance to the operations.

            Sgd C.S. Wilson
21-11-14   Lt Col R.E.
            C.R.E. III Division

"A" Form.
MESSAGES AND SIGNALS.

Appendix "C"

TO 3rd Div.

Sender's Number	Day of Month	In reply to Number	AAA
G.48	24th		

G.O.C. 14th Bde. wires as follows Begins On the departure of the 57th by RE. to rejoin the 3rd Div I should like to express my appreciation of excellent work done by Major Howard and those under his command during the week that they have been with me aaa They have worked for long hours and have spared neither time nor trouble to assist the infantry in improving the trenches taken over from the French and with the best results aaa We are all very grateful to them ends.

24-11-14

From 5th Div
Place
Time 12.5 PM

Appendix 'D'   Appendix 'D'   94

Memorandum re Loophole Plates.

III Division

I have to report with reference to the loophole plates just supplied, the loophole itself is very small & only admits of the rifle barrel, it is quite impossible to use them with bayonets fixed — As these plates are required where the enemy trenches are only a few yards away, the loophole should be large enough to admit of use with the bayonet fixed — The infantry are objecting to the present pattern on these grounds and I think the pattern should be changed, as with the enemy so close, it is essential to have bayonets fixed.

(Sgd) C. S. Wilson
Lt Col RE
C.R.E. III Div.

30-11-14

Appendix 'E'   91

Report re rabbit netting over trenches for
protection against "Minen Werfers".

II Div.
    With reference to G.H.Q. No O A 401, some rabbit netting
was put up over the trenches round YPRES but when we
left, had not undergone an actual test by 'Minen Werfers'.
Both the infantry & cavalry in the trenches objected to it on the
grounds that it prevented them using their bayonets, in which
objection I entirely concur, & consider it an insuperable
one — I think it should not be used either in fire or
support trenches, except on machine gun emplacements
& look out posts where it might be useful — It might also
be used over reserve trenches & would there also form a good
support for some form of protection against the weather.
    I do not think that any form of protection against
'Minen Werfers' can be devised for the fire trenches which
would not have the same objection to its use — As it
appears almost impossible to spot them so that they can
be dealt with by artillery, the only method of dealing
with them would seem to be to strike at them by night
or to make a sortie on the neighbourhood they are
supposed to be in.

                                Sgd. C. S. Wilson
                                    Lt Col RE
21-11-14   C.R.E. II Division

'F'   92

Memorandum on the breaking up of frozen
ground.

C.E. 2nd Corps

Sometime ago, I read some accounts (I think Japanese)
of a detonating fuze which was used for breaking up ground
                                      winter
for trenches. With the approach of ~~winter~~ such a stores if it
could be got, would be invaluable. Would it be possible to
have enquiries made as to whether it is obtainable.
Failing this it would be as well if each field Coy could
have an issue of 100 lbs of Tonite or some other high
explosive not affected by frost + 200 commercial
capes for this purpose, as this would I think be
much more suitable for this purpose than gun cotton —
and I anticipate very considerable difficulty in
carrying out any trench work in the near
future.

                    Sgd C.S. Wilson
                         Lt Col R.E.
                    C.R.E. III Division.

21—11—14

Appendix 'G'   91

Letter re issue of extra Canadian boots to
Field Coys R.E.

To III Division

There has recently been a good deal of sickness amongst men of the Field Coys, chiefly diarrhoea, which weakens the men very much [weak?], a good deal of this comes in my opinion from working daily in deep mud — As the supply of trained Field Company Sappers has now become very limited, I would strongly recommend that an issue of boots "Canada" may be authorized for the dismounted men of the Field Companies up to 50%. These could be carried by the Companies in their present transport, + would be issued to men who have to work in mud. I regard this as very essential if the Companies are to maintain their efficiency — I should be glad of a special application for the necessary authority could be made.

(Sgd.) C. S. Nelson
Lt Col R.E.
C R E III Division

21-11-14

Appendix "H"   93

Memorandum re overloading roofs over
dugouts & shelters.

III Division

I think attention should be drawn to the
inadvisability of putting heavy roofs over dugouts &
shelters, no roof that can be made in the field can hope to
keep out heavy high explosion shell or 'Minenwerfers'
& the only result when shell has fallen on or near such
shelters is that officers & men have been buried alive, there
were several cases of this occurring in the trenches
round YPRES — Overhead protection should
only be sufficient to guard against shrapnel
& splinters, it can then be made light enough
to avoid the danger of men being buried alive
under it.

       (Sgd.) C S Nelson
          Lt Col RE
22-11-14   C R E. III Division

Appendix I   92

Memorandum re Supporting Posts.

III Division

During the recent operations round YPRES, small supporting posts were made at intervals from 100 to 200 yards behind the fire trenches, they were made for all round defence with an obstacle right round & suitable for a garrison of 20 to 40 rifles. These posts proved themselves of considerable value, as when any portions of the line were forced, the enemy coming on these posts was checked, & they thus gained time for the counter attack to come up & also afforded it a very useful points d'appui. From experience they should comply with the following conditions.

All round defences with a complete obstacle, the field of fire to front & rear is not important, but the fire to the flanks must be good & effective.

Between 100 & 200 yds from fire trenches, completely concealed from the enemy's observations, at intervals of 200 to 400 yds.

The garrison should be from 20 to 40 rifles under a selected officer as these posts are expected to fight to a finish & this will only be done if they are each in charge of an officer.

The garrisons must live in the posts & should be provided with overhead cover against shrapnel, but they must chiefly trust to avoiding shell fire by concealment which is the most important point.

22-11-14   Sgd. C S Wilson
                                           C R E, III Div.

93

Appendix J

Memorandum on Improvised Mortars.

C E II Corps.

With reference to the description of the Indian Corps improvised trench mortar, I have tried since we were at BRAISNE to get wrought iron pipe to make them of at the local towns without success — What is wanted is 4½" to 5" wrought iron pipe ⅜" or thicker 15" long with a cap to screw on such as is used for water pipes. I think the chamber for the charge as shown in the Indian Corps pattern is a mistake & probably accounts for the very short range they have obtained — The original Japanese pattern had no chamber, & the charge from 1 to 2 oz of powder was in a little tissue paper envelope & gummed on to the lead bomb over the fuze. In experiments in peace time, I got a range of 600 yds with a 6 lb bomb —

Could ½ doz such lengths of pipe with caps be obtained from somewhere down country, if so, there will be no difficulty in the FL Coys making everything else

```
┌─────────────────────────────┐  W I cap      ⅜" thick
│                             │
│ <- - - - 15" - - - - >      │  4½" to 5"
│                             │
└─────────────────────────────┘
```

This would not have to be bound with wire.

26-1st-14
(Sgd) C S Wilson
Lt Col RE
C R E II Divn

II. Corps Appendix 'K'.

Considerable difficulty is being experienced in obtaining the necessary Engineer Stores for use in the trenches, at the present moment sandbags are very urgently required for the repair of trenches which have been badly damaged by "Minen Werfers" but none are immediately available, as I understand all those at ammunition railhead have been taken by another corps. The present system of supply of Engineer Stores seems unable to cope with requirements. The type of warfare we are at present engaged in approximates very closely to siege warfare, and so long as it lasts it appears essential that there should be an advanced R.E. Park from whence stores can be run out to the Divisions as required by a motor lorry at a few hours notice. Whether this should be under the A.O.D. as at present, or under R.E. management is a question that should be taken up. I would recommend that there should be an R.E. park unit at Ammunition railhead which should have a lorry available to take out stores for each division as required, and also arrange for the local purchase of such articles as wire, timber, nails etc etc as well as being able to undertake the manufacture of such things as improvised hand grenades, rifle grenades, trench mortars, saphead screens etc, which the field companies owing to the

the constant and strenuous work in the trenches are quite unable to undertake, and it considerably hampers the organization of the necessary work, when the CRE or his Adjutant has to be sent off to try and get these stores which should be supplied for them.

Amongst the stores which should be immediately available for issue, or places where they can be purchased at very short notice marked down, are the following, of all of which there should be a very plentiful supply –

  Sandbags
  Barbed wire
  Plain wire 14 & 16 gauge
  Staples for fixing of barbed wire
  6 in wire nails
  3 in wire nails
  rabbit netting or expanded metal
  Loophole plates
  Rifle grenades
  Hand grenades
  Explosives (including black powder for mines and fougasses)
  Timber 9"x 3" & Sheeting
  A reserve of entrenching cutting tools & wire cutters.
  A supply of mechanical contrivances for use with land mines would also be very useful.

The quick and ample supply of these stores would appear to be almost as necessary as that of ammunition, and can only be done by having them available at an advanced depot.

       (sgd) F.D. Wing, Maj. General
       Comdg 3rd Divn
19/11/14

C.E. II Corps   Appendix "L"   11

From what I have seen of the trench warfare we are now engaged in, I am certain that some of the portable bomb mortars as used by the Japanese in the Russo-Japanese war would be most useful in our trenches. They were fully described in one of the official volumes of notes on that war. Some 7 years ago I made one experimentally and thought it was successful, but the field companies have neither the time nor the shops to make them. Could they be made by one of the L of C units and sent up, I should like three, one for use with each Company. The only point I have to mention is, that I have noticed with the German bombs of this nature they make a big noise but the case or whatever it is, is blown to dust so that they can hardly be considered a very mankilling missile. The bombs made should therefore I think not have a very large bursting charge and should be well packed with bullets, bits of iron etc, as merely a thin shell with a full bursting charge of high explosive seems innocuous unless it bursts in contact with a man.

The weight should be such that the mortar would be easily carried by one man, as in use its position should be frequently shifted, as otherwise it will inevitably draw a heavy shellfire on itself.

Sgd C. S. Wilson Lt. Col.
C.R.E. II Division

16th Nov. 1914

III Division. Appendix 'M'   11

With reference to the operations during October, all the R.E. have done well, working at the trenches and in front of them often in very close proximity to the enemy, they have all displayed great coolness in carrying out this very trying work successfully, and it is difficult to discriminate where all have done well. I would however beg to bring forward the names of the following Officers & N.C.O. who have done particularly well during this period.

Captain CHARLES O'REILLY EDWARDS 57th Co R.E.

Lieutenant CYRIL GORDON MARTIN 56th Co R.E. for gallantry on the night the enemy got into the GORDONS trenches, a separate recommendation has been sent in as to this by the G.O.C. 8th Infty Brigade.

The following who did conspicuously good work when the enemy took NEUVE CHAPELLE and during the attempt to retake it.-

Lieutenant CLIVE-GUISE MOORES 56th Co R.E.
Lieutenant JOHN-ALGERNON-LEVENTHORPE 56th Co R.E.
No. 3160 Serjt EDWARD-WILLIAM-HINTON 56th Co R.E. (wounded)
No. 16483 Corpl PHILIP-JAMES-BULLOCK 56th Co R.E.
No. 20210 Corpl SIDNEY-TAYLOR 56th Co R.E.

(Sgd) C. S. Wilson Lt Col
CRE III Division

18.11.14

Ordnance Officer. Appendix "N" 12
, III Division

When the Division goes into the trenches again, please make arrangements to supply me at once with

    10 miles barbed wire
    2 cwt of plain wire about 14 or 16 gauge
  2000 yds iron rabbit netting 9 ft wide or as
      near that as can be got but not less than 6 ft
    56 lbs 6 in wire nails
    56 lbs 3 in wire nails
    14 cl staples for fixing barbed wire
  3000   sandbags
    25   loophole plates
  100   hand grenades

The consumption of these stores is not likely to be regular, and fresh supplies may be asked for at very short notice, some arrangements should therefore be made to have a further supply readily available at ammunition railhead or elsewhere, at least an amount equal to the above should be kept where it can be had at short notice, unless you are able to purchase locally at once.

As soon as they are available in the country a supply of rifle grenades (100) should also be obtained.

                        (sd) C S Wilson Lt. Col.
19.11.14   CRE III Division

121/3971

H⁰ Qrs. R.E. 3rd Division.

Vol I. 1 — 31.12.14

22

War Diary

R.E Headquarters III Division

December 1914

Dec 1st. Lieut MOORES killed and Capt
L.J.N NEVILLE wounded while
carrying out night work in front line.
There was a bright moon.
4 timber huts partially constructed
i.e. dug out & roofed. 4 more brushwood
and straw huts ready for use done by
57' & comps coy. Major HOWARD proceeded
on 7 days leave, Capt WELLS temporarily
taking command of 57' Coy

Dec 2nd 56 coy working on front line.
57' coy working on huts
Comps coy, working on huts and carrying
out experiments with rifle grenades
2nd coy working on second line also
employing civil labour
No1 large coy R.M R.E, working on
repairs of WESTOUTRE – LOCRE
road and LOCRE and LA CLYTTE
road.

Dec 3rd Compo Coy went to trenches with
8' Bde.
Division visited by H.M. the King.
56 Coy made a few patterns of a
device for portable wire entanglements
for use in front of trenches in front
of which it was impossible to get
out & work.

Appendix 'H'

Dec 4th 1 Sec 57 working on huts at SCHERPENBERG
2 Secs 57 ——— —— WESTOUTRE
56 Coy ——— ——

Dec 5th Very wet which caused trouble with the
huts the at WESTOUTRE which had been
dug out. Straw huts at SCHERPENBERG
very wet. Timber brought up by lorries of
2nd Corps.
Lieuts FINNIMORE and 2nd Lieut MACLEAN
joined 57 Coy and Lieut OATES joined
56 Coy.
Compo Coy returned from trenches.

Dec 6th 57 went up to trenches
56 Coy working on WESTOUTRE huts

24

Dec 7. Supply of timber for WESTOUTRE huts (22 altogether) now complete.
Roads BERTHEN – WESTOUTRE and WESTOUTRE in very bad condition owing to almost continuous wet weather. 2nd Corps asked to supply 2 additional lorries to help with work on roads.
Planks + brushwood sent up to trenches.

Dec 8. C.R.E. proceeded on 7 days leave, Major HOWARD acting for him. Night attack by Lincolns arranged. 57' Coy sent 1 N.C.O. + 3 men out with their patrol. These four did good work.

* Appendix "B" *
Just after attack failed Corpl. WILLIAMS (the 57' Coy N.C.O. with patrol) volunteered to take stretcher bearers out to wounded men in spite of heavy fire. Infantry wanted 57' Coy after attack had failed to go out in front of their trench to repair the wire entanglement. An impossible proceeding as the parapet was swept by German machine guns with such effect that the infantry themselves were not showing themselves over the parapet. The 57' during hours left before dawn made improvised entanglement and threw them over the parapet.
Two 2nd Corps lorries helping road repair

Tar obtained in BAILLEUL with which
to tar WESTOUTRE huts. Owing to rain
this work could not be done.
57' Coy from trenches.

Dec 9: 56' Coy to trenches. Tabs collected by 56'
Coy with the idea of sending them up
to the wettest trenches for men to stand
in. About 7000 sandbags had been
sent up to trenches during the last two
or three days and more are required.
From reports received from R.E. Coys
up in the trenches, a very large percentage
of these sandbags are misused or lost
by Bdes. Attention has been drawn to
this by and it is hoped that the enormous
wastage will cease.
56' Coy designed & constructed portable wire entanglements

Dec 10 More rain. Considerable difficulty is
being experienced in draining huts
at WESTOUTRE. Employed 57' Coy
and Comps Coy working on huts and
stabling for horses.

Dec 11" No 1 Seige Coy R.M.R.E still working on
roads while 42' Coy are still digging
are line as usual. 57' & Comps Coy
working on huts, straw stables and instructing
infantry in use of grenades.

Dec 12" 57 moved up to forward billet for work in trenches. Coys by working on WESTOUTRE–LOCRE road, in conjunction with MONMOUTH R.E. Coy. Enquiries made locally about professional 'pavé' layers but there are none to be found near at hand. Lieut RICHARD joined 56 Coy.

Dec 13" Coys and 56" working on WESTOUTRE–LOCRE road. N°1 Seige Coy R.M.R.E. taken from II Div and sent to BAILLEUL. Two trench mortars obtained from 1st Div with bombs

Dec 14" Coys by moved up to forward billet before dawn ready to make good ground if any gained by infantry in the attack. A little ground gained in the attack 5 B.Bde. Coys by out digging new communication trenches and entanglements. 57" Coy at work on old trenches generally. 56 Coy standing by during day with reserve Bde at LOCRE. C.R.E. returned from leave.

Dec 15" ~~Coys by and 57 Coy~~

✱ A detachment of Coys by
Appendix   under 2" Lieut DENING took trench mortars
"D"   up to fire trench by point 75 before dawn.
           30 rounds were fired during daylight
           12 of which were effective. Some degree
           of accuracy was obtained. One mortar

was blown to bits by a premature also causing casualties. Remaining mortar brought back to billets with a view to obtaining knowledge and giving instructions in its use. There had been no opportunity for this before and the mortars were only sent up the previous day owing to the fact that the Corps commander was anxious to have them in action during the attack.

Dec 15 57' and Comps Coys returned to billets. 56' Coy did some work on roads and in the evening moved up to forward billets.

Dec 16' 56' Coy started 2 saps and one point d'appui 57' Coy worked on WESTOUTRE-LOCRE road
Comps Coy flooring huts, laths making at SCHERPENBERG and experimenting with trench mortar.

Dec 17' Coys working as yesterday. A supply of waterproof canvas for covering straw huts obtained from ARMENTIERES. Boiler tubing 93 mm by 60 cm long (6 pieces) obtained for making trench mortars. 56' Coy from trenches

28

Dec 18° Coy po Coy moved up to trenches
and carried on saps and work on
points d'appui. 28 more tubs for
trenches taken up.
Two 2nd lifts steam lorries brought up
road material from BAILLEUL.
57° working on roads & flooring WESTOUTRE
huts. 56° Coy returned from trenches.
Capt P B O'Connor joined 56° Coy
Small party making trench mortars.

Dec 19° Work as yesterday, in addition 57°
Coy started work on covering straw
huts with waterproof canvas.
No more sandbags at present available.

Dec 20° 56° Coy on roads & a party on trench mortars
57° Coy on roads
Coombes Coy working on trenches & supporting
points
20 tubs sent up to trenches also two carpenters
for trial in trenches.
Brigading returns rejoined respective
Coys from Bde Ammunition Column.
Interpreter joined Coombes Coy.

Dec 21° Work as yesterday

29

Dec 22nd   Comps Cy from trenches, 57' Cy relvd d
           them, 56' Cy working on road
           (WESTOUTRE - LOCRE)
           Cheshire Field Coy R.E.(T) joined the
           Division. One section to 57' Cy with O.C.
           ———— 56 Cy
           Two sections to Comps Cy with Captain

Dec 23.   C.R.E. Inspected Cheshire F.C. Coy.
           57 at KEMMEL, 56 & Comps Coys
           working on roads and flooring
           huts at SCHERPENBERG.

Dec 24"   57' from trenches, 56' moved to KEMMEL
           Comps Cy on WESTOUTRE - LOCRE
           road. Civilian labourers on WESTOUTRE
           - BERTHEN road.

                                   flooring huts at SCHERPENBERG
Dec 25"   Work in trenches, roads, bath house at
           WESTOUTRE, sanatorium at
           BERTHEN. Divisional Cyclist
           Cy started training a 'grenadier'
           section.
           1 officer & 30 N.C.O's & men from different
Dec 26:   companies marched to BAILLEUL to
           billets.

30

Dec 26th Work as yesterday. Party at
BAILLEUL started work on making
trench braces of wood & waterproof
canvas, trench mortars & bombs
for same

Dec 27th Work as yesterday. Bath house
at WESTOUTRE completed.

Dec 28th Working Parties relieved 57th at
Kemmel. Other work as usual
(copied from note)

Dec 29th Flooring of SCHERPENBERG huts
completed. 56th & 57th working on
roads.

Dec 30th Work on roads.
Pioneer class started under 58th by
consisting of 25 men from each battalion
of 7th Bde.
R.E. park for 2nd Corps formed, Pioneer
located at STRAZEELE.
5000 sandbags obtained by advance

Dec 31st
Dec 31st Work on roads & pioneer class by 56th by
57th by relieved Lancs by at KEMMEL
(one section of Lancs by left at KEMMEL
to help with work on Fosse d'Oppine

Appendix 'A'   Report on 2nd line
—..— 'B'   —..— " good work by a/Capt
             Williams 57 Coy
—..— 'C'   Report on Revetting & construction
             of trenches
—..— 'D'   Report on trench mortars used
             in trenches 14-12-14
—..— 'E'   Report on hand grenades and
             tonite hand grenades, numbers
             required etc.
—..— 'F'   Report on Tonite grenades
—..— 'G'   Report on Hales' rifle grenades &
             suggestion that tonite grenades
             only be issued
—..— 'H'   Report on 'Knife rest' wire
             entanglements.
—..— 'J'   Report on use of loopholes in
             trenches.

6-1-15.   [signature] Lt Col
                                 C.R.E. III Divison

C.E. II Corps.   Appendix "A" Dec. 99
                                        "14"

I have now been carefully over the ground for the proposed line.

What impression one meets is the very great tactical importance of the Mt. KIMMEL. it dominates the whole area between the high ground MONT ROUGE and that of NEUVE EGLISE. practically to BAILLEUL it is most essential to retain possession of it as long as possible and there seems no good reason why it should not be used as a pivot in the event of the line to the N even as far as DUNKERQUE. its natural strength is such that it could be well maintained in a salient. provided the line to the S is still intact or nearly so, it should therefore I think be prepared in the first instance in the case of a set back on our left to connect with the FRENCH line at SCHERPENBERG.

If however there is also a retirement to the South and KIMMEL has to be given up, there is no good line in this section as it is

1 1/2

commanded not only by Mt KEMMEL itself but also by the high ground at NEUVE EGLISE.

There is also the complication that the French attach great importance to SCHERPENBERG and to join up with them effectively there, we must hold a forward line otherwise we cannot support them there properly. In any case, whether we hold a line in front of or behind LOCRE and DRANOUTRE, communication must be very exposed, and it will be very difficult to find places for reserves etc which will not be exposed to direct observation. In any part of the forward position, it will be possible to site the trenches so as to be fairly free from direct observation, and they can be also very effectively supported by artillery fire from MONT ROUGE & MONT VIDAIGNE

12/3

For these reasons the forward position is preferred as shown on the attached tracing of the $\frac{1}{20,000}$ map.

The trenches will want very accurate siting and I have only indicated the general line. The line divides itself into two sections, the Northern one from SCHERPENBERG to the DRANOUTRE - KEMMEL, road. Here the trenches are sited on the lower slopes of M⁺ KEMMEL road. Here the trenches are sited on the lower slopes of M⁺ KEMMEL and will be fairly free from direct observation either from M⁺ KEMMEL or NEUVE - EGLISE. The field of fire will be from 70 to 200 yards immediately above them. There is a bit of flat plateau. Any infantry attack across this should be readily broken up by artillery fire. Except for its communication being very exposed this

45/4

position is fairly satisfactory.

The Southern section from the DRANOUTRE-KEMMEL road will be exposed to fire MT. KEMMEL & NEUVE EGLISE but on the other hand will have rather better communications, as a good deal of cover is available from hedges &c. and by making two or 3 rows of trenches the Shell fire might be avoided by moving from one to the other.

The High ground at NEUVE EGLISE is the worst feature as it will almost enfilade the trenches on the Spur in front of DRANOUTRE, and also looks down the valley of the river DOUVE. The weakest point in the line is the portion in front of DRANOUTRE, where it has to be brought from the lower slopes of MT. KEMMEL across the valley. I think however that the disadvantage

of the line behind are
greater, they are not
supporting SCHERPENBERG
and a very bad line to get
back from there to MONT ROUGE
and the very great disadvantage
of having the two villages
LOCRE & DANOUTRE
immediately in front of the
line. The artillery support
will also not be so good.

The great advantage of
the back line is that
communication will be much
less exposed.

In short in the unfortunate
case of KEMMEL being
given up we are faced with
two bad alternatives in this
section and of the two on
the whole the forward
position is less disadvantageous
than the other.

7-12-14

Sgd C. S. Wilson
Lt Col
C.R.E. 1st Div.

Good work of
Cpl H D Williams
57' Fd Co

3rd Division Appendix 'B'
  Dec '14   18

With reference to G C 918 of 12th Dec

On December 8th when an attack was being made on the PETIT-BOIS – WYTSCHAETE, by the Lincoln Reg. No 1946 Acting Corporal HENRY DREW WILLIAMS, 57th Coy R.E, with a party of R.E, went forward and cut the wire entanglement in front of the German trenches. After the attack Corporal Williams guided the stretcher bearers to two wounded men of the Lincoln Reg and brought them safely back. Sniping and firing was still being continued.

Sgd F G S Howard Maj RE
for C.R.E III Division

13th Dec 1914

III Division   Appendix "C"   21/3
Dec. 14

With reference to your E.198A.

1. Siting of trenches — Points in order of importance.

(a) Hidden from direct artillery observation.

(b) Field of fire to be clear immediately in front of trenches and no dead ground within 200 yards

(c) Siting should provide as much cross fire as possible

N.B. If necessary to comply with
(a) a field of fire of 60 or 70 yards with a good obstacle may be considered sufficient in which case (c) becomes of greater importance

(d) screened communications to the rear

Design

(1) Each length of trench should be at least a platoon or 50 yards, should not be less than 2′6″ at bottom, with traverses 15 ft apart, if possible they should also be recessed and shelters provided under the parapet

22/4

Recesses should also be cut
back for use as latrines and for
sump pits if drainage is
difficult. Trenches 3'9" deep with a
9" parapet.

Head cover should be provided but
not overhead cover, as the men
cannot use their bayonets.

(2) Cover Trenches for supports should
be from 50 to 150 yards in rear
of fire trenches and should be
similar design. Overhead cover
should not be provided in order
that the men may get out
quickly to repel an attack
with the bayonet.

Cover Trenches for reserves should
have overhead cover, this should
only be weather and Shrapnel
proof. The roof cannot be made
proof against H.E. Shell and
any attempt to do so only leads
to men being buried alive.

(3) Machine gun emplacements should
be carefully concealed and
provided with overhead cover, or at
all events, wire netting as a
protection from grenades Etc.

Con:
they should be sited for cross and enfilade fire. If used for frontal fire they will probably be knocked out very soon.

(4) Fire trenches should be fairly continuous i.e. those for a company should have direct communication. It need not be continuously prepared for fire.

(5) Without an obstacle 300 yards. With an obstacle as little as 60 or 70 yards may be sufficient if cross fire is employed.

(6) The best line is the rear of a wood with the edge entangled. A line through a wood with a good obstacle is very good even a ditch is sufficient clearing as the attack coming through the wood is necessarily much broken up. The edge of a wood in rear is very bad as it is a good mark for artillery and the branches etc. brought down obstruct the trenches.

Cont

Buildings must be held by trenches in front with good communication to the building so that if shelled the garrison can get into the trenches

(8) Defence of hedges, nothing new learnt.

(9) Supporting points behind the trenches are very useful, they should be small closed posts with a good obstacle for from 25 to 50 men, 100 to 200 yards behind the fire trenches and must have good fire to the flanks. Their uses are to check the enemy when he has penetrated the front line and give time for the counter attack to come up and help it as pointed a spur. They should be concealed from the enemy so that they may come as a surprise, and be protected with overhead cover.

Each of these posts must be under an Officer as they are to be held to the end

Cont.

25/4

10/ Obstacles should be from 20 to 30 yards from the fire trench, if further they cannot be seen at night and would have to be patrolled, if nearer they will not keep grenade throwers at a distance. A wide low obstacle is better than a narrow high one as the latter gets very badly damaged by its own supp'g rifle fire, & machine gun cuts any high obstacle in front of it to bits. Whenever possible obstacles should be flanked by machine gun fire.

15-12-14

(Sgd) C S Wilson Dixon
CRE III Durham

C.E. II Corps. Appendix "D" 19/
Dec '14

With reference to your E.216, the following is the result of the use of the trench Mortars. These were sent straight up into the trenches, and there was practically no time for experiment — with a little time much better results would probably be obtained.

Rounds fired 30 — 14 rounds in or near the enemy's trench and considered effective, two premature one in mortar destroying it, but with no damage to personnel. One in the air half way, remainder were blind.

Cause of failure : Fuze failed to ignite 7 rounds
Wood plug with detonator fell out during flight 4 rounds
Shell on leaving jumped about and probably knocked out plug 3 rds.

Improvements required

The design of bomb wants revising

to make explosive more certain

The carriage is not sufficiently stable, it wants bolting to a wooden platform

The fuze must be new & good otherwise it is difficult to time the explosion of the Shell

Placing the charge and making up the Shell takes too long and wants improvement.

Ranging was fairly easy, the 2nd round was generally about right

Effect seemed good and better than a rifle grenade

Range 50 yards to 180 yards

I have brought the remaining Mortars in, and am going to try and improve it and remedy defects tomorrow

Sgd. C.S Wilson Lt Col
C.R.E III Division

15=12=1914

Appendix 'E'
Dec '14

47
6

With reference to letter
No. O.B. B/3016=

(a) The regulation hand grenade + the trench hand grenade are both being used, a supply is kept at Brigade Headquarters, and issued to units as required. At present the expenditure is very small, but if the troops take kindly to them, a very large amount will be required. At present I think it will be sufficient if a supply of 100 is kept at Brigade Headquarters and 1000 in Divisional Ammunition Column.

(b) If it can be devised the best form of grenade would be a special one acting by percussion, which could be thrown 30 to 40 yds. It should be as fool proof as possible and need little preparation as possible.

The regulation hand grenade is too clumsy and requires too much manipulation, withdrawing safety pin, turning head to fire position.

The Lomis Hand grenade seems an excellent pattern and as nearly fool-proof as one could be made, it is found however that it does not always go off on soft ground. Possibly the Striker could be made rather heavier or the Spring a little weaker.

(c) At present two new Coy. Company are being trained as well as a special detachment of 34 men of the Divisional Cyclists. I think at least 10% (percent) of the men and all Officers in the Infantry should be trained eventually i.e. 25 men per Coy. this will mean some good aim at grenades as each man should throw a live one, 1200 for the Division

(d) I think it is also a good plan to train all the Divisional Mounted Troops and Cyclists who are now quite fresh and would be very useful to send out parties for special little expeditions to annoy the enemy, the Infantry Grenades being used more for the actual use defence of the trenches

24/12/914   (Sgd) C S Wilson Lt Col
                     C.R.E. III Division

III Division Appendix "F"
Dec '14   25/12/1914   27

With reference to the TONITE HAND GRENADES a cause of miss-fire is that the Striker sometimes sticks — Before inserting the detonator the safety pin should be withdrawn and the grenade examined to see that the Striker runs easily in the grenade, if it does not a miss-fire will result unless the necessary adjustments are made, either by adjusting the string or removing dirt.

This should be added to the papers of instructions issued with each box of grenades.

(Sgd.) C.S Wilson Lt Col
C R E III Division

25-12-14

III Division Attendue "g"
Dec 14

50/7

With reference to my report on Grenades reference letter N.O.B. B/3016 - There have been several cases of HALES rifle Grenades mis-firing due either to the ring at the bottom being jammed or not answering during flight and also in a journey the grenade sometimes does not travel properly head first so the vanes fail to act and the lower ring does not come unscrewed.

The first cause can be remedied by passing the lower ring before firing but as if this ring is unscrewed too far the pin drops out, and the grenade is then very unsafe it is not desirable to let the men make this adjustment

The second cause appears to be that the head is too heavy for the tail to keep straight

I have tried the TONITE hand grenade with a rod instead of a wooden handle and found it worked successfully under the same conditions in which the HALES grenade was failing. I would therefore recommend to Simplify Supply that only the TONITE Grenade should be issued with rods and handles so that it can be used either as a rifle grenade and it will also avoid the risk of mixing the detonators

27/12/14

(Sgd.) C S Wilson DCol

C R E III Division

Extemporised wire obstacle

Appendix 'H' Dec '14"

III Division

The following device has been found very useful where there is difficulty in constructing the ordinary barbed wire entanglement, it is simple and easily placed by one man, if the ends are hitched into one another and two or three rows are put out, it makes quite a formidable obstacle — It could be easily made and placed by the infantry themselves

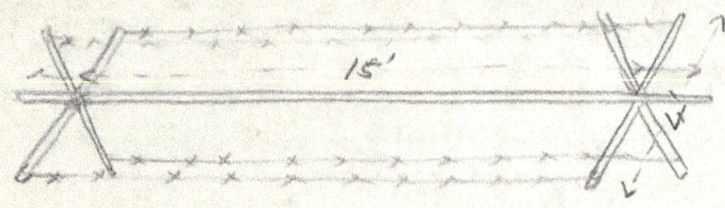

A light hop pole 15' long is taken & 2 cross pieces 4ft long bound on at each end, barbed wire is then stretched from end to end of the cross pieces.
It is quickly made & quite effective

(Sgd) C.S. Wilson Lt Col
CRE III Div

7-12-14

Appendix 'J' 11

III Division
With reference to your A.619.

Tarpaulins were tried in the trenches. Their advantage is that they keep the men fairly dry & enable them to sit down.

Their disadvantages were:-
Great weight & bulk rendering them extremely difficult to get up to the trenches, as they took 6 men to carry one & this was rather a large group & apt to draw fire.

The tarpauling when placed in the trench rather tended to destroy it as it rendered repairs almost impossible & the soft ground was pulled down underneath it.

For these reasons, it was a very partial success and I do not think any more should be provided.

(Sgd) C.S. Wilson Lt Col
C.R.E. III Division

30-12-14

SUBJECT.

No.	Contents.	Date.
	3RD DIV. R.E., H.Q. — WAR DIARY, JAN-DEC, 1916	

3rd /5 Division

121/6390

Formed 7.9.14.

Composite Coy: R.E. 3rd Division

W.I.

Sept 14
Jan 12- 1915

Sept & Dec
1914

WAR DIARY

Composite Company Royal Engineers
8th Brigade
3rd Division

<u>Formed</u> Sept 7th 1914

Capt H. M. Henderson RE

No 1 Sect	No 2 Sect
Lt C. G. Martin RE	Lt R. C. Wells RESR
&	&
No 3 Sect 56th Coy RE	No 4 Sect 57th Coy RE
40 Sappers	35 Sappers
8 Drivers	10 Drivers

<u>Total</u>

- 3 Officers
- 93 Men
- 7 Riding horses
- 21 Draught
- 2 Tool Carts
- 1 Limbered Wagons
- 1 Cooks Cart
- 1 Technical Wagon
- 1 ½ Supply Wagon
- 1 Civilian Wagonette (for Limbered Wagon)

Sept 7th Company formed at 4pm at FAREMOUTIERS
marched to CHAUFFRY arrived 9.30 pm
joined 8th Bde (Billet)

Sept 8th Moved 5am Advanced Guard action at
ORLY from 10am – 5pm
Casualties all slightly wounded
No 1 Sect Sprs Williamson – Stone – Alford
No 2 Sect Sprs Selling – Lewis
Billeted at ORLY.

Sept 9th Moved 7am Rearguard
Destroyed 51 live german shell nr CROUTTES (Lt Wells)
Searched NANTEUIL tunnel for mines (Capt Henderson)
Billeted CROUTTES at 7.30 pm
Requisitioned 1 water barrel on wheels as water cart.

Sept 10th Moved 5.30am Reserve brigade.
Cleared motor lorry & car out of road
Bivouacked at CHEZY 8pm.

Sept 11th Moved 7.45 am reserve
Billeted OUCHLY (la ville) 2.30pm

Sept 12th Moved 6am Reserve
Rubble Improved & repaired road at LES
CROUTTES.
Billeted at BRAINE 8pm

Sept 13th
    Moved 6.30 am Advanced Guard. Enemy met at
VAILLY BRIDGE. Capt Henderson & Lt Martin
reconnoitred bridges reported 36' gap in river bridge
Capt Henderson wounded in elbow at 8.30 am, sent
to Base.
    9 pm Demolished barn near bridge to obtain timber
      to repair bridge
    8 pm - 4 am with 56th & 57th Coy built pontoon
    bridge across river AISNE and made approaches

Sept 14th Crossed pontoon bridge 4 am to VAILLY advanced
    guard checked and company remained under
    heavy shell fire in VAILLY — recrossed bridge
    at 2 pm
                              Lost civilian wagonette
    Casualties 9 horses killed
      Sergt Murphy (shoeing smith) slightly wounded
      in head sent back to base.
    Billeted CHASSIGNY 8 pm

Sept 15th. Moved 3.30 am to CHATEAU LA TULERIE
    Joined 56th Coy RE. made fascines for
    heavy bridge approaches
    Bivouacked in woods near CHATEAU

Sept 16th Made fascines up to 1 pm
    Dismounted portion moved at 8 pm with
    1 limbered wagon to 8th Brigade VAILLY
    Bivouacked 10 pm VAILLY

Sept 17th
- Buried Capt Price DSO Royal Scots
  18 English } men
  1 German at 6am
- 2pm Officers went round 8th Bge position
  Men collected timber for head cover
- 7pm No I Sect built 40' of barbed wire obstacle RIRegt
  No II built redoubt for WILTS REGT
  Billeted in Hotel de ville

Sept 18th
- 2pm Both sections built splinter proof shelters for officers in firing line
- 7t Lt Wells wounded in leg - fit for duty 4.30pm
- 7pm 50' of barbed wire entanglement infront of Royal Irish Regt
  Recd first supply of Clothing

Sept 19th
- 8am Constructed 2 splinter proof shelters for Howitzer Section detachment for 6 men each
  also 2 observation posts - screened both from Aeroplanes.
- 2pm Collected posts and barbed wire
  Heavily shelled from 3-5pm
  Casualties 1 riding horse
- 7pm Dug 2 graves for 8 men each
  Received 1st Reinforcement.
   1 Lt Cpl
   9 Sappers

Sept 20th Lt Martin attended Court Martial for
           Driver Steedon   A.S.C. (case dismissed)
    8am No II Sect cleared field of fire for Howitzers
         felling trees.
    2pm Collected posts & barbed wire
    7pm 2 off & 20 men put up 50ʸ of barbed
         wire entanglement Royal Irish Regt.
         30 men cleared road through VAILLY
         of dead horses
         10 men buried 3 officers   Capt Elliot Devon
                        2 men   Lt   Rawrc
                                   Lt Boyd Royal Fusiliers

Sept 21st 8am Buried 4 horses.
           2 pm   "   6 horses.
Reinforcement 4pm collected material for constructing machine
 2 drivers   emplacement – head & overhead cover
 1 riding horse 8pm. Night Attack on VAILLY – turned out
 4 draught horses   to guard bridge Casualties 1 man wounded
                    20 men as General Doran's guard.
                    Capt Edwards took over command at 11pm

Sept 22nd 7am Buried 8 horses.
           2pm Collected wire & posts for entanglement
           7pm No 1 sect wire entanglement across gully
                infront of Devon Regt
                Prepared 2 machine gun emplacements
                   for Royal Scots
                No II Sect - 50ˣ Entanglement for Leicester
                                                        Regt

Sept 23rd
    7am Buried 1 officer Capt Dawes Leicester Regt
        2 men
    Under heavy shell fire 10am ⎫ 22nd
    Casualties 1 draught horse ⎭
    2pm Wire entanglement Middlesex Regt
    5pm Shewed officers of 12th Coy RE round
    position

Sept 24th   Handed over to 12th Coy at 3.30am
    Moved to bivouac in woods near
    CHATEAU LA TULERIE, prepared shelters
    6.30pm buried 5 horses on BRAINE-VAILLY
    road

Sept 25th   9am made Communications in wood for
    S. Lancs Regt - No 1 Sect
    No 2 Sect repaired and cleared main
    BRAINE - VAILLY Road.
    7pm. erected trip wire for S. Lancs Regt.
    12 m.n. made roadway with fascines for
    approach to heavy pontoon bridge -

Sept. 26th   7am work on BRAINE - VAILLY ROAD.
    2pm No II Sect made fascines and cut
    posts for heavy bridge
    7pm No I Sect dug ramp and carried
    fascines for heavy bridge approach

Sept 27th ~~Removed~~
    8am Took up alarm post position at N end of
        BOIS MORIN until 9am.
    6 pm No I Sect work on heavy bridge approaches
        No II Dug trenches 40^x edge of BOIS MORIN
    Camp heavily shelled at 12 noon & 4 pm.
    9 pm Sent mounted sections to BRAINE

Sept 28th 6 am Moved camp to wood S E of
    CHASSEMY.
        6 pm No I Sect Dug trenches BOIS MORIN 40^x
        No II . Work on heavy bridge approaches

Sept 29th 7am Prepared water supply for camp
        6 pm No I & II sect dug 35^x trenches and
        deepened existing trenches for 60^x

Sept 30th 6 pm. No I deepened & connected up infantry
        pits at BOIS MORIN 55^x
        No II Dug Boer trenches 45^x

OCTOBER 1914

Oct 1st 8am Cut posts for wire entanglement
        7pm Commenced march to OULCHY LE CHATEAU
        arrived 4am distance 20 miles
        Casualties 1 horse stolen from mounted
        section camp.

Oct 2nd 7pm marched to SILLY LA POTERIE
        15 miles arrived 2.30 am.

Oct 3rd 6 pm marched to CREPY EN VALOIS
        15 miles arrived 2 AM.

Oct 4th Bought 1 light draught horse
        6 pm marched 13 miles to RHUIS. arrived
        12.15 am.

Oct 5th Marched from RHUIS to entrain
        No I Sect at 10am to PONT St MAXENCE
        No II Sect at 11.30 am to LE MEAUX
        No III Sect on the road 1 mile from LE MEAUX
        at 1.15pm received verbal orders to entrain at 4pm
        at COMPIÉGNE (6 miles away) arrived there at 3.30pm.
        entrained at 12 mn.

Oct 6th No I Sect detrained and billeted at RUE
        at 8 pm
        No II Sect detrained and billeted at

CONCHIL TEMPLE at 5.30 pm.   11

Oct 7th   No I Sect marched at 11 AM to HAUT-
          VILLERS arrived 2.30 PM billeted. (10 miles)
          No II Sect marched at 8.45 am to HAUTVILLERS
          arrived 4 pm (18 miles).
          Drew 3 draught horses from Remounts.

Oct 8th   Paid men 1000 francs.

Oct 9th   Marched at 1.15 am to RAYE (12 miles)
          billeted at 7 am.
          1st Line Transport marched 5.45 pm to SAINS
          les Pernes arrived 6.30 am 10/10/14. 26 miles
          Baggage wagons marched 6 pm as above
          arrived 2 pm. 10/10/14
          Dismounted marched 6.0 pm to RÉGNAUVILLE
          (3 miles) billeted at 7.45 pm.
                                             at 2.15 am
Oct 10th marched to "HESDIN" (5 miles) arrived
          4 am, boarded motor transport 8am arrived
          PERNES 9.30 am. returned to SAINS les Pernes
          by transport 11am. billeted 12.30 pm.

Oct 11th No 1 Sect. marched 5.45 am. with Advanced
          Guard to LE CORNET MALO + billeted at 4.30 pm.
          No 2 Sect. marched 7.10 am with Main Body
          to HINGES + billeted 8.30 pm.

Oct 12th No 1 Sect. marched at 6.30 a.m. with
Advanced Guard to VIELLE CHAPELLE and
prepared house for defence covering bridge.
Billeted at 5 p.m.
No 2 Sect. marched 8.15 a.m. with main body
to VIELLE CHAPELLE & billeted 8.15 p.m.

Oct 13th Marched at 6 a.m. with reserve to cross
roads north of first E in VIELLE CHAPELLE.
Buried 1 man Middlesex Regt & 19 French
Soldiers. Billeted 5.30 p.m.

Oct 14th (10 men)
No 2 Sect. at 9 p.m. made machine gun
emplacement for Royal Scots.
No 1 Sect (12 men) at 10 p.m. superintended
construction of 200 yards traversed fire
trench for Gordon Highlanders —

Oct 15th Buried a French peasant, 19 horses, 3 cows
& 1 calf.

Oct 16th Marched at 7 a.m. to point on road
immediately north of A of LACOUTURE.
Casualty - 1 draught horse
Buried 5 horses — Billeted 6 p.m.
Received G.S. Wagon for limbered wagon without horses or harness

Oct 17th Marched 9.30 a.m. to AUBERS with reserve
Billeted 7.30 p.m, cut telegraph wires

leading from town to N.E. & S.E. at 9 pm.

Oct 18th With reserve in AUBERS. Heavily shelled
Sun   between 4 pm & 4.30 pm.

Oct 19th 7.30 am buried 4 horses –
          3 pm Collected tools for wire entanglement –
          5.30 pm ~~~~~~~~ Lt Wells & 5 cyclists
          ~~~~~ to LE PILLY & entangled road & railway
          near Royal Irish position –

Oct 20th 4.30 am company marched to HELLIERS,
          Lts. Wells & Mathin went on ahead to
          LE PILLY. Lt Mathin returned to HELLIERS
          at 6.30 am reporting no work possible at
          LE PILLY by daylight & that Royal Irish had
          plenty of tools. Lt Wells remained at LE PILLY
          to superintend construction of machine gun
          emplacement in building by men of Royal Irish.
          Company remained in HELLIERS till 6 pm.
          Heavy shell fire all day –
          Tool carts sent back to AUBERS at 4.30 pm
          were stopped by an officer of 9th Bde 23/2 picks
          & shovels removed –
          Company returned to AUBERS & then proceeded
          to RIEZ at 9 pm. Wire trenches for
          Middlesex Regt were improved & trip wires
          put up – 20 picks & 6 shovels were recovered

from 9th Bde —
Lieut Wells missing.

Oct 21st 8pm Company to LE PLOUICH
where traverses were made for Royal Scots,
trenches dug & edge of wood entangled —
4 Horses received.

Oct 22nd 11 am. made 4 ramps across ditch
running N.E. from TRIVELET & laid
out position for brigade from FAUQUISSART
to CHAPIGNY.
8 pm. Improved trenches for GORDON HIGHLANDERS
north of AUBERS - FROMELLES ROAD.
11 pm. Assisted in construction of
FAUQUISSART — CHAPIGNY position

Oct 23rd Company went into billets in RUE
DU BACQUEROT. Heavily shelled
at 4 pm. 3 men wounded — Went
into billets west of FLINQUE
at 8.30 pm. No 1 Sect made obstacle
across road on left of brigade position
& cleared 200 yards of ditch for use as
communication trench —
No 2 Section erected 60 yards wire
entanglement in front of Royal Scots position,
work stopped by attack —

Oct 24th 10 am collected posts for wire entanglement

15

Company dug cover from shell fire near billet –

Oct 24th (cont.) Company marched at 6pm to brigade position to erect wire entanglement but was stopped en route by rifle fire – Enemy broke through position – Wagon was sent back & company forward to cooperate in defence. Enemy was driven back by our infantry & company returned to billet at ~~xxxxx~~ 1.45 am. (25th).
Lt. Martin wounded –

Oct 25th Sun. Morning & afternoon, company collected & prepared pickets for wire entanglements & dug cover from shell fire near billet 5.15 pm Company erected 220 yds wire entanglement in front of brigade position + 3 sample shelters., work interfered with on right of position by enemy's fire – Lt. Martin went to hospital for base –

Oct 26th Mon. Morning, company collected & prepared pickets for wire entanglements – Afternoon, Infantry working party collected timber for pickets – 5.15 pm. Company erected 380 yds wire entanglement in front of brigade position –

Oct 27th Morning – Company collected & prepared posts for wire entanglement.
5.15 pm Company erected 380 yds barbed wire entanglement in front of brigade position & repaired some that had been damaged by shell fire –
2/Lieut B.C. Dening R.E. joined company at 8.30 p.m.

Oct 28th Morning – Company collected & prepared posts for wire entanglements
Lieut. E.F.S. Dawson R.E. joined company at 8.30 a.m.
5.15 pm Company put up 280 yds wire entanglement in front of brigade position & repaired damaged wire –

Oct 29th Morning – Company collected & prepared posts for wire entanglements & continued work on shelters
6 pm Company erected 395 yds wire entanglement in front of brigade position

Oct 30th Morning – Company collected & prepared posts for wire entanglement, made small rolls from large coils of wire & continued work on shelters –
5.30 pm Company erected 410 yds wire

17

Oct 30th entanglement in front of brigade position.
(Cont.)   Wiring of whole position completed -

Oct. 31st ~~A section~~ Morning - Company collected
          & prepared posts for loose entanglement &
          recoiled wire -
          5.15 pm. No 1 sect. collected wire & posts
          from 8th Brigade position & stacked near
          retired position -

Nov 1   Company paraded at 8 am & erected
          140 yds wire entanglement in front of
          retired position near RUE DU BACQUEROT
          also cleared foreground & worked to 5 pm

Nov 2   7.30 am to 2.30 pm Company dug
          trenches on retired position & cleared
          foreground, work stopped by shell fire.
          Paraded again 8.30 pm, marched to
          advanced position & worked on line
          to be taken up in rear of ~~2nd R~~
          2nd ~~Gurkha~~ trenches (dug trench &
          cleared foreground) -

Nov 3   Continued work till 4 am, marched
          back to billet & on to freshly filled ~~on~~
          main road ½ mile N.E. of L in
          RIEZ BAILLEUL, arrived 6 am.

Nov 3rd (cont) — No 1 Sect. paraded 7.30 p.m. & erected 290ˣ wire entanglement in front of Royal Scots Fusiliers position. Work interrupted by German attack. Returned to billet 4 a.m.

Nov 4th — No 2 Sect. paraded ~~5.0 p.m.~~ 7.0 a.m. & collected & prepared pickets for wire entanglement at B of RUE DU BACQUEROT. Returned to billet at 12 noon.
No 1 Sect re-rolled wire during afternoon.
No 2 Sect paraded 5.0 p.m. fetched wire & pickets from RUE DU BACQUEROT & proceeded to position held by Manchester Regt. Erected 440 yds of wire entanglement between Manchesters & Sikh Pioneers & in front of latter & strengthened & completed 100 yds in front of Manchesters. Returned to billet 5 a.m. (5th)

Nov 5th — No 1 Sect paraded at 8.30 a.m. Collected & prepared pickets for wire entanglement & rolled wire. 11.0 a.m. cleared hedge & started demolition of farm in front of rehired position near ROUGE CROIX.
No 2 Sect rolled wire from 12.30 p.m. to 4 p.m.
No 1 Sect paraded 5.15 p.m. & erected 175 yds wire entanglement in front of

Nov 5th (cont)   Manchesters + connected with wiring
                  party of Sappers + Miners, returned 1 am (6th)

Nov 6th   No 2 paraded 7.0 am + continued
                  demolition of farm + clearing near
                  ROUGE CROIX
                       No 1 paraded 10 am, laid out
                  shelters + assisted in demolition of farm
                       Company returned to billet 6 pm

Nov 7th   Company paraded 7.0 am continued
                  demolition of farm, clearing, barbed
                  wire entanglements + laying out of
                  shelters near ROUGE CROIX.
                  3 pm 6 men (No 1) fetched infantry which were
x also rifle   entanglements from ESTAIRES +
grenades.   delivered at cross roads north of B of
                  RUE DU BACQUEROT at 7 pm
                  4.30 pm 2/Lt Deming, 6 NCO's + men
                  assisted in superintending the digging
                  of shelters by Poona Horse near
                  ROUGE CROIX -
                  Company returned to billet
                  at 5.30 pm.

Nov 8th   7.30 am to 4.30 pm Company continued
                  demolition of farm, marked out 9
                  shelters, erected 180 yds wire entanglement

Nov 8th: & cleared foreground near ROUGE CROIX
(ct'd) 5.30 pm. 12 men N° 1 Sect. under 2 Lt Deming
proceeded to erect wire entanglement in front
of Cornwalls' trenches but proximity of enemy
prevented any work being done; returned
to billet 8.30 pm.

Nov 9th 7.30 am. Company paraded for work on
retired position at ROUGE CROIX, marked
out shelters, constructed shelter, erected wire
entanglements, levelled debris of house &
cleared foreground –
5.30 pm. N° 2 paraded & erected wire entanglements
on retired position at ROUGE CROIX. Lt Deming
+ 2 men took 7 coils patent French wire
entanglement to H.Q. Cornwalls & explained its
use –

Nov 10th 7.30 am / to 4 pm. N° 1 Sect. worked on retired position,
constructed advanced post, completed shelter, &
marked out communication trenches –
Afternoon, N° 2 cut pickets & rolled wire –
5 pm. N° 2 erected wire entanglements on
retired position
5.30 pm. French wire entanglement (11 coils)
delivered to East Surreys & use explained –
4 coils delivered to Cornwalls & splinter –
– proof shelter made for Bn H.Q. Staff Cornwalls

Nov 11th 8 a.m. No 1 worked on retired position on advanced post, marking out communication trenches & clearing of foreground.
1 p.m. No 2 worked on retired position, putting up wire entanglements & demolishing cottage.
Both sections back to billet 4.30 p.m.
6 p.m. Lt Dawson took French wire entanglement to 57th Rifles & 129th Baluchis & instructed them in use thereof.

Nov 12th 8 a.m. Company worked on retired position; marked out ~~Artillery~~ communication trenches, constructed advanced posts & abattis & cleared foreground

Nov 13th 8 a.m. Company worked on retired position; marked out communication trenches, constructed advanced posts, abattis & entanglement.
6.30 p.m. No 1 Sect proceeded to HQ Connaught Rangers for work on front line & returned to billets 10.30 p.m. work having been cancelled.

Nov 14th Company paraded 12.30 p.m. & marched to billet in ESTAIRES

Nov 15th. Marched at 10.45 am with 8th Brigade to
BAILLEUL & went into billets there at
4 pm.

Nov 16th 8 Carpenters started making wooden
frames for trench stoves.

Nov 17th 8 Carpenters worked in morning on frames for
trench stoves. ~~[struck through]~~
4.15 pm Company marched to billet 3/4 mile
north of M of RAMARIN on east side of
RAMARIN — NEUVE EGLISE road.
Arrived 6.15 p.m.

Nov 18th Afternoon, Company cut brushwood &
pickets for wire entanglement.
5.30 pm. Company marched to WULVINGHEM
& deposited brushwood for use of
Suffolk & Middlesex. No 1 Section
erected 80 yards of wire entanglement
for Middlesex & repaired existing
wire fence.

Nov 19th Morning, No 2 cut pickets & rolled wire
for entanglements
Afternoon Company cut pickets & rolled
wire for entanglements
5 p.m. Company marched to WULVINGHEM

Nov 19th (cont.)   N°1 erected 190 yds entanglement for Suffolks
            N°2   "   295 yds   "   "

Nov 20th   Morning, Company cut pickets & rolled wire for entanglement.
5 p.m. N°2 Sec (8 men) to WULVINGHEM and erected 70 yds wire entanglement for Suffolks.
7 p.m. N°1 Sec. to WULVINGHEM and erected 265 yds wire entanglement for Suffolks.

Nov 21st   Company moved to billet on main road 1 mile S.S.W. of NEUVE EGLISE + cut pickets for wire entanglement

Nov 22nd   9 p.m. Lt Dawson took party with explosives to Middlesex position for purpose of mining a disused trench. Work was cancelled on arrival

Nov 23rd   Company moved at 9 a.m. to billet at CROIX DE POPERINGHE. arriving 2.30 p.m.

Nov 24th   8 a.m. N°2 sent to SCHERPENBERG + started construction of splinter proof shelter for 3rd Div: Staff. Sites for

Nov. 24th (Cont.)	12 shelters for troops selected & marked out.
Nov. 25th	8 am N° 2 Sect. to SCHERPENBERG & superintended excavation of sites for shelters by Infantry working party. Also continued construction of splinter proof shelter. Remainder of Company moved to new billet ½ mile N of CROIX DE POPERINGHE at 8.30 am. N° 1 Sect. made charcoal, prepared materials for hand grenades & experimented with ballista also collected material for shelters.
Nov. 26th	8 am Company to SCHERPENBERG & continued construction of shelters for troops & splinter proof shelter assisted by 1 Sect from 56th Coy 1 Sect from 57th Coy & infantry party.
Nov 27th	8 am. Company to SCHERPENBERG & continued construction of shelters for troops assisted by 56th Coy + infantry party. Splinter proof shelter completed.
Nov 28th	8 am. Company to SCHERPENBERG

Nov 28th (cont.) + completed 12 shelters for troops - assisted by 56th Coy

Nov 29th Company to SCHERPENBERG at 8 am + started 4 new shelters for troops assisted by 2 Sections 56th Coy + infantry working party. 8 men No 2 Sect. made grenades + dummy grenades + overhauled tools of section. 2pm representatives of 8th Brigade instructed in use of grenades + making of charcoal.

Nov. 30th Company to SCHERPENBERG at 8 am + continued work on shelters. 3pm. No 2 Section to KEMMEL + repaired shell-hole in road.

Dec. 1st No 1 Section to SCHERPENBERG at 8 am + continued work on shelters for troops. No 2 Section to SCHERPENBERG at 11.30 am + continued work on shelters for troops.

Dec 2nd No 2 Section to SCHERPENBERG at 8 am + made pathways + steps. No 1 Section commenced erection of shelter for horses. 3.30 pm. representatives of 8th Bde. instructed

Dec 2ⁿᵈ — in use of rifle-grenades.
(cont:)

Dec 3ʳᵈ Company paraded at 3.30 p.m. & marched to billet near KIMMEL arriving 6.30 p.m. Capt Edwards & Lieut Dawson to Brigade H.Q. at 8 p.m. & afterwards reconnoitred part of line held by brigade —

Dec 4ᵗʰ Company paraded 8 a.m. & prepared [portable] barbed wire entanglement & cut brushwood (N°1 Section morning only, N°2 Sect. morning & afternoon)
Company paraded 5.45 p.m. & carried materials & stores to X roads in KEMMEL & Brigade H.Q. ½ N°1 Sect under Lt Dawson to left of Royal Scots position to assist with drainage of trenches, no possible solution arrived at. ½ N°1 Section to Suffolk
& under position dug drain for right hand trench
2ⁿᵈ Lt Denny & started communication trench towards 5ᵗʰ Div position

Dec 5ᵗʰ Company paraded 10 a.m. & prepared portable barbed wire entanglement & cut brushwood (N°2 morning only, N°1 morning & afternoon) Company paraded 5.30 p.m. & carried materials to X roads in KEMMEL —
½ N°2 Sect to Royal Scots position &

Dec 5th (cont)   assisted working party of H.A.C. to dig retired trench for occupation by men in flooded fire trench.
2/Lt Deney + 3 men to Suffolks & placed in position & fixed 90 yards portable entanglement in front of communication trench between 3rd & 5th Div trenches & superintended digging of communication trench by working party of Suffolks.

Dec 6th   Company paraded at 3.45 a.m. & marched back to billets near CROIX DE POPERINGHE arriving 6 a.m.
During afternoon work on shelters for horses continued.

Dec 7th   Paraded (Coy) at 8.30 a.m. & put up huts near WESTOUTRE. 1 N.C.O & 3 men on shelter for horses.

Dec 8th   Company paraded at 8.00 a.m. & continued construction of huts near WESTOUTRE.
Reinforcement 15 Sappers   1 N.C.O with reinforcements continued with erection of shelter for horses.
3 p.m. Representatives of 8th Brigade instructed in construction & use of rifle grenade

Dec 9th   Company (less 2 N.C.O's & 5 Sappers)
paraded 8·30 a.m. & continued with huts
near WESTOUTRE
2 N.C.O's & 15 Sappers paraded 8·30 a.m.
made thatched panels for shelter for horses

Dec 10th   Lieut Denning with 2 wagons to BAILLEUL
at 7 a.m. for timber nails &c.
Company paraded 8·30 a.m. ½ No 1 section
continued with shelter for horses.
No 2 Section & remainder of No 1
continued with huts near WESTOUTRE

Dec 11th   Company paraded 8·30 a.m. One
half of No 1 & No 2 Sections to continued with
huts.
Remainder finished shelter for horses.

Dec 12th   Company paraded 8 a.m. & made a
siding (30ft corduroy) ½ a mile beyond
WESTOUTRE on the WESTOUTRE-LOCRE
Road.

Dec 13th   Company paraded 8 a.m. continued siding
Returned to billets 2 p.m. & experimented
with two trench mortars.
6 p.m. Lieut. Denning, two N.C.O's & four
men proceeded to KEMMEL

29

Dec 14th — Company paraded 2.30 a.m. and marched to billet near KEMMEL
2/Lt Denny & party paraded at 3.30am & proceeded to trenches with 2 trench mortars for experimental purposes (returned Jan 15th)
Company paraded 3.30pm No 2 to Middlesex trenches with 10 portable wire entanglements — Traverse heightened with sandbags.
Capt Edwards with No 1 Section accompanied Suffolks to trenches where latter relieved Royal Scots. Capt Edwards accompanied O.C. Suffolks on his inspection of position including trench captured from enemy in morning. The left of this trench was connected with our original position by a communication trench dug by Suffolks — No any night work possible owing to enemy fire.

Dec 15th — Morning, Company made 20 portable wire entanglements.
9pm Company marched back to billet near MONT NOIR

Dec 16th — 2nd Lt. Denny & 3 men experimented further with trench mortars.
Company to road running east from

WESTOUTRE (8.30am) + laid 41 yards corduroy –

Dec 17th 7am G.S. Waggon to ARMENTIERES for
Willesden Canvas.
8.30am 2/Lt Dening, 1 NCO + 2 men to BAILLEUL
with trench mortars for alterations;
20 men No 1 Sect. to SCHERPENBERG to
make pathway (corduroy);
Remainder Company to huts near
WESTOUTRE, floors laid in 10 huts,
ridging put on 7 huts, 4 huts painted
or tarred.
1 draught horse received from remounts at
BERTHEN.

Dec 18th 8.30am 2 fitters to BAILLEUL to work
on trench mortars + 2 carpenters to make
range blocks for rifles firing grenades
2pm. company marched to billet near
KEMMEL arriving 4.15 pm.
6.30pm paraded + marked out sites
for 3 Supporting points + continued
work on 2 Saps – (points 73 + 76).

Dec 19th afternoon 8 men constructed wire netting shields
for sap heads
4 pm Sapping continued (3 reliefs, 4 hours
5.30pm. company started each, 5 men each

Dec 19th (ct?)	excavation of 3 supporting points with infantry working parties.
Dec 20th	Afternoon 6 men collected material for casing saps in KEMMEL
	5.15 pm. Company continued work on Saps with infantry working parties —
	4 am. Sapping continued & Saps cased
Dec 21st	Company returned to billet near MONT NOIR at 3.15 am.
Dec 22nd	7.15 am. 1 NCO + 8 men with G.S. Waggon to BAILLEUL loading timber.
	8.30 am Company to WESTOUTRE & repaired 80 yds road
	1.30 pm. 1 NCO + 17 men to BERTHEN for construction of shelter at Sanatorium
	one man all day making rods for rifle-hand grenades —
	Nos 3 & 4 Sections Cheshire Field Co. RE (T). were attached to Comp. Coy —
Dec 23rd	8.30 am Coy. paraded for work on WESTOUTRE — LOCRE road, pavée reinforced for 55 yds
	Bomb mortar fetched from

23rd (cont) BAILLEUL & experimented with
by 2/Lt Doury at 3 p.m., breech
mechanism found unsatisfactory.
Work carried on on bath house
shelter at sanatorium at BERTHEN
20 hand grenades to 57th Coy at
KEMMEL in afternoon.
2 p.m. instruction given to 8th Brigade
representatives by Capt Edwards in
grenades & grenade throwing at
Bde. H.Q., WESTOUTRE.

Dec 24th 7.45 a.m. Cheshire pontoon wagons
to BAILLEUL for timber.
8 a.m. 4 carpenters to BAILLEUL &
made 18 range blocks for rifle
grenade rifles.
8.30 a.m. Company paraded for
work on ~~relaying~~ WESTOUTRE —
— LOCRE road, also No 4 Section
Cheshire R.E. 30 yards corduroy
laid & several depressions in
pavé made good —
No 3 Section Cheshire R.E. started
erection of 2 shelters for themselves —
Work at BERTHEN continued —
2 p.m. further instruction to 8th Bde
representatives in grenades by Capt Edwards

33

Dec 25th   8am 6 carpenters & 2 fitters to BAILLEUL
for work on bomb mortars & bombs.
~~G.S. Waggon to ARMENTIERES for~~
~~Willesden canvas~~
G.S. Waggon to WESTOUTRE for bricks
& on to BERTHEN
8.30 am Company & 1 Section Cheshire
R.E. to WESTOUTRE, 24 yards
corduroy laid & holes in pavé made good
Work at BERTHEN continued.
1 Section Cheshire R.E. continued work on their huts

Dec 26th   8am Lumber Waggon to BAILLEUL
with pipes for bomb mortars.
G.S. Waggon to WESTOUTRE for
bricks & on to BERTHEN (2 journeys).
G.S. Waggon to ARMENTIERES
for Willesden canvas.
8.30 am Company to WESTOUTRE
with 1 Section Cheshire R.E., pavé
reinforced for 40 yards, corduroy
laid for 15 yards & holes in pavé
made good. Model loopholes
made near Bde. H.Q. WESTOUTRE
1 Section Cheshire R.E. continued
work on own huts.
Work at BERTHEN continued.

Dec 27th   2.30 pm Company paraded & marched

Dec 27th to billet near KEMMEL.
(cont.) Paraded 8.30 pm & worked on parallel near right of 3rd Division position & on wire entanglement & overhead cover for supporting points - also parapet of S1. Work at BERTHEN continued -

Dec 28th 8.30 am 1 NCO & 15 men collected material in KEMMEL for overhead cover 5.30 pm. worked on parallel & on supporting points with infantry working party & carrying parties. 1 man killed. Work at BERTHEN continued by 1 NCO & 15 men

Dec 29th 8.30 am 1 NCO & 15 men collected material in KEMMEL for overhead cover, & made knife rest entanglements. 2 pm. company prepared pickets for entanglement & recoiled wire. 5.30 pm worked on parallel which fell in in several places & no progress made in consequence. Work also carried on with infantry working party & carrying parties on entanglements & overhead cover of supporting points & parapet of S1. Work at BERTHEN continued.

also put up 100 yds wire entanglement behind gaps in E Group

Dec 30th 8.30 am 1 NCO & 15 men collected material in KEMMEL for overhead cover

Dec 30th (Cont)	& recoiled wire. 7 pm. work continued on overhead cover for supporting point & wire entanglements with 1 sec 57th Coy, infantry working party & carrying parties. Work continued at BERTHEN.
Dec 31st	Company returned to billet near MONT NOIR at 4.30 am. Work at BERTHEN completed.
1915 Jan 1st	8.30 am Company paraded & worked on WESTOUTRE — LOCRE road. 1 fitter made rods for rifle grenades. 1 Section Cheshire R.E. on road & 1 section putting up own hut & horse shelter.
Jan 2nd	8.30 am Company paraded for work on WESTOUTRE — LOCRE road. G.S. Wagon to BAILLEUL with canvas & back with 3 trench mortars & bombs. 2 fitters making rods for rifle grenades. 1 Section Cheshire R.E. on road & 1 putting up own hut & horse shelter.
Jan 3rd	8.30 am, Company & 1 Section Cheshire R.E. worked on repair to WESTOUTRE — LOCRE road. 1 Section Cheshire R.E. worked on own hut & shelter for horses. G.S. Wagon & 2 Cheshire pontoon wagons to BAILLEUL for timber & then to BERTHEN.

Jan 3rd (cont.) 2 NCO's + 17 men to BERTHEN for erection of hut at Convalescent Depôt
2 fitters making rods for rifle grenades.

Jan 4th 8.30 am 1 Section Cheshire R.E. on repairs to WESTOUTRE - LOCRE road
1 Section Cheshire R.E. on erection of shelter for own horses.
2 fitters making rods for rifle grenades
Work at BERTHEN continued.
2 pontoon waggons to BAILLEUL for timber + then to BERTHEN
Remainder of company on repairs to horse shelter.
1 G.S. Waggon to KEMMEL at 1pm with 5.6" logs + back with windows for huts at BERTHEN

1 NCO + 6 men experimented with trench mortars under Capt Morton R.M.R.E.

Jan 5th Company stood by to move to neighbourhood of LA CLYTTE. Move cancelled.

Jan 6th Company moved at 2.15 pm to billet between SCHERPENBERG + LA CLYTTE
All available officers inspected trenches taken over from French.

Jan 7th In billet between SCHERPENBERG

Jan 7th (cont)   and LA CLYTTE

Jan 8th   8.30 am N°2 Section Composite Coy to
KEMMEL & made 20 Knife rest
entanglements for use of Middlesex
Regt.
N°1 Section Composite Coy & N°4 Section
Cheshire R.E. worked on repairs to
WESTOUTRE — LOCRE road.
Company moved into billet in
LA CLYTTE.
8pm Lt Leitch & 2 men Cheshire RE to
Middlesex HQ to see about repair of
pump in trenches & found latter had
been removed by Suffolks so returned —

Jan 9th   8 am. Company employed on making
pathways, erecting cookhouse shelter &
generally cleaning up billet & putting
it in order. Party from Cheshire RE
worked on drainage of bath house for
8th Brigade in LA CLYTTE.

Jan 10th   8.15 am. Cheshire RE trestle wagon
with loading party of 8 men to BAILLEUL
under Lt Price Jones to procure timber
for seats in bath house —

Jan 10th
(cont.)
12 men breaking road metal for
making good holes in pavé.
12 men on fatigues in billets.
Remainder of company felling timber
& stacking it for use on corduroy
sidings on LA CLYTTE — SCHERPENBERG
road.

2/Lt Dening at 3 am to S5 to report
on field of fire from that work by
daylight, returned 6.30 pm.

Jan 11th
8.30 am. 2 men to HQ 8th Brigade
near VIERSTRAAT to repair window.
12 infantry breaking road metal &
1 NCO & 4 sappers with limber wagon
making good holes in pavé on
LA CLYTTE — SCHERPENBERG Road
12 men erecting septs & working on
drainage of bath house at LA CLYTTE
12 men on fatigues in billets.
Remainder of company with 50 infantry
making corduroy sidings on LA CLYTTE
— SCHERPENBERG road. (30 yards)

39

12th 15 men Cheshire RE. under Capt Maclvor
took down & cut up hop-poles near
LOCRE for corduroy –
No infantry under NCO. [strikethrough]
Composite Coy broke road metal –
Remainder of company made siding on
to road at SCHERPENBERG (50 yards)
(1 NCO. + 8 men loading bricks at
WESTOUTRE).
4 p.m. No 1 Section marched to
KEMMEL to rejoin 56th Coy RE.; No 2.
Section remaining at LA CLYTTE with
3 Sections Cheshire Field Coy RE pending
its absorption by 59th Coy.

*No 1 section
Cheshire RE.
joined at 1pm.

Hd Qrs RE. 3rd Division.

Vol VI. 1-31. 8. 15

War Diary

R.E. Headquarters, III Division

January 1915.

Jan 1st. 56 Coy working on roads and instructing Infantry pioneer class. Compo Coy less one section ditto. 57 Coy with one section from Compo Coy at forward billet near KEMMEL for trench work.

Jan 2nd. Work as yesterday; 1 section 56 Coy replaced Compo Coy Section at KEMMEL. Capt P.B O'Connor accidentally wounded by hand grenade (tomato) while instructing Inf. Pioneers.

Jan 3rd. Work started by Compo Coy on sanatorium at BERTHEN. 3 trench mortars, 75 bombs, 40 trench braces sent out from BAILLEUL (made by working party from the 3 Coys billeted in BAILLEUL under Capt Moulton)

Appendix 'A' Draft of 42 sappers arrived, most unsuitable as regards trades

33

Jan 4th   56th Coy replaced 57th Coy at KEMMEL
         1 section 57th left there to work
         with 56th.
         More trench stores sent up to
         depot at SCHERPENBERG.

Jan 5th   8th Bde took over part of French
         line & billeted in LA CLYTTE, Combro
         Coy were to have billeted there but
         room could not be found for them so
         remained in their old billets.
         Owing to extra line being taken over
         56th & 57th Coys have four days & up
         for trench work & 4 days out while
         Combro Coy remains with 8th Bde
         & will normally have half up for
         trench work & half out for road work
         etc.
         57th Coy had 1 man killed & six wounded
Jan 6th in KEMMEL during daytime.
         Practice with trench mortars, one
         was destroyed by a premature, this
         also damaged one of the other mortars
         slightly.

Jan 6th   Combro Coy billeted at LA CLYTTE when
         [struck through]
         [struck through] BAILLEUL
         [struck through] room had now been found.
         Mortars returned to BAILLEUL for when

34

Jan 7th. Doors made for WESTOUTRE huts.

Jan 8th. 57th Coy relieved 56th Coy at KEMMEL.
4 trench mortars & bombs under Capt
Moreton sent to KEMMEL at night.

Jan 9th. 90 rounds fired from trench mortars
vide Capt. Moretons report.
Appendix New trench mortar and bombs made
"C" in ENGLAND fetched from BAILLEUL

Jan 10th. Trials carried out with home pattern
trench mortar.
Coys working on roads or up in KEMMEL
for trench work.

Jan 11th 1 section of 56th sent up to KEMMEL
to help 57th with supporting from
Pad of Compre & 56 Coys working on
roads.
Capt. G. E. Sopwith joined 56 Coy.

Jan 12th Party working on Trench boxes at BAILLEUL
returned back to their Coys. 139 boxes have
been made & no more Wilkinson canvas
obtainable.
56 relieved 57 at KEMMEL
Compo Coy broken up, one section
returning to its original Coys. Establishments
joined up with those. Lt Jennings &56.

35

Jan 13°   More trials with home pattern
trench mortar. Mortar destroyed
by premature. Report on mortar
attached.

Jan 14°   56 Coy working on S₁, S₂, S₃
supporting points at night.
57 on roads & carrying party.
Cheshires Coy working on roads
and 1 ration with 8 Bde for
work on trenches.

Appendix 'F'   French howitzer from home destroyed by premature.
Jan 15°   Ditto.

Jan 16°   57 Coy relieved 56 Coy at KEMMEL
Capt Nation, Lieuts Dawson, Richards
and Finnimore promoted.
Appendix   Cheshires working on roads.
'G'   Compass by finally broken at. Capt Edwards - L'Dawson & 57½

Jan 17°   57 Coy found it possible to have a
small party of men working by
day at S₁.
Notes from A E Paul taken
direct by Comm Post to KEMMEL
instead of SCHERPENBERG.

— 18°   Trench mortars used on F₂ trenches
Appendix   vide report. Searchlight also used
"H"   vide report.
Appendix
I

36

Jan 19th Timber obtained for new huts at LOCRE. 20 huts to be built. Wood frames about 1'6" above ground level covered with corrugated iron. Ends & sides boarded, floor dug out about 1 foot & boarded over. 20' x 15' Cheshires at this work assisted by infantry carpenters & working party.

Jan 20 56 Coy relieved 57 Coy at KEMMEL. Sappers sent to supporting points to remain there during the four days tour of duty to keep them in good repair. Sandbags filled with brick being used at many places for parapets. 57 Coy

Jan 21st 56 Coy working on supporting points and trenches. 57 Coy on roads and assisting Cheshires with carpenters on huts at LOCRE.

Jan 22nd Work as yesterday. Lieut J. A. LEVEN-THORPE killed while constructing machine gun emplacement at E.1. C.E. II before visited some of the trenches and supporting points.

37

Jan 23 Work as yesterday

Jan 24 57' relieve 56' at KEMMEL
        work carried on.

Jan 25 Same work as before except that
        part of 56' Coy was employed on
        concrete bed for 9.2" howitzer
        at BROOZE.

Jan 26 Work as yesterday

Jan 27 57 relieved 57' at KEMMEL
            5-6

Jan 28 2 trench mortars under Capt Willis went
        up to F.4. before daylight. After about
        10 rounds, 1 trench mortar burst &
        so damaged the other in doing so that
        both it was rendered useless. A faulty
        detonator is thought to be the cause
        of the premature.

Jan 29 Positions for machine guns in
        neighbourhood of E, finally decided.
        Owing to frost work could not be started
        on the new positions
        LOCRE huts completed.

Jan 30   56° Coy did a certain amount
of work on 2nd line. Checkurs
still working on roads & carrying
hop poles for wiring. Our
gang working on WESTOUTRE
- MONT NOIR also asking for train
for same purpose.

Jan 31st 56° Coy relieved by 59° Coy.
         2nd Lieut A D PANK joined
         56° Coy.

The following Appendices are
attached.

Appendix 'A' Complaint re trades of new
                drafts.

Appendix 'B' Report on 'Blastine'

— " — 'C' Report of trench mortar action
            in trenches under Capt Macelwee RMRE

— " — 'D' Report on desirability of
            forming Divisional Bridging
            train from equipment of
            Div. Field Coys.

Appendix 'E' Report on mechanical trays lighters

— . — 'F' Report on 3".7 trench howitzer sent out from home.

— . — 'G' Disbandment of Composite Field Coy.

— . — 'H' Report of trench mortars in action under Capt Willes.

— . — 'I' Report on 14" (oxy acetylene) Field searchlight

— . — 'J' Report on necessity of CRE having two 3 ton lorries.

— . — 'K' Report hand grenade, double cylinder

— . — 'L' General report on trench mortars

— . — 'M' Application for Cheshire F'd Coy to be authorized to draw two more double tool carts to complete.

9-2-15.

G. Willes
Capt RE
Adj & Sub'ty
for CRE

Copy

Appendix "A"

III Division

I have the honour to forward the following complaint as to the composition of the reinforcing draft of 42 men which from No 3 General Base Depot today. II Corps wire D832 of 18.10.14. laid down a suggested proportion of trades for reinforcing drafts for Field Companies R E which was concurred in at the time, and no further action has accordingly been taken in asking for men of particular trades.

In the draft referred to there is not a single carpenter, mason or smith, while over a third are of absolutely useless trades Photographers Printers, Surveyors etc who will probably be quickly knocked up by the hard manual labour demanded from the Field Companies, or a superfluity of comparatively useless trades such as engine drivers painters etc.

The draft appears to be made up without any attempt to comply with what was suggested by A G- GHQ in the above quoted wire, and without any reasonable intelligent anticipation of the Field Companies requirements.

I should be glad if Steps could be taken to ensure a reasonable proportion of the really useful trades especially carpenters in future drafts as otherwise the general utility and efficiency of the Field Companies must be seriously impaired.

3-1-15

Sgd. S.S. Wilson Lt Col.
C R E
III Division

Copy Appendix "B"

III Division

With reference to ii. Caps O 6359 I ...
... E in bombs for French
... very safe explosive will not
... low, and does not catch
... ges in which it is made
... make it a very convenient
... aking up charges. Its
... guncotton in these bombs.
... is not so violent he
... I think it is quite
... like to have some more
... arly used up the original

... d. L S Wilson Lt Col
      C R E
         III Division

About Blastine.
It is said here not to
detonate by a violent
blow (but it does to
as a matter of fact from
the impact of a bullet)

E...
7/4

Copy   Appendix "B"

III Division

With reference to II Corps O 6359 I have now tried BLASTINE in bombs for Trench Mortars. It seems a very safe explosive will not detonate by a violent blow, and does not catch fire easily. The cartridges in which it is made up and its consistency make it a very convenient form of explosive for making up charges. Its effect seems superior to guncotton in these bombs as though the detonation is not so violent the effect appears greater. I think it is quite successful, and would like to have some more supplied as I have nearly used up the original 100 lbs.

                          sgd. G. S. Wilson Lt. Col
                          C.R.E.
5.1.14   III Division

"A" Form.
Army Form C. 2121.

MESSAGES AND SIGNALS.

| Prefix | Code | m. | Words | Charge | of Message |

Office of Origin and Service Instructions.

Sent
At
To
By

TO CRE

Sender's Number   Day of Month

Jun

I went
with 4 trench
wet and muddy.
The parapet is
being made so,
and is being done
traversed. Trench
I used
about 90 rounds.
bombs failed to
I then stopped fir
about an hour
During the day
parties in the Ger
and one at 250 —
bomb was dropped

From
Place
Time

The above may be forwarded as now corrected

3662 M. & Co. Ltd. Wt. W929/519—100,000. 6/14

Trench mortar
See also Appendix F.
and L.
7/4

"A" Form.

MESSAGES AND SIGNALS.

Prefix	Code	Words	Charge		
Office of Origin and Service Instructions		Sent At ___ m. To ___ By ___	*This message is on a/c of:* ___ (Signature of "Franking Officer.")	Service	Date ___ From ___ By ___

TO — CRE III Division

Sender's Number | Day of Month: Jun 10th | In reply to Number | **AAA**

I went up to F2 yesterday with 4 trench mortars. I found F2 wet and muddy but draining fairly well. The parapet is not bullet proof but is being made so, and a lot of work has been and is being done in the trench, it is well traversed. Trench boxes are needed.

I used the 4 guns all day and fired about 90 rounds. During a heavy storm four bombs failed to detonate owing to wet fuze. I then stopped firing and started again after about an hour and had no more failures. During the day I saw three separate working parties in the German lines, two at about 150x and one at 250–300 yards. In the first one bomb was dropped, in the second two and in

From ___
Place ___
Time ___

The above may be forwarded as now corrected. (Z)

Censor ___ Signature of Addressor or person authorised to telegraph in his name
This line should be erased if not required.

"A" Form.
MESSAGES AND SIGNALS.
Army Form C. 2121.

the third three. These last three were fired simultaneously and burst practically together, one in the trench and two on the parapet on which the men were standing. Work in all three cases was suspended and did not start again. The German trench had a thick lattice work fence in front and I destroyed a long length of this together with the parapet. The mean error of shooting I judged to be at the most 10 yards either in front or behind, but the great majority of shots were direct hits. One man was seen in a house (ruined) two shots were fired one through the roof and one through the door-way, both burst well inside. No trouble occurred owing to length of firing fuze, the shots all exploding well

"A" Form. Army Form C. 2121.
MESSAGES AND SIGNALS.

Prefix	Code	m.	Words	Charge	This message is on a/c of :	Reed. at	m.
			Sent			Date	
Office of Origin and Service Instructions.			At	m.	Service.	From	
			To				
			By		(Signature of "Franking Officer.")	By	

TO — (3.

| Sender's Number | Day of Month | In reply to Number | AAA |

and usually on graze. I have given orders for two alterations in gun-platform – spikes should be longer and bolted on as the screws came out, and secondly I have given orders for a traversing arrangement to give about an inch play on each side. It is a simple one, but greatly needed owing to the difficulty of moving guns slightly and not losing a good bed when found. 2nd Corporal Halewood 57th Coy. and Cap: Otton Compo: Coy: thoroughly understand the working of these mortars and the latter has done especially good work both in workshops and in the trench. I should like to report that the 27th Division are now using our bomb-shop to work in, and there is not room for all.

From
Place   S. Thonton
Time   Capt R.E.

The above may be forwarded as now corrected. (Z)

Censor. Signature of Addressor or person authorised to telegraph in his name
*This line should be erased if not required.
9662 M. & Co. Ltd. Wt. W929/549–100,000. 6/14. Forms C2121/10.

Appendix "D"
Copy

C.E. 1; Corps

With reference to 2nd Corps the detaching of the Pontoons and Trestle Wagons from the Field Companies to form a Divisional Bridging Train is a reform I have long been in favour of.

The bridging wagons are a great nuisance to a Field Co, as they cannot move with them, but have to march with the Train or Divisional Ammunition Column, and if they have to move up at the end of the day's march it will be some time before they find their own Unit, and the next day they have to be left behind to join up again with the Train as best they can. — This leads to both personnel and equipment being badly looked after.

In this Division the Pontoons etc have been attached to the Divisional Ammunition Column, who have looked after the personnel, as an Officer could not be spared from the Field Companies. But it is hardly fair to ask Officers of other arms, who have their own work to do, to do this. Still the system has worked well, and the Pontoons have always been on the spot when wanted, as they can easily be sent up, and it is difficult to imagine a case in which their possible use could not be foreseen in time.

Now that we have three field Companies, the size of the Bridging Train warrants an Officer to look after it, and with the   work that is thrown on the Field Company Officers, it will be very difficult to spare one. I think therefore that a small additional personnel should be asked for and the unit duly authorized and formed. Three extra Officers will be invaluable to the C.R.E. for use as Field Engineers, and looking after the large number of services that at once requires carrying out behind the actual fighting line whenever the force halts.

I would suggest the formation of a unit as shown in the attached table, where I have suggested how the personnel should be provided distinguishing what can be formed from the Companies and what will have to be provided additional.

DIVISIONAL BRIDGING TRAIN
Proposed Establishment

Personnel	Established 17th Fd	Found from Companies Dis-mntd	A Co	B Co	C Co	To be provided Extra	Total	Remarks
Captain	1	–	–	–	–	1	1	
Lieutenant	1	–	–	–	–	1	1	
a/ C.S.M.	–	1	1	–	–	–	1	The 5th sergeant from A. Co.
a/ C.Q.M.S.	1	–	–	1	–	–	1	Mounted sergeant from B. Co.
2nd a/ds Corporals	3	1	1	1	2	–	4	2nd Cpl from C Coy dismounted.
Sappers	–	12	4	4	4	–	12	4 batmen, cook, cook's mate & wheeler.
Drivers for vehicles	28	–	10	9	9	–	28	
" span	2	–	–	1	1	–	2	
" Batmen	3	–	–	–	–	3	3	
Shoeing & Carriage Smith	1	–	–	–	–	1	1	
Attached { ASC	2	–	–	–	–	2	2	For water cart & supply wagon.
{ RAMC	2	–	–	–	–	2	2	For water cart.
					2 officers	& 56 men		

Horses

	Established	Dis-mntd	A Co	B Co	C Co	Extra	Total	Remarks
Riders	8	–	1	1	1	5	8	3 officers chargers, 1 rider each for a/C.Q.M.S., shoeing smith & 3 mounted L/e Corporals.
Draught	56	–	18	18	18	2	56	2 for cook's cart.
" span	3	–	1	1	1	–	3	
Attached from A.S.C.	4	–	–	–	–	–	4	For water cart & supply wagon.
						Horses	71	

Vehicles

	Established		A Co	B Co	C Co	Extra	Total	Remarks
Bridging wagons	9	–	3	3	3	–	9	
Cook's cart	1	–	–	–	–	1	1	
Attached (water cart	1	–	–	–	–	1	1	
from ASC (supply wagon	1	–	–	–	–	1	1	
						Vehicles	12	

* As it is very undesirable to take mounted NCOs from the limited establishment of the Field Companies if it can possibly be avoided, it would be advisable that the 3 mounted Lance Corporals & their horses should also be provided extra.

10.1.15.

Copy   Appendix "E"

C E II Corps

Mechanical Fuze Lighter

Two types of mechanical fuze lighter have been received:-

-a- NOBEL'S This is simple safe and apparently certain, it is easily attached worked in the dark and would appear to fulfil every requirement

-b- BICKFORD'S It is simple and certain, it has the great disadvantage of requiring a special pair of pliers to set it off & not being self-contained. There would also appear to be some risk of setting it off if it has to be nipped on to the fuze ready for carrying

Mechanical fuze lighters have long been badly wanted for the equipment of field units. I would recommend that NOBEL'S pattern be adopted and a supply of 200 carried by each Field Company and a proportionate amount for other Field units R E and the Cavalry

               -sgd- C S Wilson Lt Col
                     C R E
                        II Division

12-1-15

Copy

Appendix F

III Division

The 3.7 inch M.L. French Howitzer received from ENGLAND was destroyed to-day by a premature after about 25 rounds had been fired.

The Howitzer is of a very similar pattern to those we have made locally, but being made at the ARSENAL is of much better finish.

The defects of the design are as follows:-

1. The howitzer is very inaccurate, as much as 100 yds variation was found in the range using the same charge, the same elevation and under the same weather conditions. This is due to the excessive windage. In our local pattern the windage is much less and much less variation of range is observed, generally rounds are within 10 yds of one another.

2. The vent is too far forward in the powder chamber, with the result that the charge cannot be pricked after the bomb is loaded as detailed in the instructions, and the vent sealing fuze does not always in consequence ignite the charge, as apparently the fuze plug of the bomb comes under the vent. The destruction of the Howitzer was due to this cause, the firing fuze did not light the charge but did light the bomb fuze with the result of a premature.

3. The bomb fuze projects too far from the plug and is occasionally cut by the discharge with the result of a premature sometimes close to the muzzle. This has been remedied in the local pattern by doing away with the wooden

plug. The detonator & fuze cut to length is inserted in the bomb and coiled in the plug hole, so that only a quarter of an inch projects through a tin plate used to cover the hole. The hole is stopped with putty or mud, the end of the fuze placed in a hole in the tin plate & the plate secured. Since this method has been adopted no prematures from this cause have occurred.

4. The carriage is very unsteady and needs resetting after each round, and the quadrant is very clumsy. If it is intended as I gather from the instructions to always fire at an elevation of 45° it would be better to have a carriage with a good base which would take the gun at this angle. The base can be set up quite level enough by eye. The best range results are however obtained with the howitzer at elevation of 40° or 50°.

-sgd- C. S. Wilson Lt Col
C.R.E
III Division

13-1-15

Copy   Appendix "9"

Draft for Routine Orders

The Composite Field Company will be broken up on the 16th inst. sections re-joining their original companies.

Its place will be taken by the Cheshire Field Company, which will be affiliated to the 8th Infantry Brigade.

            sgd. L.S. Wilson Lt Col.
                C R E
                III Division.

14=1=15.

Appendix "H"

C.R.E.

Report on use of Trench mortars in F2 on 18-1-15.

1st round was fired at 7.20 AM, target being German trench (straight to front of F2) on the parapet of which a shovel had just been seen in use. A salvo of 4 mortars was then fired at the same spot. The shovel appearing & disappearing over the crest of the parapet was the only movement seen in the German lines during the day. The front German trench was searched with bombs to the right to the ruined house which was well plastered inside & out.

As our own artillery started to pay attention to this ruined house, I worked back along the trenches in front of F2 firing bombs in pairs throughout.

Early in the day there was a premature which blew one mortar to bits & temporarily damaged another. This premature was due to (I consider after investigations) the fact that the time fuze in the bomb had not been bent at all so that the shock in the zinc plated came direct over detonation thus making a straight flash up time fuze in detonator.

54 bombs were fired of which 2 were blind. Apparently trench mortars were located by enemy as shell fire was opened on the trenches early in the afternoon and parapet struck three times without doing any damage. During shell fire, trench mortars were not fired & after discussing question with O.C. trench, I decided not to open fire again.

It was of course impossible to see whether any real damage was being done to enemy trenches, but the shooting appeared to be fairly accurate & there was no doubt that some of the bombs dropped into fire trenches or communicating trenches. A traversing gear would greatly facilitate working of the mortars. A periscope is almost essential as it enables steady observations to be made.

19-1-15.

G. A. Mills
Capt RE

Copy   Appendix I

III Division

Report on 14in (Oxy acetylene) Portable Field Searchlight

The light was first of all tried in billets, where it was found from near the light some 200 yards could be seen, but an observer 200 yds in front of the light could see about 200 yds. The beam was very small, and had a good deal of diffused light surrounding it.

From this experience a position was selected about 180 yds behind the fire trenches and an emplacement constructed for the light, the total distance to the enemy's trenches being from 350 to 400 yds.

The emplacement was concealed by an old French trench a little in front.

Some men stated they saw a German working party, and opened fire, but others stated they could see nothing.

An attempt to control the light by flashlight from the trenches was made, but was not successful. From the light itself it was quite impossible to control it, or see what was happening.

There was a slight mist on both occasions it was tried which was of course against the light.

The old trench in front of the emplacement was lit up by the diffused light of the beam & was struck 3 or 4 times by rifle bullets.

The conclusions come to were:—

The light should not be more than 300 yds away, this necessitates it being very close to or in the fire trenches, this is I think inadmissable as at such short range the light will probably get knocked out at once, and the diffused light from the beam would show up the trenches and draw fire

If the light is behind the trenches as it should be, some form of communication with the trenches by telephone or buzzer is essential, as though you can signal back with a flashlight you cannot signal forward

The beam is rather too small for any practicable purpose—

What appears to be wanted is a larger and more powerful beam, which could be set up some 300 yards behind the trenches, and would illuminate objects for the men in the trenches 300 yds away. The diffused light round the concentrated beam should be got rid of if possible

Further trials will be made on a quite clear night when one is to be found. The apparatus appears to be altogether too gimcrack to stand the work in the trenches, and will be very difficult to keep clean and in working order, even carrying it in a springless cart necessitated several slight repairs before it could work.

It is fairly portable, it took six men to carry it and they could, owing to the heavy ground, only go very slowly and with frequent halts, it is rather high and conspicuous and might easily be seen as it is being carried up by the light of star shells etc, as turning it hurriedly on to its side on the

3

ground is likely to lead to damage.

The whole apparatus strikes me as being too much of a toy and I do not recommend any further provision until more extensive trials have been made.

I think the provision of an electric light mounted on a small motor car whose engines could drive the dynamo would be much more useful. There should be no difficulty in getting a site for this some 100 yds or so from the trenches, its safety depending on a constant shift of position every time it was used. In any case these lights should be used sparingly and with caution.

Special R.E. personnel should be provided with each light. 4 men are required with this one.

23-1-1915.

(sgd) L S Wilson Lt Col
C R E
III Division

Copy   Appendix 'J'

III Division

With the absolute necessity of the C.R.E being provided with at least 2 Thornton lorries being brought forward

At present these are required every day, often I want five or six, and the only method of obtaining them at present is to go round begging.

As a rule at present I get two lorries by favour of Camp Commandant at BAILLEUL nearly every day and sometimes can borrow from II Corps Signals but these lorries have to return to BAILLEUL every day and much time is lost in going and coming, and orders as to when and where they are wanted have to be sent there. Besides the road work, there are always stores of sorts to be fetched, and they would be very fully employed if I got them. On the march they would carry the Sandbags and barbed wire which are often wanted at a minutes notice in action, at present I have one county cart told off for this which is utterly inadequate

I regard the provision of 2 lorries for the R.E of each Division as quite essential. The present conditions impose a very severe hardship on the carrying out of any work, which owing to the difficulty of getting Stores is absolutely already sufficiently hard to get done in reasonable time

31-1-15   sgd. C.S. Wilson Lt Col
                                           C.R.E
                                           III Division

Copy.   Appendix "K"

III Division

Report on Grenade, Double Cylinder.

Except for its weight which is nearly double & rather better finish this appears to be identical with the extemporised jam pot grenades I had made and used successfully at YPRES. It has the same disadvantage that it requires a time fuze to be lighted thus practically ruling out its use in any small adventure such as crawling up and bombing an enemy saphead or trench, as the light even if a mechanical fuze lighter is used will give the men away.

It has the further very serious disadvantage of weight though of course this increases its man killing power. An ordinary man will with difficulty throw it 30 yds. and the pieces can wound at 40 to 50 yds. anyone using it must therefore must get under cover, its use is therefore very restricted, as it could not be used against an attack without very nearly as much risk to the men standing up and using their rifles as to the enemy.

If made light so that it can be thrown 30 to 40yds. it would be useful in case the supply of percussion hand grenades giving out, but it is so very easily & quickly extemporised, that I think the special manufacture & supply of them is quite unnecessary.

(sgd) G.S. Wilson Lt Col
C R E
III Division

23-1-15

P.A. Trench Mortar

Appendix L

III Division

With reference to 2d Army G 711. The Trench Mortars used in the 3d Division have, except for minor differences, been practically of the same type as the 3.7 M.L. Trench Howitzer. Whilst these have produced good results in action against the enemy's trenches, they can in their present state only be regarded as rather dangerous playthings. As an extempore makeshift, which has been made with some difficulty and scanty appliances in the field, they may pass muster, but they are very far from fulfilling requirements, and should be greatly improved before they are standardized.

The use of Trench Mortars is, I take it, to carry out work which cannot be done by the Artillery owing to the proximity of the enemy's trenches or some such reason, what is required is a Trench Mortar fulfilling the following conditions.

Weight Each component part should be readily portable by one man & should therefore not exceed 30 lbs.

Range 50 to 300 yds.

Charge Smokeless powder.

Bomb At least a 10 lb bomb, with a possibility of using a double bomb. This has been tried with the present pattern and is quite feasible.

Carriage should have a firm platform, it was found a wooden platform with spikes to stick in the ground was very suitable, the iron legs of the existing pattern shift when firing necessitating relaying after every round.

The mortar should be reasonably accurate, and safe enough to stand up to it when serving it.

As far as the gun is concerned there should be no difficulty in making a 5in mortar within the weight, nor if it is made breech loading as far as the charge is concerned, in using smokeless powder & percussion lock, which

2.

? will do away with the present great disadvantages caused by the smoke of discharge and also from the safety fuze at present used to fire it.

: The present type of mortar appears quite safe as far as the gun itself is concerned, the whole cause of failure lies in the bomb. This has two great faults. The projecting length of fuze is apt to be cut on discharge, causing a premature often very soon after leaving the muzzle. This however has been remedied by protecting the fuze with a tin cap. The service safety fuze is also hardly reliable enough for this purpose. Secondly there is a liability to a premature at the moment of discharge, which destroys the mortar, this was at first thought to be due to the flash of discharge reaching the detonator, careful measures to obviate this were taken and some 150 rounds were fired without any accident, but since then under precisely similar circumstances and cause two more prematures have occurred, and I am inclined to believe the fault may lie with an occasional extra sensitive detonator which will not stand the shock of discharge.

This liability to accident necessitates very considerable care in the use of trench mortars, which means that unless special emplacements are made every time, the trench has to be cleared for some 15 to 20 yds on each side, so that a mortar in action takes up 30 to 40 yds of trench, which is often impossible to get, whilst if emplacements have to be made, their utility is limited, as they cannot readily be moved from place to place to reach another target or to avoid drawing shell fire by always firing from the same spot. It also necessitates their being handled by technical troops (R.A and R.E) whereas it is most desirable that infantry should be able to use them, as occasional rounds may be most useful in dispersing a working party, or stopping sniping. For any more important work such as the regular bombardment of a trench by a battery should be available to be sent up to the trenches with a regularly trained personnel either RA or RE, or specially trained infantry.

So far 8 Trench Mortars have been used in this Division and between 300 & 400 rounds fired, with the result that 7 have been put out of action.

The causes of failure were:

1. The 3.7 M.L. Trench Howitzer made in England. Premature due to charge not igniting whilst the bomb forged ahead, the cause of this was that the vent was too far forward, the bombs had to be moved in the barrel to allow the charge to be pricked.

2.3.4.5. Local pattern. Prematures at first thought to be due to the flash of discharge reaching the detonator, but now thought to be possibly due to too sensitive detonator.

6.7. Local pattern. Damaged beyond repair by the neighbouring mortar being burst by a premature.

I am now experimenting with a breech loader, for smokeless powder and a safer arrangement of bomb which will I hope prove a success.

So far I do not think the present pattern justifies any standardization at present, but its results have most undoubtedly shown that a larger and safer pattern would be an extremely valuable and useful weapon.

30-1-15

[signature]
CRE III Division

Copy. Appendix "M"

III Division

The CHESHIRE FIELD COMPANY - R.E. on arrival here was found to have been equipped with 2 G.S. Wagons in lieu of 2 double Tool carts.

The Officer Commanding was at once instructed to demand 2 Tool Carts, but has been informed that they cannot be issued without the authority of the DIRECTOR OF TRANSPORT.

As these G.S. Wagons, which have only a quarter lock, are quite unfitted in every way for use as tool carts, being difficult to turn in a confined space, impossible to get across country, and too conspicuous to accompany the men on advanced guard duties &c, may the question be strongly represented and the necessary authority obtained for the issue of two double Tool carts to complete the proper equipment of this unit.

31-1-15

-sgd- C.S. Wilson Lt Col
C.R.E.
III Division

121/4664.

H.Q. 2nd R.E. 3rd Division

Vol VII 1 – 28.2.15

40

War Diary
R E Headquarters.
III Division
February 1915.

Feb 1st. Lt Col G D Close RE 13 Div joined RE Hd Qrs for 4 days. Major Wolff R E 72nd Fld Coy joined 57 Coy for 4 days at KEMMEL
Road maintenance behind approx 2nd Line handed over to 2nd Corps.

Feb 2nd. Owing to 5 divisions making use of timber yard at BAILLEUL, timber scarce a search was made for another timber yard but there are none within 20 miles of KEMMEL

Append "A" — Handle-less hand grenades with Carlos trued

Feb 3rd. 57 Coy working on supporting points. 56 Coy fitting up boring plant for trial doing pontoon drill. 1 section on 9.2" howitzer bed.

Feb 4. Lt Col Close & Major Wolff left for home. 2nd Lieut A.R.R. Woods joined 56 Coy RE 57 Coy relieved by 56 at KEMMEL
1 Sect 57 billetted at LACLYTTE to work on wire entanglements 2nd Line on misty days & on huts on clear days.

41

Feb 5 2012 sheets of corrugated iron received
at BAILLEUL station & sent out
to site for the 50 new huts at
LA CLYTTE
56 Coy relieved 57 Coy at KEMMEL
Support trench for g₁ + g₂ machine guns, also
fire trench between K + J₃ also work on S₄(a)
1 Section 57 left at LA CLYTTE in wiring 2nd line.

Feb 6 56 Coy as yesterday, also working on
2nd line trenches.
57 carrying out work with boring
machine

Feb 7 Experiments tried with fresh pattern
of trench mortar which is fired by
trigger + cap. Breech loader as regards
charge which is put in ordinary
12 bore cartridge case. Smokeless powder
tried without success.
Party of 57 Coy working at saw mill
in BAILLEUL cutting up timber (⅞")
for flooring LA CLYTTE huts.

— 8" Further supply of nails purchased.
— 9" 57 relieved 56 Coy. 1 section of
56 left at LA CLYTTE to carry on
wiring of 2nd line

February [?] [?] 56 [?]
KEMMEL
Feb 10" 57" Coy working in firing line
         + on second line
         56" Coy - 1 section wiring 2nd line
         remainder at pontoon drill, hut
         building + [?] wood repairs

Feb 11" Work as before. Concrete for 9.2"
         howitzer laid. 56" Coy carried out
         experiments with rifle rest and
         "[?]scope"
         More boiler piping for trench mortars obtained

Feb 12" 56" Coy conducted experiments
         with wiring machine.
Append   Work as yesterday
  'C'
         Feb 13" 56" Coy relieved 57" at KEMMEL
         the latter Coy leaving 1 section at
         LA CLYTTE for wiring 2nd line.
         Cheshire F[?]y working on fire
         trenches (1 section) and on new
         huts at LA CLYTTE as usual.

Feb 14" 56" Coy managed to work on 5.5 during
         day. Other Coys building at
         LA CLYTTE and LOCRE

43

Feb 15 — Nights recently very dark
rendering night work on trenches
& supporting points difficult and
slow.
Work as on previous days

Feb 16 — Work as yesterday, in addition
pursuers made for road & bed for
15" howitzer. WESTOUTRE huts
covered with paper.

Feb 17 — 56" Coy returned from KEMMEL
and 57" went up, but owing to
9" Bde leaving Dvermen, 7" Bde
remained in trenches so 56" Coy
went back to KEMMEL and 57"
returned to MONT NOIR.

Feb 18 — Work on supporting points, 2nd line
and huts at LA CLYTTE and
LOCRE.

Feb 19 — Work as yesterday.
Huts for 1 battalion finished at
LA CLYTTE. 4 huts and mess hut—
for officers to be erected therein.

44

Feb 20   Work as yesterday
         Lieut Seabrooke joined 57 Coy

Feb 21" Work as yesterday
         New trench mortar from HARVE
         tried.
         Capt Dawson left 57 Coy for 23rd Coy
         2nd Lieut N.D.R. Hunter joined 57 Coy

Feb 22nd 57 Coy relieved 56 Coy. The latter
         leaving 1 section at LA CLYTTE
         Work on :- Front line, supporting
         points, wiring 2nd Line, huts at
         LA CLYTTE, LOCRE, & making
         fascines for bed for 15" howitzer
         Lieut Seabrooke left 57 Coy for 1st works

Feb 23" Work as yesterday.
         Morning cases got from R.E. Park
         3 trench mortars completed at
         bomb factory at BAILLEUL.

— 24'   Work as yesterday except 2 sections
         of 56 Coy got in some pontoon
         drill

— 25'   Replacing of straw huts at
         SCHERPENBERG started. Another
         20 huts started on LOCRE-BAILLEUL
         road

Feb 26ᵗʰ Experiments carried out with
Arnaud Ammonal.
56 Coy relieved 57 at KEMMEL
Work on reserve trenches & on S, S₂ S₃

Feb. 27ᵗʰ 56 Coy work as yesterday. Cheshire
Field Coy working on front trenches
and huts at SCHERPENBERG.
57 Coy working on huts at LOCRE and
carrying out experiments with
ammonal

Feb. 28ᵗʰ New trench started across angle
of G trenches.
Party of infantry from 85ᵗʰ Bde
started training in pioneer work
Experiments carried out with
new bomb for trench mortar. Fuze
is in fund of bomb & converted by
instantaneous & time fuze through
bomb. Results satisfactory
Lieut C G Martin D.S.O. joined
56 Coy.

10-3-15

G.H.Wells
Capt & Adj R.E.
III Divl Engineers

Appendices War Diary
February 1915

Append A Report on service pattern hand
              grenades without handles

   —   B. question of R.S.M. for Divl
              Engineers

   —   C   Report on horizontal boring
              plant

                                    [signature]

Copy   Appendix A

III Division

With reference to II Corps O.b.7 of 24-1-15.
The 6 Grenades in question have been drawn and tried

They can be thrown and used at very much the same distance as the regulation grenade with cane handle, but require very good footing & room to swing, they are therefore quite unsuited for trench work, as in a properly constructed trench there would be no room to swing the grenade, and any attempt to do so would be very dangerous, If not swung the grenade can only be thrown a very short way, it is also not so ~~economical~~ convenient to carry as the handled grenade. I very much prefer the handled pattern and can find no advantage in this pattern who adoption I do not recommend.

(sgd) C S Wilson Lt Col
C R E
8-2-15   III Division

Copy   Appendix B

III Division

Now that there are 3 Field Coys allotted to a Division I should be glad if the question of a Regimental Staff could be taken up – at present the O.C. Divisional Engineers has none except an Engineer Clerk and the want of a responsible Warrant or N.C. Officer is severely felt. Promotion to Warrant rank is very difficult for the S.M's of the Companies as there are hardly any appointments open and I should recommend that the Divisional Engineers should have a Sergeant Major who should be a mounted man – He would be of the greatest assistance to the C.R.E. and would give a much needed impetus to the promotion available to the men of the companies. I would recommend that the Establishment of the Headquarters Divisional Engineers should be increased by 1 Warrant Officer (Mounted)
                Regt Sergt Major
                1 Riding Horse
                1 Driver (Batman to R.S.M.)

                    sgd. L. L. Wilson, Col.
                    C.R.E. III Division

Report on Boring Plant
unsatisfactory

bored in 8 days, an average rate of 2 ft per day of 8 hours, a fitter who has had experience of boring plants was in charge.

There was no difficulty in boring and lining the first 8 feet, after that it was found very difficult to work, the pipe augur had to be withdrawn after every few inches, and finally the screw augur had to be used. A small piece apparently of soft sandstone was struck about 14 ft in and held up the boring a whole day before it could be got through.

A length of 9 to 10 ft was found necessary to work the plant, so that if used in a trench a recess would have to be made and blinded.

A firm base to the rig is essential, at least 5' x 4' otherwise the rig is apt to tilt back and the base gets out of line.

The pipe augur appears to be of particularly bad design, a small hard stone met with in the bore will effectually stop it.

Only one jack is supplied, two are required for drawing the pipes.

In thick clay soil, I doubt its being possible to bore much over 30 ft with this apparatus.

Copy   Appendix D'C

C E

II Corps

I have to report as follows on the earth boring plant.

The plant was erected and boring started in a stiff clay soil. 16 ft has been bored in 8 days an average rate of 2 ft per day of 8 hours. a Sapper who has had experience of boring plants was in charge.

There was no difficulty in boring and lining the first 8 feet, after that it was found very difficult to work, the pipe auger had to be withdrawn after every few inches, and finally the screw auger had to be used. A small piece apparently of soft sandstone was struck about 14 ft in and held up the boring a whole day before it could be got through.

A length of 9 to 10 ft was found necessary to work the plant, so that if used in a trench a recess would have to be made and blinded.

A firm base for the rig is essential at least 5′ × 4′ otherwise the rig is apt to tilt back and the base gets out of line.

The pipe auger appears to be of particularly bad design, a small hard stone met with in the bore will effectually stop it.

Only one jack is supplied, two are required for drawing the pipes.

In this clay soil, I doubt it being possible to bore much over 30 ft with the apparatus.

2

The apparatus requires men experienced in boring work to get any result

The whole process is desperately slow, much slower than ordinary mining would be

Boring 1 ft — 1 hr to 1½ hrs

Taking blast adrift and cleaning drill ½ hr to 1 hr

Fixing blast ready for drilling ½ hr

Driving tube about 1 hr to ½ ft

i.e. it takes about 4 hours to bore a line 1 ft This time will be very considerably increased as the bore increases in depth.

The plant has been given a very fair trial, in soil such as would be met with in the trenches and the opinion I have come to is that it is utterly useless for any purpose in the trenches here

Possibly it might be useful in a very light sandy soil or in sand, but in clay it is a failure

I should be glad of instructions as to the disposal of the apparatus, as I have no use for it

E. S. Wilson Col
C.R.E. W. Div.

15/5/15

Hd. Qrs. RE. 3rd Division.

Vol VIII 1 - 31. 3. 15.

War Diary

R.E. Headquarters
III Division

March 1915

March 1st 57' Coy relieved 55' Coy at KEMMEL
Major J.J.H. Nation O.C. 56' Coy at present
on leave is to remain at home as B.M. S.M.E.
56 Coy working on G trenches & on
reserve line

March 2nd Timber for 2' x 3' cases and
12" x 2" sheeting obtained
for mining purposes
Class for pioneers of 85' Bde. Officers
of 85 Bde instructed in grenade throwing
Halting at LOCRE. Work on reserve trenches
G & F trenches

March 3rd 1000x of support trench dug to 6"
deep by night to mark it for
infantry working parties the following
night

March 4th. 2 Officers (2nd Lieuts. Musgrove 6th Bn. KOYLI and H.C.B. Ackhleny R.E) with 14 sappers and motor lorry joined Divl Engineers being part of 172nd Coy R.E (mining) Attached to 5th Coy for time being.
No organisation, no warning of the arrival of this party.
57th relieved 56th at forward billet

— 5th Men selected as under to join 172nd Coy for mining purposes
23 Royal Scots
13 South Lancs
4 Worcesters.
172nd Coy moved to billets in KEMMEL & party went up to commence mine from G.1
1 section 56 Coy out to put out infantry working parties onto 2nd line of supporting trenches and then marked out 3rd line of supporting trenches 6" deep.

— 6th Trench mortar class for 1 Officer and four men from each of infantry Battns started under adjutant.
Old pattern mortars out. New ones from England arrived but no ammunition
Major Barnediston joined & took command of 56th Coy. Work as yesterday. the 4th line of support trenches dug out to 6"

49

March 7th Coys worked as follows
  56 by 3 sections on stables & two
  new huts. 1 section wiring reserve
  line.
  57 by. Marking out & supervising digging of
  new trenches by infantry. Breaking out saps
  Chatham ½ on LOCRE huts & ½ on front line trenches.

March 8th Work as yesterday for all three
  Coys. Mining progressing and another
  shaft started on on E trench.
  Trench mortar class continued
  in better weather. Class now quite
  capable of working the mortars them
  -selves.

March 9th New pattern 3.7" trench mortars
  (12 twentyfive) from England tried
  with success. These mortars are fired
  mechanically & use guncotton as charge.
  & are much easier to load do than
  our own make.
  Following officers in Inf Bdes trained in
  use of Trench mortars.
    Capt. H F Dawes 3rd R.F.   85 Bde.
    1st Lieut Cole Hamilton R.S.   86 Bde
    2nd Lieut Thomson 2nd S. Lancs 7th Bde
  Coys working as on 7th inst.

Appendix A.

March 10th: Two trench howitzers handed over to 85th Bde with supply of ammn.
Some trench bridges 16'0" long, sent out from BAILLEUL and sent down to KEMMEL.
2nd Lieut A.D Parke left 56 for 2nd Field Squadron
Lieut R.W Oates went sick

March 11th: 100 trench bridges sent up to trenches
56th Coy moved up to take up position in assembly trenches ready for the morrow's attack.
57 Coy also moved up into trenches
Trench bridges taken up & put in position. Openings prepared through our own wire entanglements.

March 12th: Attack made by Wilts and Worcester. Not successful.
Following arrangements made jumping off trench had been previously dug below. Trench bridges were put
See attached report Appendix 'B'

Appendix 'B'

March 13th 56 Coy returned to MONT NOIR
            57 remained up.

March 14   56 Coy to KEMMEL, 57 to MONT
           NOIR.
           Major G F Evans took command of 56 Coy

March 15   Work:- hutting, fascine making
           for 'Mothers' lock. E, bank revetment
           wiring reserve line, building
           laundry & disinfector shed at LA
           CLYTTE

March 16   56 Coy marched to RENINGHELST
           to join 27 Div. South Midland
           Field Coy formed from 27 Div
           & was split up with 57 Coy to
           form two Coys

March 17   Usual work on Trenches, hutting
           etc

March 18   Lt Col. Wilson CRE back ordered to
           be CRE 27 Div in addition
           to being CRE of this Division

March 19   Principal work on trenches at
           present is constructing of communications
           2. Lieut A.C. Brooks joined 56 Coy

March 20. Work on Molteno tr[ench] being
carried on. Other work as usual.

March 21 }
" 22 }   as above

March 23. 57' Coy moved to DICKEBUSCH
South Midlands Coy to go to
5' Division.
New home made 5" trench mortar
tried with success. Detonation in head
+ lit by instantaneous fuze through
bomb. Work on Dramondi huts
stopped.

March 24. 56 & 57 Coys working on trenches
on 3rd Div new front with
approx 800 infantry. Much
work to be done in strengthening
old firing line and making a
supporting line.

March 25. As above except that 2 sections
57' Coy were employed on
hutting - for themselves + for
Divisional army head quarters.

March 26. As above. Supply of loop holes
for knife rests being gradually
accumulated at DICKEBUSCH

March 27: Store at SCHERPENBERG is being gradually vacated & 27' Div old R.E. Store being taken over and used by Div.

Require 20000 sandbags a day but cannot get more than 15,000 whilst 5000 are the normal divisional allowance.

D on& is on 26'

March 28' Work as above

March 29: Supply of timbers sent to R.E. Store for use in hutting & trenches.
Work as above
Major G.F. Evans wounded.

March 30th Work as usual
2n 2nd Lieuts Finnimore & Whitestone joined 56 Coy.
2nd Lieut Dyer joined 57 Coy.

March 31st Capt Finnimore transferred from 57 Coy to 56 Coy.
Mining by 172 Coy has been progressing steadily since Div took over new line.

Appendix 'A'   Report on 3.7" trench mortar
— . — 'B'   — on attack 12-3-15

G.P. Wells
Capt A/C.R.E.
II Div Hqrs

Appendix A

III Division

The 3 new Trench Mortars of improved pattern have been drawn and tried, and were found to be a great improvement on the first issue. The smokeless charge and percussion fireing worked well, but it was found the way the charge was put in made a considerable difference to the

Report on Trench Mortars

flight.

The accuracy of these new Trench Mortars was much better than the old pattern.

Sd. C.S. Wilson Lieut-Colonel
C.R.A. to 3rd Division.

10/3/16

Appendix A

III Division

The 3 new French Mortars of improved pattern have been drawn and tried, and were found to be a great improvement on the first issue. The smokeless charge and percussion firing worked well, but it was found the way the charge was put in made a considerable difference to the range, if quite loose the results are better than if squeezed up when put in. The baffle plate appears to act satisfactorily.

The carriage and bombs are the same as the original issue, and are open to the same objections which have already been reported on.

Out of 30 rounds fired, there were 2 blinds due to the detonator plug dropping out during flight.

The accuracy of these new French Mortars was much better than the old pattern.

Sd. G.S. Wilson Lieut-Colonel
C.R.A. 3rd Division

10/3/16

Appendix B   1

Notes on operations on 12-3-15

The attack took place in accordance with operation order attached. JM

Preliminary arrangements. assembly trenches were dug were dug for 2 in rear of C & F sectors. These trenches were 2'6" wide and 3'6" deep with a step and berm in front so that the troops could get out easily. Assembly trenches were partially dug 2'6" wide & 2' deep for 2 battalions in rear of C sector and for 2 battalions in rear of S₂ & S₃. These would have been deepened and used had more troops been available. As it was they might seem as a blind for the real point of attack. Bridges for crossing both our own trenches and old disused ones were made 16' long & 2'6" wide strong enough to carry 4 men at once. 500 yds of portable knife rest pattern barb wire entanglements were made & a supply of sandbags etc. collected.

Conferences of the staff, R.A & R.E were held and the duties required from R.E were carefully explained to the Company officers by the C.R.E

The 57th Co. R.E. with an infantry battalion as a carrying party were in charge of the preliminary arrangements. Their duties being to get the bridges, knife rests, sandbags etc up to their proper places, and to have 2 sections

2

in the trenches to be crossed by the attack, these sections were to make the necessary gaps in our own entanglements & to place the bridges in position during the preliminary bombardment. Gaps were also to be made for some distance on each side of the point to be assaulted with a view to deceiving the enemy, as to the real point of attack. They were also charged with the duty of organising working parties from the troops in the trenches to start opening up communication forward as soon as the assaulting column has succeeded in capturing the enemies position.

The 56th Co. was detailed to the assault and it was forcibly impressed upon them that the closest and most cordial co-operation between the R.E. & Infantry was essential.

Their duties were explained to be to have parties with the leading troops of the assault for the following purposes.

(a) R.E. to improve gaps in wire made by artillery fire to enable the supporting troops to get up easily.

(b) R.E. & Infantry under an R.E. officer to double block the enemy's trenches right and left of the attack after clearing them as far as possible. These parties to be armed with hand grenades

and carry sandbags.
   (c). Similar parties as in (b) to be held in readiness under an R.E officer whose duty it would be at once make a search for the enemy's communication trenches push down them and double block them at least 40 yds from the front trenches.

The remainder of the company was to have an infantry working party (2 Co) with picks and shovels told off to be under their orders, their duties were as soon as the enemy's trenches were captured to open communication trenches back to our trenches & get into touch with the parties opening communication forward from them.

They were also to assist the infantry in reversing the parapet putting the captured trenches in a state of defence, and bringing up the knife rests and collecting any obstacle as soon as possible, but at all events as soon as it was dark.

The actual detailing of the parties by the units concerned was left to the discretion of the C.O. in consultation with the infantry.

The attack was not successful owing chiefly to the long wait in the cold and wet assembly trenches necessitated by the heavy fog. Some of the sappers with a few infantry succeeded in penetrating the enemies trenches and held on there until dark. The leading sections of the 56th Co. behaved with great gallantry practically all the leading parties who were not hit pushing right up to the German trenches.

The casualties were :—

	Killed	Wounded	Missing	
56th R.E. Officers	—	3*	—	Mjr. Barnardiston
" R.E.	5	11	2	Lt. Martin D.S.O
57th R.E. R.&F	2	1	—	" Denning

121/5254

H.Qrs. R.E. 3rd Division

Vol IX 1 – 30.4.15

54

War Diary
==========

R. E Headquarters
III Division

April 1915

April 1st. Cap~~tain~~ ~~transferred from 57 by~~
~~to 6th.~~ 2nd. Work on repair of DICKEBUSCH
huts taken in hand. Floors are being put
into these huts which are on boggy land.
Work on trenches:— Joining up Q3 to P5.
communications trenches to P5 & Q3
to Q2 started. Work on S6 progressed
well. Progress made on saps N3 N4. good
progress on M sector main communication
trench & drainage. M1 connected 6 M2
by 27 yards of new trench. 70 yards of
communication trench dug in L sector.
Good progress made on revetting & wiring
of subsidiary line, ditto on 2nd line.
Infantry provided large working parties
for the above works carried out under
R E supervision.

April 2nd. Work as yesterday. new supporting points
~~pressed~~ sited & also line for new
communication trench through wood
reconnoitred.

April 3rd Trench work as before - Joining up of
Q 3 to P.5 completed. Drawing of
communications improved. Laying
out of communications. M5 improved.
No working parties from 27 Div
available for 2nd line. Work on huts
progressing.

April 4th Reconstruction & wiring of S7 commenced. Sites
for new supporting points in wood
reconnoitred. No progress made on
subsidiary line owing to civilians not
working being Easter Sunday.

April 5th 57 Coy left Division to join North Midland
Division. Capt Edwardes left behind with
Cheshire field Coy for 6 days to assist them
and 6th Bde. Lt Richardson Ches Coy to
hospital. Very heavy rains interfered
greatly with work in trenches, however
good progress was made on wiring S7
and subsidiary line. Materials got
up for S7.

April 6. Light work interfered with by rain. New work begun :- Connecting T_1 & T_2. Old work continued.

April 7. Hd Qrs moved to RENINGHELST. Whole of 42nd Coy R.E. placed under Division for work & administration. Old work continued. New supporting points laid out.
During the past week of month timber has been obtained from BAILLEUL for huts and for trenches. 15,000 sandbags have been drawn & used nearly every day. Corrugated iron & barbed wire have also been drawn daily & used in large quantities for trench work. Mining at St ELOI has also progressed well.

April 8. S_6 & various subsidiary lines completed. Other work continued.

April 9th Work as yesterday

April 10th Trench howitzer emplacement in M4
completed. Subsidiary line reconnoitred
& laid out. Work on shelter made
good progress.

April 11th Work as follows:-
On T1 - T3 & main communication trench
On S7 Communication trench to BOIS CARRÉ
Draining communication trench near
BRASSERIE. Deepening & widening L
communicating trench. Draining & improving
part of subsidiary line. Draining G & J
2nd line. Part of 3rd line & switch. Work also
continued on various huts, making microscopes
training infantry pioneers etc. Water supply
question of Dumonell billeting area
investigated in conjunction with R.A.M.C.

April 12. Work as usual.

April 13. New work started. Flanking breastwork from BURNT FARM. Other work continued.

April 14. Drain for new redoubt completed. Germans exploded mine opposite heavy from fire which interfered with working. Mine somewhat buried but shaft & gallery practically uninjured.
R.E. stores from Park & timber sent up to DICKEBUSCH & LACLYTTE daily; nails purchased locally owing to shortage at Park during the last week.

April 15. Work on trenches as usual.
A commencement made on removing huts at WESTOUTRE, 7 to be added to DICKEBUSCH huts and 15 to be added to ROSENHILL huts. Timber supplied

for bath house etc at convalescent home at WESTOUTRE. 7° F⁰ Ambulance are to provide necessary labour for erection.

April 16° A large supply of square wood pickets arrived at BAILLEUL & are sent up to DICKEBUSCH in 9 lorries. These pickets are new wood and it will be necessary to paint or stain them before using for wire entanglements. Work on subsidiary line handed over to Div¹ Cyclist Coy. Trench work carried on as usual.

April 17° During 4.5 D.W. attack, work was somewhat interfered with on the left. Other work carried on as usual.
All huts at WESTOUTRE have now been removed & are in course of re-erection.

April 18. Joining up of K, to J₃ hut in hand. Scheme for small dam, filter and reservoir to supply LA CLYTTE and neighbourhood got out. Dam to be made in KEMMELBEEK. Other work as usual. CANADA huts are being covered with rot proof canvas as original tarred paper put on rough boarding is badly torn rendering huts very leaky.

April 19. 2ⁿᵈ Lieut B.F. WHITESTONE, 56 by, wounded. Further supply (2000) picketts arrived at BAILLEUL & were sent to DICKEBUSCH. Bombs and some local pattern trench mortars handed over to 5 Division. Work continued on communication trenches and draining thereof. S & progressed with. Work of connecting up J₃ from K, continued.

April 20. Amm Park lines withdrawn from STRAZEELE. Much difficulty in borrowing lorries to bring up stores. Communication trench in K sectn very wet, work of draining it progressing. Good progress with other communication trenches & drainage.

April 21. Still trouble in obtaining transport
to bring up stores from Park and
two truck loads of pickets. 8 lorries
eventually obtained from D. Amm Park.
Work as before. Wiring of subsidiary
progressing well as is also the
2nd line.

April 22nd. Two more truck loads pickets
arrived at BAILLEUL. Sent up to LA CLYTTE
and DICKEBUSCH. Supply of timber
for 3 36ft × 16ft huts for F.W. Amb.
at LA CLYTTE obtained.
Lt C G MARTIN awarded V.C.
Work in hand:— Medical huts at LA CLYTTE,
DICKEBUSCH huts, removing of Canada
huts, repair of ROSENHILL huts. Communication
trenches to St ELOI, C.T. near BOIS CARRÉ.
Subsidiary line, 2nd line, S.8, J.10
drainage of C.T. L sector.

April 23rd. Divisional cyclist company sent up
to DICKEBUSCH to provide daily
working party for work on
subsidiary line. Work on C.Ts
continued as before.

62

April 24. Chinkin Coy sent up to bridge canal somewhere in I.19 a. & b. Canal dry, three trestles used, one of which with superstructure was borrowed from N. M. Div. The above was done for 5ᵗʰ Div. Work on C. trenches continued. Cyclist Coy employed on wiring.

April 25ᵗʰ. Infantry of 9ᵗʰ Bde given instruction with trench mortars (3.7" Bethier with p. rifle mechanism).
Work as before.
Civilian carpenters employed on LA CLYTTE medical huts as all R.E labour is required for night work.
2ⁿᵈ Lieut H.F. STRANGWAYS joined 42ⁿᵈ Coy R.E

April 26ᵗʰ More trouble with reference to getting up stores from R.E. Park owing to withdrawal of 4ᵗʰ Ammn Park lorries. Division at present requires at least 15000 sandbags, about 200 sheets corrugated iron & 200 coils of barbed wire daily. Corrugated iron is mostly being used for revetting harbours extensively by the 42ⁿᵈ Coy on the G.H.Q line.
Work on trenches etc as usual.

April 27. Some lorries have now been left
at the disposal of R.E. Park, STRAZEELE
in which to send up stores. Demands
need now only be sent to R.E. Park.
This arrangement should work well
so long as park have sufficient
transport at their disposal to send
up all stores required.
Work on C. trenches, G.H.Q. line +
subsidiary line continued.

April 28. 2nd Lieut A. W. GORDON joined the
56 Coy. Sites for new supporting
points in BOIS CARRÉ sited. Work
still being continued on S.8.
Besides usual infantry working parties
for trenches etc., R.A. are also
providing a working party of 100 strong.
Work on various supporting points,
trenches, C. trenches + wiring continued
by both field coys, 42 Coy, Cyclist Coy
+ various infantry working parties.

April 29. Work as usual on trenches etc.

April 30. 650 yards of subsidiary line dug.
Work on S.8 continued. Wiring
of 2nd + subsidiary lines continued

Pr [pairs?] made with clean [?] &
drainage. Trench between Ridge wood
and ELZENWALLE nearly complete,
wiring of this portion of G H Q line
completed. Good progress made with
trenches round about VIERSTRAAT.

Appendix 'A'. Re want of fairly senior
R.E. officers.

" 'B'. Report on explosion of
German mine near St ELOI.

" 'C'. Re coloured sandbags.

" 'D'. Recommendations for
awards etc.

4-5-15.

G H Wells
Capt & Adjt
3rd Divl Engineers.

Copy   Appendix A

III Division

     Now that the Divisional Engineers are reduced to 1 Regular and 1 Territorial Field Company, and in addition the four regular subalterns are all very young and inexperienced the want of another fairly senior Regular R.E. officer or two is very severely felt. This is especially the case with the Territorial Field Company, for though the Officers are keen and willing they are severely handicapped by a want of military training and knowledge which tends to make them have an unnecessary lack of confidence in their own opinions, and to be shy of expressing them, especially if they find they do not coincide with those of the Regular Infantry Officers and Staff they are dealing with. I think every Territorial Company should have a Regular R.E. Captain attached to it. Under present circumstances it is impossible to arrange for this in the Division, and I request that two Regular R.E. ~~Officers~~ Captains may be

                       posted

2.

posted to me for duty until I get back the second Regular Company. I regard this as very important for the efficiency of the Divisional Engineers, and would suggest that if no other R.E. officers are available 2 might be lent me for the time being from the Field Squadrons or other units not at present employed in the front line.

(sgd.) C.S. Wilson
Lt. Col.
C.R.E. III Division

15-4-15.

Copy.　　　　　　　Appendix 'B'

III Division,

　　　An enemy mine was exploded during the night of the 14th-15th April against the defended house and left of Q1 at ST. ELOI. The house collapsed and part of the trench fell in. From subsequent examination it would appear that the enemy had driven a gallery from the house 66 yards away along the road in their lines, and having reached about ⅔rds of the way across probably heard our working and hurriedly loaded their gallery with a large charge and fired it, hoping to destroy our workings. Fortunately, although the shock of the explosion caused a good deal to fall in, it was not near enough to do any very serious damage, and our workings, except for being rather choked with debris are quite intact. The crater made was some 70 ft. x 60 ft. x 25 ft. and a large quantity of blue clay was thrown up which was only found at a depth of 13 feet. The centre of the crater was 60 feet from the front of the
　　　　　　　　　　　　house.

2

house. From this it is inferred that the enemy gallery was probably 20 ft. deep, and a charge of some 500 lbs of high explosive was used. This would bring our workings a few feet outside the radius of rupture, and corresponds with the state of our shaft and heading. Such a large charge must have been placed in a gallery, and not in a bored mine. From all I can learn the men of the 5th Fusiliers who rescued the buried men in the ruined house must have done very good and gallant work. One of the R.E. party was killed and ten injured most of them only slightly.

The probable result is a delay of 48 hours for us, and most probably a very considerably longer delay for the enemy, as their gallery must have been destroyed for some distance, and in any further advance they will have to go round the area of the explosion, which will interfere very slightly with our proposed direction

(sgd) C. S. Wilson
Lt. Col.
16-4-15. C.R.E. III Division

"Appendix 'C'"

Copy.

C.E. II Corps,

Where as at present we have much building of breastworks to do, the ordinary white sandbag is very conspicuous — The Germans use a proportion of black ones with very good results. I would suggest that a good proportion of the sandbags supplied should be dyed in the primary colours - red green and yellow - this would make works much more difficult to spot, and as we now find with the German trenches also makes loopholes practically impossible to see.

(sgd) C.S. Wilson
Lt. Col.

28/3/1915

C.R.E. III Divⁿ

Appendix D. 36

III Division.

In forwarding lists with the names of officers, NCOs and men whom I wish to bring to notice in accordance with your A/2557 of 18.2.15 I would wish to emphasize the trying nature of the duties the officers and men of the Field Companies have been called on to carry out during the winter months of trench warfare. The duties though not often affording instances for special recommendation have been uniformly trying and arduous and have called for a high standard of coolness and gallantry, and the character of the work may be judged by the casualties which have been fairly heavy. Under these circumstances I would urge that recommendations for continued good & gallant work covering considerable periods might be regarded as equivalent qualifications to those when rewards are granted for some specific instance. The officers NCOs & men of the Field Companies have all done exceedingly good work carried out often in arduous and dangerous conditions with a coolness gallantry and thoroughness that deserves all possible credit.

20.4.15.
J. Richardson
GOC III Division

2   32

Recommendations.

Captain GUY FRANEY WELLS Adjutant Divisional Engineers
Has been of great assistance to me since he joined on 21.9.14.
and has done consistently good work especially with trench
mortars with which he has done good work in the trenches.

56 Captain GEORGE SOPWITH.
Has done very good & valuable work since he joined on 13.1.15
During most of the time he has commanded the company with
success & has done especially good work since the Division
took over ST ELOI. — Brevet of Major.

56 Lieut BASIL CRANMER DENING
Has done consistently good & gallant work since he joined
on 26.11.14 and has shown a constant example of cool
gallantry to his men. He was wounded whilst gallantly leading
his men in the attack on SPANBROEK MOELLEN on 12.3.15
— Military Cross —

57. Captain CHARLES O'REILLY EDWARDS.
Has done consistently good & gallant work and set a
fine example of coolness and devotion to duty. His
work throughout since he joined on 21.9.14 in command
of the Composite F.d Co and afterwards with the 57th Co has
been good & thorough, and he has frequently made
good reconnaissances in front of our lines. D.S.O. or D.C.has

Clerk of Works ARCHIBALD LEITCH.
Has done consistently good work since he joined
the Division on 22.12.14

3   33

St. 17220. Capt. FREDERIC HEATH.
Has done conspicuously good work throughout the campaign and has on many occasions set a fine example of coolness & resource under fire. D.C.M.

St. 16174. Capt. SIDNEY. PARNELL. SKINNER.
Has done conspicuously good work throughout and has on many occasions shown a fine example of coolness and gallantry, especially on 12th March 1915 when in the attack on SPANBROEK MOLEN he got into the enemy's trench and did good work with hand grenades and in holding the trench. D.C.M.

Sl. 19762. a/Lce Cpl. MATTHEW. McCLOSKY.
This mi's name has already been put forward for gallantry in the attack on March 12th. He has done very good work and frequently been conspicuous for his courage and gallantry. D.C.M.

St. 23712. a/Lce Cpl. ERNEST SHREOUBER.
Sl. 10647. a/Co SM ROBERT. PERCIVAL. WILLIAM. WHITE.
Have done consistently good work and shown a good example of coolness & gallantry in trying circumstances.

St. 13836. a/Sergt JAMES. FREDERIC HADLOW.
Has done consistent good work and set a good example of coolness & energy to his men.

St. 14572. a/2nd Cpl. WILLIAM. JAMES. HADLEY.
Has done consistent good work, and has always set a good example of coolness and energy under fire.

4

57. 28934 Sgt. WALTER. EDGAR. WYATT.
Has done consistently good work, and has on several occasions displayed good coolness and gallantry under trying circumstances giving a fine example to his men. — D.C.M.

17 3673 Sergt. WILLIAM - JOHN - HENWOOD.
Has done consistently good work since the beginning of the campaign and shown a fine example of coolness & gallantry to his men when under fire. — D.C.M.

57. 1659. Sapper. SAMUEL WALTER MEOPHAM.
Has done consistently good work under trying circumstances, and has always set a fine example of coolness and energy whenever there was any dangerous work to be done. — DCM.

57. 33   Corporal. GEORGE NORTHOVER
19722 Corporal. EDWARD. JOHNSTON.
10431 Sapper. JOHN - WILLIAM. KNIGHT.
21110 Pioneer WALTER - CANTER.
18550 Sapper. FREDERIC. REYNOLDS.
Have done consistently good work and shown a good example of coolness & gallantry under trying circumstances.

Cheshire Co. 4 Sergt JOHN ARMSTRONG.
26 Sgt JOHN. RICHARD. HUGHES.
76 L/Corpl THOMAS CHALLONER.
57 L/Corpl DAVID JONES.
Have done consistent good work since the

5

Company joined the Division on 2.12.14 and have shown an example of coolness and energy to their men.

[signature]

In the Field

26.4.15.   CRE 3rd Division

Hd Qrs RE. 8nd Division

Vol IX 1 — 31.5.15.

65

War Diary   May '15

R.E. Headquarters 3rd Division

May 1st. Work continued on trench along BALLHARTBEEK on S_6 and S_6^{+58}, on drainage of in BOIS CARRE Wiring continued in front VOORMEZEELE across the St ELOI road. New communication trench from Q3 towards Cont Trench from VOORMEZELE to P.5 dug out from P.5. Wiring of subsidiary line behind M continued. Parapet of enclosed work in M sector built up & barricade built up across NEUVE EGLISE - YPRES road. Cont Trench in K sector improved by draining, deepening & widening. Traverses rebuilt on K 2 a. Dug outs in M, rebuilt.
Wiring of 2nd line between RIDGE WOOD and ELZENWALLE nearly completed. Trenches & breastworks also continued between these two points.

May 2nd. Work generally the same as yesterday. Small parties of Cheshire Field coy worked during the day on certain front line trenches.

May 3rd — Efforts were made to find a water supply by the DICKEBUSCH huts & the LA CLYTTE huts by the help of a water diviner (Col Rore, Camp Commandant 3rd Corps). Slight indications found at spots near both lots of huts.
Work on front trenches, comn trenches, subsidiary line, 2nd line continued.
Div'l Cyclists still working under C.R.E.

May 4 — Supply of wooden trench boards arranged for from timber Yard BARGELL. Still very necessary in the Com.Trenches.
Work at night considerably hampered by heavy rain, however extra stores were taken up to various places ready for use in future.

May 5 — Well started at spot indicated by water diviner by DICKEBUSCH huts by means of N.Frenchmen. Surface spring by LA CLYTTE discovered. Filter bed & tank near LA CLYTTE on KEMMELBEEK marked out. A large amount of wiring was done on subsidiary line during the night. Work on trenches generally continued.

May 6. Wiring & work on Coin Trenches, front line trenches, subsidiary line & 2nd line continued. S6 by owing to infantry reliefs were unable to get through as much work as usual.

May 7. It has been found necessary to paint the 4"x4" wood pickets, used for high wire entanglement, green as they are new & very conspicuous. Paint is obtainable locally. Work as usual. Owing to growth of undergrowth Sg has now lost much of its usefulness & it will be necessary to increase length of branch at side of wood to remedy this.

May 8. Tank & pillar bed down LA CLYTTE, progressing slowly. Greatly delayed by amount of night work that has had to be done by Fd. Coys lately. Wiring between BOIS CONFLUENT and Sg completed. Other work carried on as usual.

May 9. Wiring in front of Nq round S6a and S6b completed also that on N.E side of BOIS CONFLUENT. Trenches on N.E side of BOIS CONFLUENT dug now, surfaced by go mm. Other work continued.
Lieut A. Leitch Churchin Field by wounded.

68

May 10th — Wiring thickened up in many places on subsidiary line. Tunnel work continued by 42', Chesham Coys. Comn. Trench dug between Mortar garage & new support trench.
2nd Lieut Eastwood Chesham F Coy wounded.

May 11th — No special comments. Work as heretofore continued.

May 12th — As above. Lieut C.A. Moore joined this F Coy

May 13th — Whole of 56 Coy & 1 section of Chesham Coy went up to 5" Divn to march out & dig new switch line from ZILLEBEEKE to Hill 60. Wiring also started from the left of switch. 42', Chesham Coy (2nd) & Coy Shot Coy carrying on work as usual on subsidiary & 2nd lines.

May 14th — RE HQ quarters moved from RENINGHELST to WESTOUTRE where it combined with RA HQrs for messing purposes.
1 Section 56 Coy & 1 section Chesham F Coy went up to 5" Divn to continue last night's work of wiring. Their time was mostly wasted owing to failure of 5" Divn to provide the necessary material on time. Other work carried on.

69

May 15th. Well at DICKEBUSCH huts now down
to 18'-6". Solid blue clay, no sign of
water. 50 other Coys. now provided with
150 respirator each. Considerable amount
of wiring done on subsidiary and GHQ
lines. Communication trenches boarded
and parapets built up with sandbags
so that reasonable good lengths
of C.Ts are now 7 to 8 ft. from
top of parapet to bottom.

May 16. Difficulty in getting stones up from RE
Park owing to break down of lorries, finally
3rd Div Supply Column were able to
produce 3 for this purpose. Work continued
on filter & tank at LALLYTTE which is
being lined with brick built or with cement.
Work on wiring, C.Ts continued.

May 17. Bad weather interfered greatly with
work, however large quantities of stones were
carried up to various sites ready for use.

May 18. Weather still bad so work was
confined to putting up wire entanglements.
Claim for cut trees investigated. Laid.

May 19. Huts started near DICKEBUSCH for
172" by R.E. which finds DICKEBUSCH too
unsettling for as a resting place between
reliefs owing to shelling etc.

May 19. Again owing to wet, most of the work consisted of building up wire. A few traverses were built up in trenches on right sector.

May 20. Wiring in front of support trench from VERMEZELE to BOIS CONFLUENT completed. Building up of sandbag revetments on various C.T.s continued by 2nd South Lancs, now acting as pioneer Bn to division. Work continued on support trenches behind the BALLAARBEEK. Wiring also done in front of trench N of VIERSTRAAT - WYTSCHAETE road. Wiring of subsidiary line improved. Work continued on G.H.Q. subsidiary line by 42nd Coy assisted by 2 Coys of Belgians and 150 Belgian civilians.

May 21st Fresh supply of timber arrived at Mrs Dufour Aerts yard at BAILLEUL, a large proportion of which was purchased for this division. Claim for hop poles by farmer at KEMMEL settled. Work continued on trenches - wiring as usual.

May 22nd Nothing special to note. 30000 sandbags are now required daily for use of division. Timber/brushwood? for building revetments to C.T.s etc as general as possible is still very wet just below the surface.

May 23rd Work as usual, 56 Coy, part of Cheshires & men of S. Lanc. working on ɛ railway line trenches on our left which was really work of 5' Divn who however were unable to do it.

May 24th Heavy attack aided by gas made round YPRES. Gas drifted across country and 56 Coy had to take to respirators, otherwise no harm done to R.E. of this division. C.E. 2nd Corps visited front trenches by day in BOIS CONFLUENT. Work as usual. Great portion of main C.T's are now boarded and have permanent working parties in them to keep them in good order.

May 25th Numbers working on G.H.Q. 2' line with L.2' Coy R.E. have now been raised to approx 700 Belgian soldiers and 1050 civilians. Work is considered urgent in view of state of affairs round YPRES. Other work carried on as usual.

May 26th 8' Bde took over part of line S.East of YPRES from 2t Divn. R.E. Adjutant accompanied this Brigade to help them with work to be

to be done on their new line. 56" Coy
carried on work as usual, ditto 42 & Chatham
Coy.

May 27" Chatham Coy moved up to join S' Bde also
2" South Lancs went up to assist S' Bde
as previous Billeting. 2" South Lancs dug
1200 yards of C.T. from Front line back
to G.H.Q. line which had been marked
out by party of 38 F[ld] Coy the previous
night. 56 Coy working on old line as
usual.

May 28" Chatham F[d] Coy and 2" South Lancs worked on
S' Bde line wiring, digging support and
C.T. etc. 38 Coy also worked on their part of the
line marking out another C.T. running
back to G.H.Q. line from left of S' Bde.
56 Coy worked on old line.

May 29" O.C. 56 Coy went up to HOOGE to see what
work was required as Div. taking over this
front shortly from Cavalry.

May 30" 56 Coy worked at HOOGE. Chatham and
SOUTH Lancs on S' Bde line. R.E H.Q. Qrs.
moved from WESTOUTRE to place on
RENINGHELST - POPERINGHE road about
1 mile N of former place.

73

May 30th   Suffolk Bde dug C.T. marked out of
             3rd F.[?] by on 8th Bde left.

May 31st   Cheshires by working with 8th Bde and
             56 by, having moved up from DICKEBUSCH
             to near VLAMERTINGHE worked on
             trenches in the neighbourhood of HOOGE.

           ———

Appendix A   Recommendations for Russian
              Devotions

                              J. Wells
                              Capt & Adjt
9-6-15   3rd Divl Engrs

Aberdeen A

3rd Division

With reference to yours a/2771 of 2-5-15 I have the honour to submit the following recommendations

For the cross of the order of St George 4th Class

No 823 A/Regt Sergeant Major ALBERT GEORGE PALMER. was C.S.M of 56 Coy R.E. he was awarded the DCM for great gallantry & coolness at the battle of LE CATEAU on 26 August 1914 in assisting Lt MARTIN to hold his men at their exposed post at CAUDRY which had been found untenable by the infantry. He has since done consistently good work & always shown a fine example of coolness & gallantry to his men, which has been very marked on several occasions.

For the medal of St GEORGE 2nd Class.

No 5509 Sergeant ALFRED EARNEST SMITH – 57 Coy R.E. was mentioned in despatches for conspicuous gallantry & devotion to duty at the battle of MONS on August 22nd when he assisted Capt WRIGHT in his efforts to complete the demolition of the bridge at MARIETTE and again at VAILLY, he was assisting the same officer in repairing the pontoon bridge under a very heavy fire whilst the 5 Cavalry Brigade was retiring over it — Capt WRIGHT was awarded the V.C. for his gallantry on these occasions. He has since shown a fine example of coolness & gallantry on several occasions until he was wounded & invalided.

For the medal of St GEORGE 3rd Class

No 3690 Lce Cpl. JAMES DUFFY, 56 Coy RE – Has been prominent on many occasions in giving a fine example of coolness & devotion to duty in trying circumstances. He also led his party in a most gallant manner in the attack on SPANBROCKEN on

2

March 12th 1915 and did good work in collecting parties of infantry, who had lost their officers & NCOs, only desisting in his efforts when the infantry finally retired.

For the medal of St GEORGE, 4th Class

No 16590 Sapper FREDERIC REYNOLDS – 57 Coy R.E. has constantly shown a good example of coolness and gallant work. This was particularly conspicuous on Dec 8th 1914 in the attack on PETIT BOIS when he went forward before the attack to cut the wire entanglements & afterwards assisted in getting in wounded men under fire

(Sgd) C.S. Wilson
Lt Col
C R E 3rd Divn

2-5-15

12/5992

3rd Division

HdQrs RE, 3rd Division

Vol XL   1 — 30.6.15

War Diary   June 1915
R.E. Headquarters III Division

June 1st. 53rd Coy worked on conversion of C.Ts behind HOOGE and all round fire trenches. Was rather afoot owing to find that HOOGE and neighbourhood had been bombarded for 15 hours continuously during the day and the garrison, cavalry, did not seem to know quite what had happened. Cheshires Coy with Suffolks & ½ Bn South Lancs wiring, digging support trenches, repairing damages to 1st Gordon trenches also heavily bombarded, digging and improving communication trenches.
Adjutant rejoined C R E from 8th Bde.

June 2nd, 3rd. Work on improving trenches.
June. 6.7th. Cavalry relieved by 7th Brigade.
— 7.8th. 50th Divn relieves 9th Brigade.
     171. RE No 2 Seig. Co. R.A.B.E. No 4 Sig Co. R.M.R.E. attached to 3rd Division on 8th.
— 9th. 10th. Steady work going on on upkeep and of trenches my etc.
    11th. Assembly trenches begun for attack on BELLEWAARDE.
    12th.   ———— carried with aid of 11th Bgde the pioneer battalion of the 10th Division.

15th Were in assembly trenches not completed owing to the 11th Divn having been scattered by shell fire. Captain and adjutant Lt WELLS was severely wounded on his way to the trenches and died of his wounds the next morning

16th HQ in YPRES remnants 7th & 9th Brigades with Cheshire Rgt to attacked BELLEWAARDE the others were used for consolidating the position won. Casualties some 20 officers and 2 minor. In the evening the 5th & 2nd South Downs sent down to assist in consolidating the position gained, but owing to the confusion after the action & relieving little could be done. 8th Brigade relieved

17th During the night the position was consolidated and some further German trenches occupied & the whole wired and communications made.

18th Hooge again taken over by 7th Brigade no work has been done or attempted since we left and the defences are in a bad condition.

19. 9th Brigade relieved by 14 Division & 7th Brigade takes over remainder of old front from HOOGE to S of SANCTUARY WOOD

20. Considerable work required at HOOGE put in hand.

23. An attempt was made to capture German redoubt at HOOGE by 2 Cos of Wilts supported by 1 Section 56th Co R.E. The bombardment was however not effective & numerous machine guns opening on the troops as soon as they left their trenches the attempt was abandoned

28. G. C O'R. EDWARDS - RE joined as adjutant. **76**
29. 200 men of 9th Argyle sent up to Sanctuary Wood as an additional working party.
30. Recommendation of Each Patrol to Shelters and Hooge conferred

Appendices.

A. Recommendations for St Georges 2nd Bn.
B. Orders for RE attack on 16.6.15
C. Recommendation for in white road for 16.6.15
D. Work of 2/3rd Lancers as Pioneers.

5.7.15   Philip [illegible]
         Ch 23° [illegible]

3rd Division   A

With reference to your Q.322 of 12.6.15. I have the honour to submit the following names—

For St. George's Cross — 4th Class

No. 3976. Lce Corpl Charles Alfred JARVIS. 57th Co. R.E. now invalided and believed to be at home.

For displaying great gallantry and coolness in successfully firing the demolition charges. He worked for an hour and a half under very heavy rifle and machine gun fire at close range with only very partial protection from the bridge itself.

Lce. Cpl. Jarvis was awarded the V.C. for this act.

For St. George's Medal — 4th Class

No. 25712. Sapper, A/Lce Cpl. ERNEST SANGROUBER 57th Co R.E. Has done consistently good work, and has on every occasion of difficult or hazardous work set a fine example of coolness and gallantry.

(Sgd.) C. S. Wilson
Lt. Col.
C.R.E. 3rd Divn

13/6/15.

B

Operation Order by R.E. 3rd Division

With reference to Div. Operation Order No..
the following preliminary work will be carried out
O.C. CHESHIRE Fd Co. will form the Depôts at each
end of CAMBRIDGE road, each Depôt to consist of –

    3800 sandbags
      50 coils French wire
      20   " barbed wire
     200 iron pickets
     200 spades
       6 mauls (muffled)

He will also see that the ladders (300) for
getting out of the fire trenches are carried up and
distributed.

O.C. 56 Co. R.E. will relieve the detachment of
CHESHIRE Fd Co. on the pontoon bridge at the SALLY
PORT the day before the operations and will have
2 pontoons and superstructure at the SALLY PORT
to repair damages.

The 56th Field Co. will go into the ramparts
the night before the operations following a
battalion of 7th Brigade. Tool carts will be
brought up and horses sent back. The O.C.
57 Co. R.E. will be responsible for the maintenance
of the pontoon bridge, and new footbridge
during the operations.

3. The O.C. Cheshire Field Co. will report to the G.O.C. 9th Brigade and inform him of his proposed arrangements. The two sections for making communications are to be detailed beforehand, and the ground carefully reconnoitred by the officers. The communication to Y wood should be begun as soon as the wood has been occupied. The best line will probably be S and under cover of the hedge & line of trees. The communication trench from RAILWAY wood should be begun as soon as the enemy trenches E of the wood are occupied. As the troops move forward this section should be moved round to RAILWAY WOOD in readiness for its work. The O.C. Cheshire F.C. on the ground having been reconnoitred will arrange direct with G.O.C. 9th Brigade for any infantry working parties required.

The O.C. with the remaining two sections will move forward with the 2 reserve battalions and do everything in his power to consolidate the captured positions and put them in a state of defence. Wire should be got out as soon as possible.

The O.C. will arrange for the men to carry the necessary tools, 100 rounds ammunition and rations for 2 days. Packs & greatcoats will not be carried.

4. The O.C. Cheshire Field Co. will ascertain from G.O.C. 8th Brigade the arrangements for making gaps in our own wire and in the hedges. He will lend any necessary assistance in carrying out this.

5. The O.C. Cheshire Field Co. will arrange direct with G.O.C. 9th Brigade as to getting into the assembly trenches. The Company will be between the two battalions of the 2nd line of the 9th Brigade.

(sd) C.S. Wilson
Lt Col
C.R.E. 3rd Divn

III Division

I have the honour to bring forward for immediate reward the name of a/Corporal No 290. ARTHUR. JAMES. BYRNE. Cheshire Field Co R.E. (T.F.) for a conspicuous example of courage and devotion to duty in the attack on BELLEWARDE on 16-6-15. He was wounded in the hand as the troops were getting out of the assembly trenches but refused to have it dressed and went on with his men, he worked hard himself and kept his men at it in the 2nd line trenches at BELLEWARDE and when driven out of there in the German first line trenches only giving up late in the evening some 13 hours after he was wounded, by which time his wound prevented him doing any work himself, and the crowded state of the trenches prevented any more work being done on them.

(sd) C.S. Wilson
Lt. Col.
C.R.E. 3rd Div'n

19-6-15.

D.

3rd Division

I have the honour to bring to your notice the very excellent work that has been done by Lt Col DUDGEON, the Officers, N.C.Os and men of the 2nd SOUTH LANCASHIRE regiment during the period they have been acting as pioneer battalion for the Division. All ranks have shown a very commendable zeal and interest in their new role, and have done their best with excellent results, in spite of the work being often of a trying and arduous nature, and being attended I regret to say by a considerable number of casualties.

C.S. Wilson
Lt Col
C.R.E. 3rd Divn

22/6/15.

Hd Qrs R.E. 3rd Division

July 15

War Diary   July 1915
R.E. Headquarters 14 Division

1st to 4th   56th Coy with 200 infantry continued
work on HOOGE defences.
Cheshire Coy continued work on
supporting point South of ZOUAVE
WOOD & on 1st commenced work
on splinter proofs for stretcher
cases in SANCTUARY WOOD.

5th   Work continuing as above.
Lieut A.R.R. WOODS 56th Coy killed.

9th   Work continuing as above.
Lieut W.T. LEFEUVRE joined 56th Coy
Work on first new supporting point
west of YPRES was begun.

10th   Work on second new supporting point
west of YPRES begun.
New main communication trench
from MOATED GRANGE to
SANCTUARY WOOD started.

11th   2 motor lorries received from 3rd Army.
Sub Park for work under C.R.E. making
4 in all. Employed on carting stores

from ABEELE to 3rd Div Park.

12th — Work continued on defences of HOOGE, dug outs in SANCTUARY WOOD, Supporting points and communication trenches.

13th — Cheshire Coy started carting timber collected in YPRES to 3rd Div Park.

14th 15th — Steady progress at HOOGE, and on dug outs, Supporting points, & main Communication trench.

16th — Two Supporting points east of YPRES commenced by Cheshire Co.

17th — Work progressing well at HOOGE and on Supporting points, main Communication trench & dug outs.

18th — 2 Motor lorries returned to 3rd Amm Sub Park and 2 received from Army Troops Supply Column.

19th — We exploded a mine at 7 p.m. under the enemy's trenches opposite BULL FARM and afterwards an attack by 8th Bde occupied the crater and a length of

German trench on either side. Two sections 56th Coy starting immediately after the assault worked through the night on communications between our old line and the crater and the captured trenches. By dawn these communications were passable in daylight. 56th Coy casualties 3 killed 9 wounded. (See Appendix   ).

20th.21st   Good progress with consolidation of captured position and other work at HOOGE & on supporting points & main communication trench.

22nd   Capt J. WAYNE MORGAN joined Cheshire Field Coy R.E.

23rd   Cheshire Coy moved to new billets at H 22 d 6.3. Movement of 3rd Divn R.E. Park to H 27 C 4.7 was begun. Front handed over to 14th Divn & taken over from 5th Divn.

24th   Two motor lorries received from 3rd Amm. Sub Park.

25th   4th S. Lancs Regt became pioneer

battalion of division & was placed under CRE. for orders and administration. Two motor lorries returned to 2nd Army Troops Supply Column. Movement of RE. Park completed.

26th 6 Carpenters from Cheshire Coy and a party of civilian Carpenters started work on erection of huts for HQ. 3rd Division at RENINGHELST. 56th Coy moved to new billets at H 27 b 6.2

27th Two sections Cheshire Coy. moved to dug outs in wood I 34 to assist with front line work of 8th Bde.

28th Two Foden steam lorries received.

29th Capt. H.W. FLINT joined Cheshire Coy, R.E. Two motor lorries returned to 3rd Amm. Sub Park. This left 2 Foden lorries & 2 motor lorries working for CRE. between ABEELE & 3rd Divn Park.

30th Work progressing on front line & supporting points West of YPRES, also on RENINGHELST Huts.

81

31st H.Q. 3rd Division moved to
RENINGHELST. One Foden lorry
moved to 3rd Divn Park to work between
5th Corps Park & 3rd Divn Park carrying
timber – 2 Companies 4th S Lancs
went into bivouacs in wood in H29D –

Appendix A   Application for experienced
             officer, regular if possible to
             command Cheshire Co R.E.

Appendix B   Report re brigade pioneers
             & pioneer battalions.

Appendix C   Report on mining operations at HOOGE

Appendix D   Recommendation in connection
             with operations at HOOGE 19th-20th
             July

Appendix E   Re. Shortage of material for
             front line trenches

Appendix F   Operation Orders 18.7.15.

4.8.15

C.R. Edwards
Capt.
Adjt 3rd Divl Engrs.

COPY. Appendix A

3rd Division

May an urgent request be put forward please for an experienced officer, Regular if possible, to command the Cheshire Field Co. R.E. (T.). It was understood that an officer was applied for to replace Major MARQUIS who gave up the command on the 19th ult. but nothing has been heard of his successor. At present the Company is commanded by a young subaltern who has been out with it all the time, but he has under him five young officers who have only been out a short time and have had little or no previous training or experience. The result is naturally that the company is not at all efficient. There are now only two Field Companies in the Division and it is essential that this Unit should be commanded by an efficient officer, otherwise the very important and urgent work on the trenches must inevitably suffer seriously.

(sgd) C.S. Wilson
Lt. Col. R.E.
C.R.E. 3rd Division

3/7/15.

Copy.   Appendix B.   98.

3rd Division
    With reference to 2nd Army there is no doubt the establishment of R.E. are unable to cope with the amount of work required. It has been found perfectly possible to get assistance from other units by selecting men & Officers. This has been in practice in the 3rd Division since last Christmas and has been found to work very satisfactorily. The system is not quite the same in the different brigades, but the best way is for each brigade to select an officer as Brigade Pioneer Officer, if one who has been a civil engineer is available so much the better, 25 men under the pioneer sergeant are taken from each battalion, as many as possible being carpenters. The whole were then trained in Field Engineering by the affiliated Field Company whilst the Brigade was out of the trenches. The men still continue to live with their units though working as a whole for the Brigade under the Pioneer Officer. At the same time each unit has the call on its own 25 pioneers for any work in the front line. Brigade workshops are established by the Pioneers where any articles required for the trenches are made. In this way a very great deal of urgent work has been done, and a

very great help given to the R.E.. I think however that these pioneers should remain with their Brigades, as this system works much better than trying to get them together as Divisional Troops, which would mean forming a new unit. Personally I am very averse to having sections attached to the Field Companies, and so are all my Field Company officers. The men would not have the same training or be used to the same discipline, and there would be difficulties as to pay etc. unless the men were transferred to the R.E., in which case they would be lost to the Infantry, whereas under the present system of Brigade Pioneers they can always be used as infantry in an emergency.

In addition the Divisional Cyclists have been used and had a good deal of training as pioneers, as well as one battalion which has done very good work as a pioneer battalion when not required in the firing line.

By this means it is possible to organise the work in the Division fairly well. But it would not be possible to withdraw them from the Division without seriously impairing its efficiency, they should therefore remain Divisional and not become Corps Troops.

There is certainly however an urgent need of pioneers for Corps troops,- as these however would not as a rule have to work under fire; it is suggested that pioneer battalions for each corps could easily be raised at home, officered by civil engineers - the men being partly artisans but mainly navvies - they would want little or no training provided they are enlisted and put into uniform so that they come under Military Law. They need not be armed and would be of the greatest assistance.

(sd) C.S. Wilson
Lt. Col.
C.R.E. 3rd Division

7-7-15.

SECRET.

3rd DIVISION OPERATION ORDER NO: 19.

18th July, 1915.

1. The mine which has been prepared under the southern redoubt at Y.21 is to be fired at 7.pm. on 19th July.
   The G.O.C., 3rd Division intends to take advantage of the explosion to improve our position in this locality.

2. The G.O.C., 8th Inf Bde will, with this object, seize and hold the mine crater and the trench to the west as far as point (H), connecting this front with the HOOGE defences as soon as circumstances allow.
   To cover this work it will be necessary to block the three trenches which run from (C), (E) and (Y.20).

3. The troops for this attack will be detailed from the 8th Inf Bde.
   In addition two sections 56th Fd Co R.E. will be placed at the disposal of the G.O.C., 8th Inf Bde to assist in placing the captured line in a state of defence and in the preparation of communication trenches.
   No: 24 Trench Mortar Battery is also placed at his disposal.

4. The 2nd Group H.A.R. and Howitzer Batteries of 3rd Divl Artillery will open fire at 7.pm. and will bombard the following points from 7.pm. to 7-30.pm.

   (a) Two 9.2" Howitzers - ANNEXE & Trench junction (C).

   (b) 130th Battery - Trench junction at (D), one section on (Y.19).

   (c) One 9.2" Howitzer - Trench junction (Y.19).

   (d) Two 6" Howitzers - Half way between (B) and (C).

   (e) Four 6" Howitzers (14th Division) - Y.20 to half way between Y.20 and (K).

   (f) Four 60 pdrs - (F) and (G).

   (g) Four 4.7" - Y.22 to MENIN Road.

5. Field batteries of 3rd Division will be ready to open fire if required as follows :- One Brigade on front (A) - (B) - (D). Two Batteries on Y-19, (F), and (G). The object of these batteries will be to prevent the approach of hostile reinforcements after the Heavy Artillery has ceased fire.

6. It is anticipated that the crater formed by the explosion will measure about 30 yards in diameter and that debris will be piled up in a ring of about 10 yards in width round the outside of the crater.
   To avoid falling debris assaulting troops should not advance for 40 seconds after the mine has been fired.

7. Troops holding the Stable Buildings and ISLAND POST should be withdrawn from those places as the explosion may cause falls of masonry. For the same reason no men should be in dug-outs at that time.

8. Acknowledge receipt by wire.

P.T.O.

Lieut-Colonel,
General Staff, 3rd Division.

Copies to :-

       7th Inf Bde.
       8th Inf Bde.
       O.C.Sig.Coy.
       C. R. A.
       C. R. E.
       A.A.Q.M.G.
       A. D. M. S.
       Div Mtd Troops.
       2nd Group H. A. R.
       5th Corps.
       14th Division.
       46th Division.

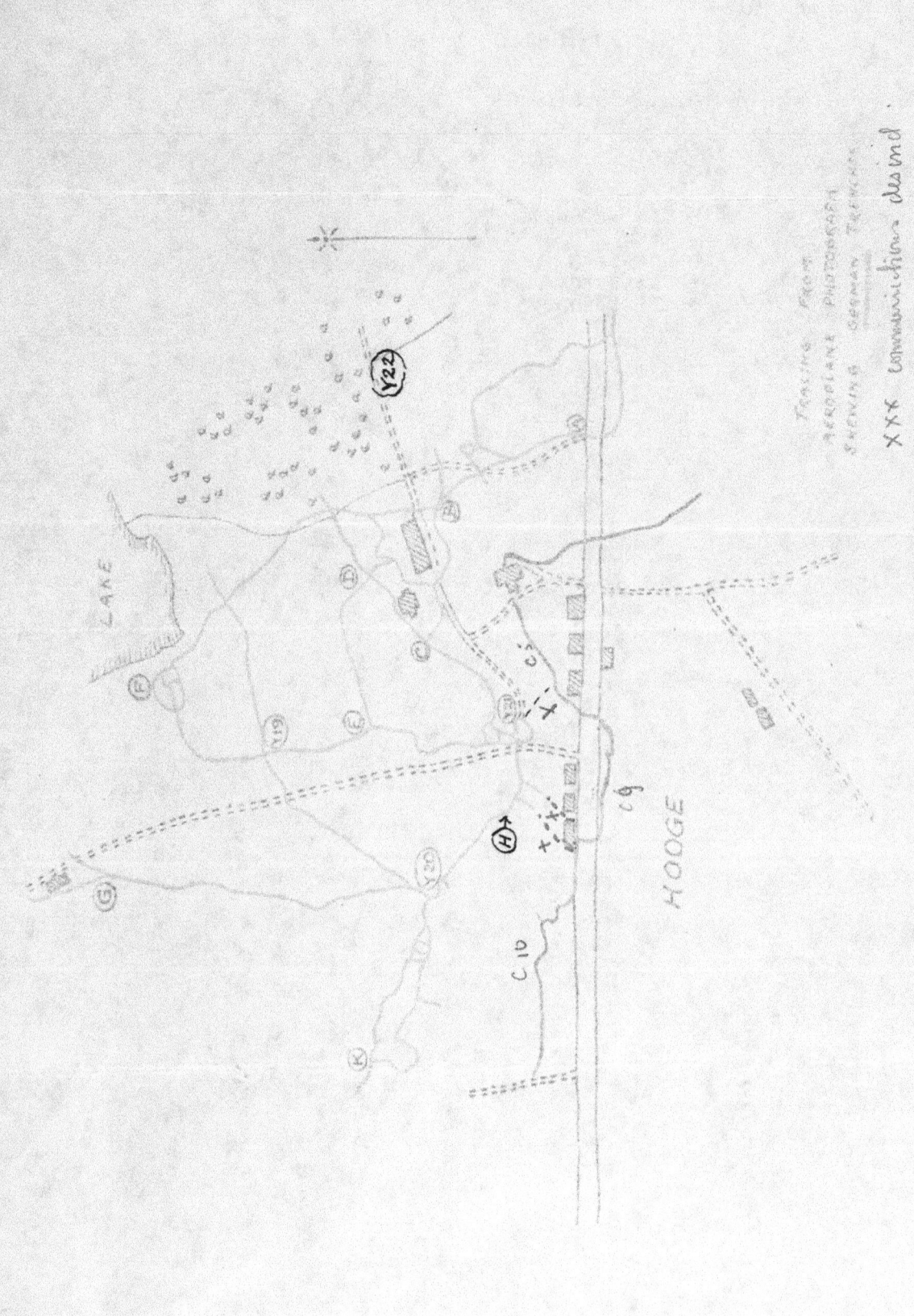

Copy.   Appendix C.

3rd Division,
Mining Operations round HOOGE.

After the enemy had dug in round the CHATEAU and REDOUBT it was decided to resort to mining, two shafts were started, one in the STABLES against the CHATEAU, and one in BULL FARM against the REDOUBT on 9-6-15. The STABLES shaft got into running sand and collapsed, and had finally to be given up. The BULL FARM shaft in spite of difficulties with water and considerable interruptions from bombardment especially with minenwerfers was successfully sunk and a gallery 200 ft. long driven under the REDOUBT reaching approximately to the further side of this small work. The depth of shaft was 20 ft. and the depth of gallery at the end was calculated as 20 ft.

On night of orders for the attack the gallery was loaded with 3,000 lbs of Ammonal and well tamped, the charge was successfully fired at 7.0 p.m. on 19-7-15, and produced a crater some 140 ft from lip to lip and 24 ft deep, this was rather larger than had been calculated on. Some 150 yds of enemy trench was destroyed and much more badly damaged. Our own trenches suffered very little. I think possibly the charge was rather too large, and a rather smaller one would have been equally successful. There was a second explosion North of the mine possibly a bomb store which the concussion of the mine exploded.

Credit is due to 2nd Lt G.R. Cassels and the Officers & men of the 175th Tunnelling Co R.E. who carried out the mining operations successfully under some difficulties. When the assault took place 2 sections of the 56th Co. R.E. were told off to accompany the assaulting troops and make communications back from the captured trenches, this work was successfully carried out under fairly heavy fire, a separate report has been sent in mentioning the names I wish to bring forward.

(sd) C.S. Wilson
Lt Col. R.E.
C.R.E. 3rd Division

23-7-1915.

COPY.   Appendix D.

3rd Division

With reference to the operations at HOOGE on the night of the 19th/20th July 1915 - I beg to bring to your notice the good work done by the two sections of the 56th Field Co. R.E. under 2/Lieut ALBERT COLLUM BROOKS and 2nd Lieut DAVID KEITH FINNEMORE. These sections got to work on the communications back from the crater as soon as it was occupied - the work was successfully carried out, the first part in broad daylight under a heavy rifle fire from short range by the enemy's trenches in front of the CHATEAU. The men all worked steadily and well in spite of fairly severe casualties - 3 N.C.Os killed, 2 N.C.Os and 7 Sappers wounded out of some 50 men. In addition they were frequently called on to leave their work and carry up grenades & ammunition to the infantry - In this connection I would wish to bring forward the names of No. 10568 a/Sergt. J. SMITH and No 2570 Sapper T. SEDDON, who whilst carrying up grenades were knocked over by the explosion of a heavy shell in the open, they picked themselves up, collected the grenades, and carried them up to the infantry. As Sergt SMITH was also doing very good work by the gallant example he showed his men in their hazardous task in digging in the open, I beg to submit his name for immediate reward.

I also wish to bring forward for mention the name of 2nd Lt. G.R. CASSELS 175 Co. R.E, who was in charge of all the mining operations, for his good work.

(sd) C.S. Wilson
Lt. Col.
CRE. 3rd Division

23.7.15.

Appendix E.

3rd Division

The supply of materials from the R.E. Parks is not nearly sufficient for preparing the front line trenches for the winter. This question unless strong steps are taken at once is going to be very serious, as not only will the trenches themselves suffer and defence become more difficult, but the winter conditions will cause a very heavy wastage from sickness, such as was experienced last winter. I think it ought to be very strongly represented to higher authority, that the need for the supply of materials at once is vitally important. The country itself is practically stripped of everything useful except for a certain amount of timber that can be obtained from houses wrecked by shell fire, we are therefore dependent on what arrangements for supply of materials can be made by the higher authorities. In the meantime I consider that no more material of any kind should be put into 2nd lines or works of defence still further back until the requirements of the front line have been satisfied. The principal stores required are timber, corrugated iron, expanded metal & sandbags — of all materials required the supply of wire plain or barbed alone appears to be adequate.

(sd) C.S. Wilson
Lt Col.
C.R.E. 3rd Division

28/7/15.

Appendix F.   Operation Order by CRE 3rd Division
                                                    18.7.15

With reference to 3rd Division Operation
Order No.19 of 18.7.15 attached.

1. O.C. 175 RE will arrange to join the mine
at 9.0.p.m. on 19.7.15. Two officers are to
be in charge of the firing arrangements, and
are to compare watches with the officer in
charge of the assault (Major BRIDGEMAN
The MIDDLESEX regiment). The 2 explosions to
be used simultaneously.

2. The detachment 175 RE in SANCTUARY WOOD
will be withdrawn during the night of the
19th/20th.

3. O.C. 56 RE will detail 2 sections to
report to O.C. assaulting troops at HOOGE.
One section should be close behind the
assaulting troops and at once try to
connect the 2 safes to ISLAND POST and C.10
The other section will as soon as darkness
permits connect the crater with C.5 North
of BULL FARM.
Ladders to enable troops to get out of C.6

... taken up forward and placed in
position by the Infantry.
An ample supply of sandbags is to be
available for consolidating the ground won
and for reposes to new or existing trenches. This
will probably be especially required, in the STABLE
C.6, ISLAND POST and East end of C.10.

4. Distribution:-

       OC 56 RE
       175 RE   CRE 3rd Division

121/6754

3rd Division

Hd. Qrs. R.E. 3rd Division

Vol XIII

August 15

WAR DIARY

R.E. Headquarters 3rd Division
August 1915.

1st Work on H.Q. huts at RENINGHELST carried on — Supporting points in H 15 C & H 16 d continued & improvement of communication trench from VOORMEZEELE to R 7 started on by 56th Coy and 4th S. Lancs. Cheshire Coy working on front line 8th Bde Sector.

2nd Work continued as above 200 men 8th Bde assisting with S.P. in H 16 d. 100 men 4th S Lancs helped 2nd S Lancs rebuild parapet of R 3

3rd As above — 200 men 4th S Lancs assisting 2nd S Lancs
56th Coy less 1 section detached to 6th Corps temporarily for tactical purposes

4th Work continued on hutting, S.P. in H 16 d, communication trench, + front line 8th Bde Sector. 2 Companies 5th S Lancs worked on R 3.

5th, 6th Work continued on front line, hutting,

5, 6ᵗʰ Supporting points & communication trench.

7, 8, 9, 10 Work as above progressing well – Civilian carpenters also employed at R.E Park (since 5ᵗʰ) sawing timber & making trench boards.

11ᵗʰ Work continued as above on communication Trenches, supporting points & front line. Also on Hutting at Reninghelst and civilian carpenters making trenchboards at R.E. Park.

12ᵗʰ, 13ᵗʰ & 14ᵗʰ } Work as above continued
15ᵗʰ }

16ᵗʰ, 17ᵗʰ & 18ᵗʰ ——— Do ———

19ᵗʰ 9ᵗʰ Brigade took over SANCTUARY WOOD position from 46ᵗʰ Division. 56ᵗʰ Coy returned from 6ᵗʰ Corps – Work continuing on Supporting Points H 16 D (infantry party) & H 15 C (4 S Lancs), Cheshires working on 8ᵗʰ Brigade line at The BLUFF. Hutting continued at RENINGHELST and civilian carpenters making trench boards at R.E Park –

20, 21, } Work carried on on hutting, supporting
22, 23 } points H15C, H11D, + civilian
carpenters making trench boards.
1 officer + 50 O.R. 4/5 Lancs. to billet near
ABEELE to make hurdles. Cheshires
supervising construction C.T's on S bank
ZILLEBEKE LAKE + from ZILLEBEKE
to MAPLE COPSE.
N° 2 Siege Co R.A.R.E. came under
orders of C.R.E. 3rd Division for work on
23rd

24th, 25th } 7th Bde took over HOOGE position (24th)
26th, 27th } from 6th Division. 8th Bde handed
over its line to 46th Division & came
back (24th). Work continuing as above
56th Coy working on defences in
neighbourhood of HOOGE + on
dug outs for 7th Bde H.Q.

R.A.R.E. working on dug outs for
3rd Div. Battle H.Q.
1 officer + 50 O.R. from the
Division proceeded to CLAIRMARAIS
FOREST to cut timber for corduroy on 27th

28th-29th } 56th Coy started making dug outs
30th-31st } under MENIN road

and one Company 4th S.Lanc asked reclaiming F1 on 28th. Work proceeding as usual on Supporting points H15C & H16D, hutting, making of trench boards, Communication trenches near ZILLEBEKE hurdle making, & timber cutting at CLAIRMARAIS FOREST. Cheshires working on supporting point near MOATED GRANGE with infantry parties

---

Appendix A   re unfitness of CAPT. H.W. FLINT for command of Cheshire Field Co RE.

" B.   re shortage of men in Cheshire Field Co RE.

" C.   Recommendation of CAPT C.E. SOPWITH for appointment of Divisional CRE.

4.9.15.

C.H. Edwards
Capt.
Adjt 3rd Div Engrs.

Confidential   Appendix A.
3rd Division   Copy

       I have to report that
Captain H.W. FLINT, has been sent out
from ENGLAND to command the
CHESHIRE Field Company RE. This officer
is quite unfitted for the command
of a field unit, as he possesses no
technical knowledge or experience, and
has not been used to managing men,
nor is his physique equal to the
strain imposed on a Field Company
Officer. These facts he quite appreciates
himself, and I would recommend
that he either be sent back to his home
unit, or employed on some
administrative duties on the Lines
of Communication. Under instructions
from G.O.C 3rd Division I have
relieved him from command of
the unit pending further instructions.
May these be obtained early please
as this officer is of no use to me,
and unfit to be with a unit in the
Field.

                        (Sgd) C.S. Wilson
1-8-15.   Lieut Colonel.
                         C.R.E. 3rd Division

Appx in B.

Copy.

3rd Division

The Cheshire Field Company are still 53 Sappers under strength – May the draft for this unit be hastened please – They have now been very much under strength for quite two months now, and with only two companies in the Division the necessity for keeping units up to strength is urgent.

4-8-15

(Sd) C.S. Wilson
Lieut Colonel
CRE III Divn

Appendix C.

Copy.

3rd Division

Your "G" 354.

I have the honour to put forward the name of Captain G.E. SOPWITH 56th Coy R.E. as a suitable officer to fill the appointment of divisional C.R.E. He has a very excellent power of organisation, and has now had a good experience as a Field Company Commander, as which he has done excellent work.

(Sgd) C.S. Wilson
Lieut. Colonel.
C.R.E. III Divn

14-8-15

$\frac{121}{7145}$

3rd Division

H^d Q^rs R.E. 3rd Division
Vol XIV
Sep! 15

87

WAR DIARY

R.E. Headquarters 3rd Division

September 1915.

1st Work continued on Supporting point H15C by 4th S.Lancs. who also worked on trenches F1 & C1. 56 Coy worked on new dug outs at HOOGE in support & communication trenches & Craters, also on dug outs for 7th Bde H.Q.
Infantry party worked on ZILLEBEKE switch. Cheshire Coy with infantry parties worked on Supporting points near MOATED GRANGE, & DORMY HOUSE communication trench. Hutting continued at RENINGHELST & civilian carpenters making trench boards at R.E. Park. ~~Transfer of R.E.~~ Hurdle making near ABEELE & cutting of timber in CLAIR MARAIS FOREST carried on. No 2 RARE working on Battle H.Q. for 3rd Division.

2d Work as above continued but much interfered with by rain. HOOGE heavily bombarded & much damage done. Transfer of R.E. Park to H16d11 commenced

3rd Forward Companies of 4 S Lancs making telephone cable trenches I.17.d. Cheshires worked out new C.T. from junction REGENT STREET & OXFORD STREET to MAPLE COPSE. Other work going on as usual but much interfered with by rain.

4th Cheshire Coy working with infantry on new C.T. above, DORMY HOUSE LANE & PROMENADE. 56th Coy working on 7th Bde H.Q. dugouts, repair of trenches at HOOGE damaged by bombardment, and with infantry on ZILLEBEKE SWITCH. Work again interfered with by rain. R.E. dug outs in SANCTUARY WOOD damaged during bombardment. Other work as usual.

5th Forward companies 4 S Lancs finished cable trenches & worked on Appendix. RARE on repair of Canal Line on ramparts and 3rd Div H.Q. dugouts, also A.A. battery dugouts MAPLE COPSE. Other work as usual.

6th Cheshires superintended infantry party on supporting points near MOATED GRANGE. 56th Coy. started bombardment slits at HOOGE. Other work as usual. Capt. G.E. SOPWITH wounded. Forward Coy. 4 S Lancs on Appendix 4 F.

89

7th   Work as above. Movement of Park completed
8th   Capt. V.P. SMITH joined 56th Coy & took over command – Work as usual
9th   Work as above – R.A.R.E. started dressing station in MAPLE COPSE
10th   Work as usual
11th   R.A.R.E. started on dressing station in KRUISSTRAAT – 8th Brigade miners, working with 56th Coy continued dugouts under MENIN ROAD. 56th Coy carrying on with bombardment slits & other work in & around HOOGE – Forward Coys. 4 S. Lancs started work on trenches eastward from F.1. Other work as usual.
12.13th   Work as above
14th   Hutting for division begun by a party of 12 R.E., 15 infantry ~~and civilians~~. Other work proceeding as usual.
15th   R.A.R.E. started making dugouts in ramparts at YPRES – Other work as usual. 10 more infantry + 14 R.A. on huts
16th, 17th, 18th   Work as usual (Trench tramway from SANCTUARY WOOD started on 16th)
19th   Forward Coys 4 S. Lancs on Appendix & new C.T. S. of MENIN ROAD – Other work as usual –

20th 1/1 East Riding Field Coy. joined 3rd Division.
25 more infantry on huts - Work as usual

21st 22nd 23rd } Work going on as above
24th } 2 Sections E Riding Coy attached to 56th Coy for work and 2 sections to Cheshire Coy.

25th 3rd Div. in conjunction with 14th Div. attacked at 4.20 am enemy and captured several trenches but were unable to retain them. Four mines successfully exploded under enemy trenches opposite B4 just prior to assault.
2 sections each of 56 & Cheshire Companies took part in the operation. After dusk remaining 2 sections of each company and 4 S. Lancs went up to assist in repair of our trenches which were damaged during operations.

26th } Field Coys & 4th S Lancs working on front
27th } line and main CT's

28th 56th Coy working at HOOGE
S Lancs on UNION STREET
Cheshires working in SANCTUARY WOOD, also working on DORMY HOUSE LANE and repairs to transport road KRUISSTRAAT to ZILLEBEKE

29th   56th Coy working at HOOGE and on ZILLEBEKE dug outs.
S.Lancs working on UNION STREET and started corduroying transport road at KRUISSTRAAT.
Cheshires on DORMY HOUSE LANE and repairs to transport road.
Enemy gained a footing in B4.

30th   56th Coy working on Upper Grafton Street, Regent Street and ZILLEBEKE dug outs.
Cheshires wiring in SANCTUARY WOOD
S.Lancs on new fire trench in SANCTUARY WOOD + corduroy of transport road.
Hutting going on, also hurdle making near ABEELE + wood cutting at CLAIRMARAIS. Civilian Carpenters continuing on trench boards at Park.

Appendix A,   Recommendations, 2nd Lt McKELVIE, Cpls YOUNG and HANLEY 175 Coy and Cpl KING 1st Lincolns.
"   B,   Recommendation, Capt. G.E. SOPWITH 56th Coy RE.
"   C,   Notes on preparation of Stable Standings
"   D,   Recommendations, 56th + Cheshire Coys.
"   E,   CRE 3rd Div Draft Operation Orders d/- 22-9-15
"   F,   Operation Order by C.R.E. 3rd Div d/- 23.9.15

Appendix G,   Application for a draft for the Cheshire Coy R.E.
Appendix H,   Recommendations in connection with the operations of 25th September 1915
Appendix I,   Report on Operation of 25th September 1915 -

11-10-15

C.O.R.Edwards
Capt R.E.
Adjr 3rd Div Engrs.

3rd Division.   Appendix A

I have the honour to bring to your notice for immediate reward the following N.C.Os.

Nº 10222 Corporal F.R. YOUNG. 175 Co. R.E.
Nº 14113 Corporal E. KING. 1st LINCOLNS.

These N.C.Os were at the mine shaft with the outgoing and incoming reliefs on the night of September 4th/5th when the front trenches were destroyed by heavy minenwerfer there were several casualties out of the small party, 1 killed, 4 missing and 13 wounded. The shaft was cut off by the trenches being destroyed, and the enemy opened rapid fire and a bombardment, These N.C.Os of whom Corpl YOUNG was himself wounded, brought in the wounded men to cover under the very trying circumstances existing, and displayed conspicuous gallantry and ability.

Nº 79992 Corporal H. HANLEY, 175 Co. R.E. also assisted in the above work, and afterwards accompanied the officer in charge, 2/Lt D. McKELVIE in an examination of the mine galleries, a service of very considerable risk as the shaft was then exposed and under bombardment and might have been blown in at any time whilst they were making their reconnaisance.

2/Lt D. McKELVIE showed great coolness and ability in his reconnaisance and getting the shaft and gear covered up to prevent discovery until the

trenches could be built up again and I should recommend that his name should be noted for mention in despatches.

(sgd) C.S. Wilson.
Lieut-Colonel
C.R.E. 3rd Division.

7.9.15.

Appendix B

3rd Division.

I have the honour to bring forward the name of Captain GEORGE. ERNEST. SOPWITH, 56th Co. R.E, this officer has commanded the unit with very conspicuous success and ability for some six months until he was wounded on 6-9-15. During this time his services have been of very great value to the Division, his careful arrangements and work were of great assistance in the attack on SPANBROEK MOELEN on 12.3.15, where the company did very good and gallant work, and also in the attack on BELLEWARDE on 16.6.15. when it was largely due to his personal reconnaissance and initiative when in charge of working parties the night after the action, that more enemy trenches were held and consolidated than would otherwise have probably been the case. In view of the fact that he has now been wounded and invalided, I would request that if practicable his name might go forward for immediate reward, and I have the honour to recommend him for the D.S.O. which his consistently good and gallant work under often very trying circumstances, have in my opinion well gained for him.

(sd) C. S. Wilson, Lieut-Colonel
C.R.E. 3rd Division.

7-9-15.

Appendix C.

Notes on preparation of Stable Standings.

Standings should be 12 ft wide and 4' 9" in length for each horse. They should be made either where a hedge or trees will act as a wind screen, or at all events so arranged that the horses tails are towards the prevailing wind (S.W.).

They should be laid with a slope of about 1 in 15 to the rear for drainage.

The site should be levelled to this slope, and covered with a layer of a few inches of sand, which can be obtained from SCHERPENBERG; to prevent the mud working up between the bricks.

Boards or logs should be picketed to keep the edges of the standing from breaking down.

The bricks should then be laid in carefully as paving, whole bricks on edge being used, and packed with sand.

The standing being laid, the cracks between the bricks should be raked out and run with a grouting of 1 part cement to 3 of sand.

(sd) S. C. Wilson, Lt-Col
C.R.E. 3rd Divn

Appendix D

Confidential

3rd Division.

With reference to your A 5160/1 I have the honour to bring forward the following additional names from the R.E. I have no names to add to the list already sent in for the 4/SOUTH LANCS.

For MENTION. Officers.

Lieut ALEXANDER, WILLIAM, GORDON, 56th Co. R.E. has done consistently good work since he joined the Company on 23.4.15, and has set his men a fine example when dangerous work was to be done. His work was particularly good on the night of 16th June when his party was heavily shelled on their way down to work with gas shells.

For D.C.M.

No 17220 Sergt. F. HEATH, 56th Co. R.E, this N.C.O has done conspicuously good work throughout the campaign, he has always displayed great confidence and initiative, and has set a fine example of coolness and courage on the very frequent occasions when dangerous work has had to be carried out.

No 2570 Sapper T. SEDDON. 56th Co. R.E. in addition to the gallant action already reported on 23.7.15, at HOOGE on the night of the 19th/20th July. Whenever there has been dangerous work to be done he has always shown great coolness and courage and taken a leading part in it.

For MENTION.

P.T.O.

	Nº 10973 Sapper E. WHALE	56th Co. R.E.
2	Nº 22721 Sapper F. PREECE	56th Co. R.E.
4	Nº 19548 Sapper R. LIDDELL	56th Co. R.E.

These men have done excellent work and have been conspicuous by their coolness, gallantry & energy on the many occasions in which dangerous work has had to be carried out.

6 Nº 63 C.S.M. T. QUIGLEY. Cheshire Field Co. has done very excellent service as C.S.M. since the unit arrived in the country in December 1914.

3 Nº 4. Sergt. J. ARMSTRONG Cheshire Field Co.
5 Nº 523 a/Corporal W. N. HIGSON. Cheshire Field Co.
7 Nº 11 a/Lance Corpl E. HUGHES. Cheshire Field Co.

These N.C.O's have done consistently good work and have set a good example of coolness and gallantry whenever any dangerous work had to be carried out.

I have numbered the recommendations for Divisional Engineers in order of merit, but not the others who have been working with us.

Reference recommendation of Lt CASSELLS for affair at HOOGE on 19th/20th July, he has since been awarded the Military Cross for this, his name may therefore be cancelled.

(sd) C. S. Wilson.
Lieut Colonel,
C.R.E. 3rd Division.

19-9-15.

Appendix E.

C.R.E. 3rd Division. Draft Operation Order.
Reference 1/10,000 HOOGE (linen) and 1/5,000 Special Map.

1. 3rd and 14th Divisions will attack and occupy the enemy's front line from J.19.a.6.8. to I.12.a.0.4. Dividing line between Divisions will be ECLUSETTE STREAM which flows West from BELLEWARDE POND at I.12.d.2.5.

2. The following main communication trenches are reserved for west-bound traffic ZILLEBEKE STREET PROMENADE. CASTLE STREET. All other main C T's will be for east-bound traffic.

3. Task of 3rd Division is to occupy enemy's line Q 5.16.15.9.91.30-27-43-47-42-41-40.56 60. West edge of BELLEWARDE POND as far as outflow of stream.

4. Tasks allotted Brigades.
   9th Brigade cover right front of attack and find 4 battalions for Divisional reserve. Left battalion 9th Brigade will assist by attacking Q 5 and will join up the right of the captured trenches to our present line.
   8th Brigade seize and occupy enemy's line Q 5 inclusive Q 16-15-9-91-30-27-43-47-42-41-Q 40 inclusive.
   7th Brigade seize and occupy the enemy's line Q 40 exclusive Q 56-60. West edge of pond to outflow of stream. Keeping touch with right of 14th Division.

5. The chief objectives are as follows:—
   (a) Trenches enclosed by points Q 16-15-9-11.
   (b)   "   "   "   Q 22-20-91-30-27-43-
                                   26-25-24-23.
   (c)   "   "   "   Q 36-42-41-40-39.
   (d)   "   round CHATEAU in area Q 55, 56, 59, 90
   (e)   "   in area Q 59, 60, 65, 62.
   The main attacks will be delivered against these objectives and the intervening spaces cleared by bombing.

6. Front attacked will be bombarded from 3.50 a.m to 4.20 a.m. guns will lift gradually from front to support trenches commencing 4.5 a.m. Two mines will be exploded under Q 12 at 4.19 a.m and two under Q 14 at 4.19½ a.m.

7. Assault will be delivered all along the line at 4.20 a.m.

8. 7th and 9th Brigades with 2 battalions 17th Division attached will furnish trench garrisons.

9. Reserves. 1 Battalion SANCTUARY WOOD
             1 Battalion ZILLEBEKE SWITCH & POND
             2 Battalions H 23. b.

11. 2 Sections Cheshire Field Co are allotted to the front of attack Q.16 to Q 17. Their task will be 1 Section dig communication trenches from crater and captured trenches to B 4 and help consolidate craters. A working party of 50 infantry from 8th Brigade will be attached. 1 Section dig communications back from Q 18 and Q 22 to our assembly trench East of C 1.

a working party of 50 infantry will be attached to this Section from 8th Infantry Brigade.

This section will also be prepared to assist in clearing obstacles for which purpose they will have 8 BANGALORE torpedoes prepared; and have them on the spot ready with leads & exploders.

2 Sections 56th Field Co will be allotted to the front of attack from Q 24 to the left of the Divisional front. Their task will be :—

1 Section with working party of 25 men from 8th Infantry Brigade attached, dig communications from about Q 86 N of MENIN ROAD to captured trenches.
They will also be prepared to clear obstacles for which purpose they will have 4 BANGALORE torpedoes prepared and have them on the spot ready with leads and exploders.

1 Section with working party of 50 infantry attached from 7th Brigade, dig communications from our line to Q 94 and 92. They will also be prepared to assist in clearing obstacles with grapnels and the arrangements for using them if necessary must be made beforehand. Grapnels, pulleys and wire rope will be available in R.E. PARK today.

All ranks must be impressed with the utmost importance of getting covered communications through to the captured trenches as early as possible, as the fate of the bombing fight will largely depend on it.

Officers are reminded that there is often a short calm immediately after the assault, if this occurs advantage must be taken of it to get out an obstacle for which purpose each section should have some French wire and iron pickets with it.

The remaining sections of the two Field Cos and the 4/SOUTH LANCS will be in the YPRES ramparts in reserve and will be available to assist in the consolidation of the captured position after dusk. East Riding Fd Co will be in reserve in its billets H.9.d.8.6

56th Co will be responsible for maintenance of pontoon bridge at SALLY PORT and will arrange to have material for repair available on the site.

CHESHIRE Field Co will be responsible for maintenance of footbridge from South SALLY PORT.

Toolcarts will be brought up to ramparts and teams sent back.

O.C. 56th Co will be with 7th Brigade H.Q. and O.C. Cheshire Field Co with 8th Brigade H.Q. These Officers should take any opportunity of making themselves acquainted with the situation as it develops and will be prepared with proposals for the best employment of their reserve sections and the pioneer battalion after dusk.

Pioneer battalion and infantry working parties will be distinguished by a bow of white tape on
12. the shoulder straps.
13. Collecting stations for wounded will be at :-
    N.E. corner of MAPLE COPSE
    LILLE GATE
    KRUISSTRAAT dugouts H.24.a.5.9.

13. Depots of R.E stores will be formed as under:—
   (a) B 4 S
   (b) in rear of C 1
   (c) Culvert under MENIN ROAD I.18.a.2.7.
   (d) SANCTUARY WOOD dump.
   Each to consist of 5,000 sandbags
                     100 pickets
                     50 coils barbed wire
                     50 coils French wire
                     100 shovels
                     25 picks
                     10 mauls.
   56th R.E will form c and d. Cheshire Fd Co a & b.
14. HQ 9th Brigade   S.E. corner of MAPLE COPSE
    HQ 8th   "   N.E corner of MAPLE COPSE
    HQ 7th   "   HALFWAY HOUSE
    HQ 3rd Division and C.R.E & C.R.A. in the casemates in YPRES ramparts, South of the SALLY PORT.
15. Dates, hours & march tables will be communicated later.
16. Acknowledge.

(sd) C. S. Wilson.
Lieut-Colonel.
C R E. 3rd Division

22. 9. 15.

Appendix F

SECRET.   Copy no 3.

Operation order by C.R.E. 3rd Division.

Reference 1/5,000 special map.

1. In addition to the two sections already detailed, The O.C. Cheshire Field Co will detail a party of 8 men under an officer to report to G.O.C. 9th Brigade at MAPLE COPSE in the evening of 24th. Their task will be to assist the attacking battalion of the 9th Brigade by dealing with the wire about I.19.a.6.7. to 7.9. For this purpose they will have wire cutting tools and two of the Bangalore torpedoes already ordered to be prepared.

(sgd). C. S. Wilson
Lieut Colonel
23. 9. 15.   C.R.E. 3rd Division.

Copy no 1. Cheshire Fd Co.
Copy no 2. 9th Brigade
Copy no 3 office.

Appendix G.

3rd Division.

With reference to my letter of 4.8.15. May a special request be made for a draft for the CHESHIRE Field Co. R.E. This unit in addition to ordinary wastage had many casualties in the actions of 16th June & 25th Sept. and is now 70 sappers under strength and has had no draft for months. The necessity for a draft is urgent with the very large amount of work that has to be done, and it is rapidly growing so weak as to be of little use.

(sgd) C. S. Wilson
Lieut. Colonel.
C.R.E. 3rd Division.

28.9.15.

Appendix H
Confidential.

3rd Division.

I have the honour to bring to your notice the names of the undermentioned Officers, N.C.O's & men in connection with the operations on 25th September 1915.

For immediate reward.

2nd Lieutenant GILBERT. FRANCE. WATSON- Cheshire Field Co. R.E. for very conspicuous resolute courage and devotion to duty. On the night of the 24th/25th September he made a close and excellent reconnaissance of the enemy's wire. On the 25th when wire was reported by a scout he crawled out with 2 men before the assault and cut it successfully. As soon as the assault commenced he got his party of 12 sappers and 25 infantry to work on a communication trench to the captured position, 80 yds of trench were completed in two hours under heavy machine gun and shell fire during which time 70% of his party became casualties. The work being completed as far as possible he reported to the 4/GORDONS headquarters for instructions and on receipt of them took the remains of his party up into the captured positions and worked at consolidating them until we were forced to withdraw, he got back to our original trenches with only a Sergt. who was killed almost at once and 3 or 4 men & finding they were not manned he collected some 25 of the 4/GORDONS and manned a portion of the trench, holding it until

relieved after dark by the MIDDLESEX regiment.
   Recommended for D.S.O.   O.C. Cheshire Fd Co. C.R.E. 3rd Divn.

Nº 527 Acting Lance Corporal R. BARKER. Cheshire Field Co. R.E.
   For gallantry, good work and initiative. On the 25th September 1915 he was with his section in the salient of SANCTUARY WOOD, in the rush of the assault he got separated from his party, he however at once assisted & superintended a party of the Royal Scots FUSILEERS who were digging themselves in, and on completion went back on his own initiative and collecting a party of infantry started opening out a communication trench from our line to the captured position; he persisted in this work under heavy machine gun & shell fire until it became impossible to continue when he was the last man to leave the work.
   Recommended for D.C.M.   O.C. Cheshire Fd Co. C.R.E. 3rd Divn.

Nº 522 Corporal MARTIN. J. Cheshire Field Co. R.E.
   For conspicuous gallantry. On 24th he accompanied 2nd Lt WATSON in his reconnaissance of the enemy trenches and on the 25th he displayed great gallantry and spirit in keeping the men at work under very heavy machine gun and shell fire, all the other N.C.Os of the party and 70% of the men being casualties, and was of great assistance to his officer.
   Recommended for D.C.M.   O.C. Cheshire Fd Co. C.R.E. 3rd Divn.

For mention.

Lieutenant LESLIE. ALBISTON. HALSALL
Cheshire Field Co. R.E.

On the 25th September 1915, he went out with a small party from the salient in SANCTUARY WOOD and though discovered before the work was completed succeeding in placing and exploding two torpedoes in the enemy's wire entanglement under rifle fire, making two gaps which materially assisted the success of the assault.

Recommended for mention. O.C. Cheshire Fd Co. C.R.E. 3rd Division.

2nd. Lieutenant CHARLES GATTENS. 56th Co. R.E.

On 25th September when in charge of his section and a working party, showed gallantry and resolution in getting his men at work in spite of heavy casualties until the failure of the attack compelled him to desist. This officer has done very good work since he joined the Company on 27th July 1915.

Recommended for mention. O.C. 56th Co. R.E. C.R.E. 3rd Division.

No 331 Sapper G.W. JONES Cheshire Fd. Co. R.E.

On 25th September he assisted Lt WATSON in going out and cutting the enemy's wire entanglement and afterwards when the party were having heavy casualties, he was conspicuous by his untiring energy and the cheerful spirit with which he encouraged the rest of his party.

Recommended for mention. O.C. Cheshire Field Co. C.R.E. 3rd Divs.

No 508 Sapper H.S. SIMS. Cheshire Field Co. R.E.
No 563 Sapper G.B. SWINBANK. Cheshire Fd Co. R.E.

These two men showed great gallantry in going back from the captured trenches over the open under heavy rifle and shell fire and bringing up supplies of sandbags during the action of 25th September.

Recommended for mention. O.C. Cheshire Fd Co. C.R.E. 3rd Divs.

(sgd) C.S. Wilson
Lieut-Colonel.
28. 9. 15. C.R.E. 3rd Division.

Appendix I

Report on Operations on 25-9-15.

As soon as it appeared probable that offensive operations might be undertaken by the DIVISION, it was decided to assist the attack by mining, the only point that appeared to offer any chance of success in the time available was in the salient of B4, where two listening galleries had already been run out about 40 ft, work was at once started on that nearest the enemy's lines, distance 180 ft and a branch gallery broken out against an important trench junction further SOUTH, distance 320 ft. An officer and 20 men were obtained from the 175 Tunnelling Co. R.E and with the assistance of the 9th Brigade Mining Section, the work was pushed forward with the utmost energy, and the ground being favourable the progress made was excellent, though the work was interrupted by bombardments which caused fairly heavy casualties in the personnel, and at one time they were cut off from the shaft for nearly 48 hours owing to the front trenches being blown in. As more time became available two other galleries were driven & the second listening gallery connected up so as to give a second access to the mines. Four charges were laid from 10 to 30 ft inside the enemy's front line trench, charges of gunpowder were calculated for about 3½ tons craters and 4 tons intervals. It was hoped to destroy the network of trenches and communications for about 150 yards by 50 yds. The mines were successfully fired in two groups at 30 seconds interval so that the debris would just have time to come down before the moment of assault. The result was very successful, the 4 craters were 30 to 35 yds from lip to lip and over 150 yds in length by 60 yds in depth of the enemy's trenches were destroyed and blocked. The attacking troops were enabled to reach the 3rd line trench with practically no difficulty and the attacks on each side were greatly facilitated. The enemy's loss must have been heavy as their trenches here were a close network and included some important communication trench junctions, added to which it had been noticed during previous bombardments that a great many men crowded up there to get away from it. The enemy casualties were most probably at least 200 and very possibly 300 men.

Lt D. McKELVIE superintended the work throughout, displaying great skill & resource as well as resolution, he was ably seconded by his sappers and by 2/Lt STUBBS of the LIVERPOOL SCOTTISH and the 9th Brigade miners, and all ranks worked magnificently under trying and anxious conditions.

The Field Companies & Pioneer Battalion were very fully employed in carrying out & superintending the necessary preliminary work in reclaiming our old trenches and making new ones, and all worked hard and well in endeavouring to get the work done in time.

Before the attack certain points where the wire was reported to be a serious obstacle were reconnoitred by R.E. officers and it was decided to try to clear a gap at two places with explosives. Two BANGALORE torpedoes were successfully placed and fired by Lt HALSALL and a small party of the Cheshire Field Co. on South of the salient in SANCTUARY WOOD, though the enemy were throwing up flares and the party were under rifle as well as shell fire, as they were seen before they had finished - Two gaps were made in the wire.

The other attempt near the wall was unsuccessful, there was no cover and the enemy were keenly on the alert, the officer in charge & most of his party were shot down at once.

Parties of R.E. with infantry working parties were told off at different points along the front to open up communications with the captured trenches and assist in consolidating the position.

From B4 this was partially done but the heavy shell & machine gun fire prevented its completion before dark.

From C, the party under Lt WATSON of the Cheshire 7th Co and 4th GORDONS did excellent work immediately after the assault they got to work and in two hours under a very heavy shell and machine gun fire they got a trench 80 yds long through from the appendix losing 75% of their number in the process. The remainder then went up and helped consolidate, when the troops were finally compelled to withdraw, there were only 1 sergt and 3 men left, seeing our original trenches not manned, Lt WATSON collected some 25 men of the 4/ Gordons and manned a portion of B8 maintaining his position there until relieved in the evening by the MIDDLESEX. In addition before the assault a scout having reported some wire, Lt WATSON with 2 men crawled out and cut it successfully.

The sections with the left of the attack got to work at once but owing to the failure of the assault were unable to do anything, both R.E and the working parties of the

1st Gordons & R. Irish Rifles suffering heavily.

In the evening the remaining sections of the Field Co's and the Pioneer Battalion were sent out to work, the sappers got out a certain amount of wire, and the 4/South Lancs did excellent work in clearing and rebuilding the very badly damaged trenches in the salient of SANCTUARY WOOD, in spite of the conditions and wet state of the ground they filled and laid 12 sandbags a man, a very creditable piece of work.

During the attack 2 officers 4/South Lancs were in charge of the grenade supply and did very good work.

The 4/South Lancs machine guns were with the 7th Brigade and their bombers with the 8th Brigade.

The casualties in the R.E with the attack and their working parties were I regret to say very heavy, as well as in the Machine Gun and bomber detachments of the 4/South Lancs but all ranks carried out their duties with great courage and resolution.

The attempts to cut the wire show again that this is only possible where some form of cover exists by aid of which the enemy wire can be approached, or where the enemy look out is extremely bad, any attempt to do this across the open especially with a moon is impracticable and means the loss of officers and men engaged in the attempt.

The marking of R.E. and working parties with a distinguishing badge in the shape of a knot of white tape on the shoulder strap was found most useful, and I strongly recommend that this should always be adopted in the future, it was very readily recognised both by day and night.

The officers who got into the German trenches report that only the front lines showed much signs of damage the 3rd line & communications were practically intact, the trenches were wide, well constructed and revetted, a similar type to our own, the communication trenches were 8 or 9 ft deep and very narrow, not more than 2 ft wide, they had a wooden box drain running along the bottom under a flooring of small logs. Dug outs were off communications trenches in most cases stepped down with 12 ft of cover & wooden flooring over a big sump, all were heavily & very well timbered. Where the dug outs were in the fire trenches they were in the parados which was exceptionally high, so much so as in some cases to make reversing the parapet a difficult operation. A few bomb stores were noticed in the front parapets in one case made in concrete.

I am sending a separate letter re the officers and men whose names I wish to bring to notice.

(sgd) C. S. Wilson
Lieut Colonel.
C.R.E. 3rd Division

29.9.15

121/7496

HQ - RE - 3rd Divn

Oct, 15

Vol XV

93

WAR DIARY.
R.E. Headquarters 3rd Division

October 1915.

1st 56th Coy working on trenches at HOOGE and ZILLEBEKE dugouts – one section to live in dugouts in REGENT STREET.
4 S. Lancs on trenches in SANCTUARY WOOD and corduroying Transport Road from KRUISSTRAAT.
Cheshire Coy. wiring in SANCTUARY WOOD. Party of infantry cutting timber for corduroy in CLAIRMARAIS FOREST –
Party of 4 S. Lancs making hurdles near ADEELE.
Divisional hutting progressing – Civilian carpenters making trenchboards R.E. Park.

2nd Work as above. One company of 4 S. Lancs to cellars in YPRES.

3rd 2 Sections East Riding Coy to 7th Bde & worked on FOSS WAY
9th Bde miners started again on MENIN ROAD dugouts.
4 S. Lancs started work on REGENT ST.
Other work going on as usual.

94

4th Work as above   50 men RARE continued work on ~~party~~ dugouts in RAMPARTS YPRES.

5th Cheshire ~~working~~ parties on wooden tramway to SANCTUARY WOOD and on ZILLEBEKE STREET. Other work as usual.
103 Co. RE, 24th Division attached for "instruction"; one section attached to 56th Coy and one to Cheshire Coy.

6th Div. Cyclists wiring in ~~~~ SANCTUARY WOOD.
Party of Cheshires on bomb stores in MAPLE COPSE.
Other work as usual.

7th Two sections of 103 Coy not with 3rd Div Field Coys worked on defences of KRUISSTRAAT ~~with~~ and BELGIAN CHATEAU with 500 infantry of 24th Division.
E. Riding section with 7th Bde wiring in SQUARE WOOD.
Other work as above.

8th ~~~~ Wooden tramway from SANCTUARY WOOD to ZILLEBEKE Completed ~~~~

9th, 10th Work going on as usual – Sections of 103 Co with 3rd Div 7th Corps changed on 9th
(H.Q. + 2 Coys)

11th No 2 Entrenching Bn attached to CRE 3rd Div for administration and work – 103 Coy rejoined 24th Div – Work as usual

12th Work as usual. Entrenching Bn. provided parties for work on ZILLEBEKE SWITCH under 56th Coy and under Cheshire Co for supporting points at MOATED GRANGE. ~~and at HOOGE~~

13th East Riding Coy started work on steel tramway from KRUISSTRAAT to ZILLEBEKE. Other work going on as usual. Lieut. LE FEUVRE, W.T., left 56th Coy for England 2 Lieut GIBSON, J.P.B., left 56th Coy to join 63rd Coy –

14th } Work as usual. E. Ridings started
15th } laying wooden tramway from ZILLEBEKE to ZOUAVE WOOD on 15th –

16th Entrenching Bn unable to supply working parties as they are reduced to some 40 men after sending away large drafts. Work as usual.

17th Work as usual. 2nd Lt. E.P. WARNER
joined 56th Coy –

18th E.Riding worked on wire entanglement
at S.P. at MOATED GRANGE.
Other work as usual

19th Work as usual

20th Cheshire Coy supervised 200 infantry
on extension of ZILLEBEKE STREET
to west end of LAKE. E Riding Coy
moved with 76th Bde to POPERINGHE.
Other units working as usual.

21st Work on extension of ZILLEBEKE STREET
carried on –
E. Riding Coy. with 76th Bde to EECKE
~~as before moved~~ 56th Coy working as usual

22nd Cheshire Coy with 8th Bde to STEENVOORDE
~~others~~ ~~~~
4th S Lancs to BERTHEN.

23rd H.Q. RE to STEENVOORDE after
handing over to CRE 17th Div –
56th Coy with 9th Bde to GODEWARSVELDE

24th ⎫ RE. Companies & 4th S Lancs drilling &
to   ⎬ training & instructing infantry in trench
31st ⎭ construction &c. Special instruction to

24th to 31st 5th Bn London Regt & 50 men each from
4 new battalions of 8th & 76th brigades
given by 56th Coy RE.

6.11.15   C R Edwards
                              Capt RE
                           Adjt 3 Div Engrs

Appendix A   Asking 5th Corps for material
              for road repairs.

Appendix B   Drawings of 'Dug outs'.

8-11-15   H S G   Capt RE.
                           Adjt: 3rd Div. RE.

C.E.
5th Corps.

Appendix A

The road up to the trenches from KRUISSTRAAT over bridge 14 is nearly impassable, and no material practically for corduroy is coming in. This road will practically be useless unless material for corduroying comes up quickly and in considerable quantities. Most of the stuff we get is so crooked as to be useless for making a road.

A report was sent early in July stating approximate requirements as 30,000 11ft logs. This I understood was to be cut and supplied but so far practically none has been delivered.

(sgd) C. S. Wilson
Lieut Colonel
C.R.E. 3rd Division

1.10.15

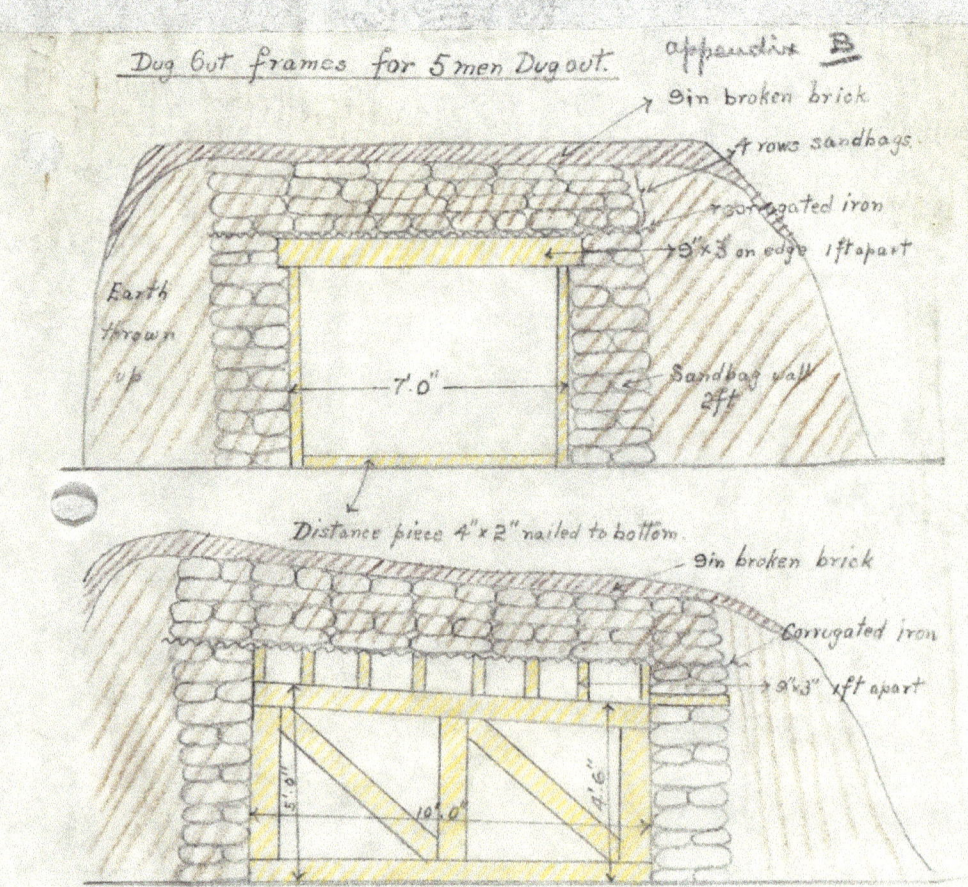

Dug Out frames for 5 men Dugout.   Appendix B

Frames to be set up 7 ft apart and 4"x 2" distance pieces nailed to bottom. 3"x3" fixed on top 1 ft apart and a 2 ft sandbag wall built up. Corrugated iron should then be laid on covering dugout and sandbag walls. A roof of 4 rows of sandbags should then be put on and the whole earthed well up and covered with a 9 inch layer of broken brick.

12/
7694

WAR DIARY
H.Q. R.E.
3rd Div.
Vol. II
November 1915

1st to 5th — R.E. Companies & 4 S. Lancs drilling and training. Also instructing Infantry in trench construction. Special Instruction to 5th Bn. London Regt.

6th — As above. Capt C.O.R. Edwards leaves to command 57th Coy. R.E.

7th — As above. Capt H.G. Pyne R.E. joined as Adjutant.

8th – 11th — As above

12th — As above. Lt. Brooks 56th Coy. leaves for England.

13th – 17th — As above. Preliminary orders to relieve 24th Div.

18th — As above. ii Lt. R.H.H. Watson joins 56th Coy.

19th — Operation orders for relief of 24th Division.

20th–23rd	Relief in progress
24th	56th Coy working at dugouts in VOORMEZEELE. 1st E Riding laying double tram lines. S. Lancs. working on communication trenches and defences. Capt V.B. Smith 56th coy wounded.
25th	Field companies revetting front line and repairing tram lines. S. Lancs revetting communication trenches
26th	Work as above
27th	Work as above. Hutting party started work.
28th	" " "
29th	Companies work with 2 sections each at Front line, & 2 sections preparing material S. Lancs and companies laying tram lines. Remainder of S. Lancs revetting trenches and making dug outs.
30th	Work as above

H S Gynn Capt RE
adj. R.E. 3rd Div.

Tactical

3rd Div
G.46

O C 172 RE

I understand that your company is responsible for the whole Division front i.e. from P. to 35 inclusive. Apparently the officer in charge North of the canal thinks his responsibility stops short at the RAVINE. There is a listening post beyond this in 34 which the infantry man, but it should be henceforth looked after and inspected by your officer up there.

P. Wilson Lt Col
C R E 3rd Division

28.11.15.

C.R.E. 3rd Division.

This company is responsible for the whole Division front, from P. to 35.

An officer has inspected the listening posts in 35. One is full of water and is now being pumped. The other is too shallow to be of any value as a defensive gallery, but we have listeners posted.

The post in 34 will now be included.

G. A. Symes. Lt.
O C 172 Co. R.E.

The plastic roller to guide the K 75's
Bayeh. 1/2 to an expansion for the roller
division is good.

[signature]
Cu 9 9hr
30.11.15

754 24 8k
Please order + return

30.11.15
Alcatraz
Dist 5,5

3 Dw.
Notes & returns.
Hip Rom thy
1-12-15. for Riga
Case 76 Bey

H.Q. R.E. 2nd Div.
Dec.
Vol. XVII

Army Form C. 2118.

WAR DIARY
INTELLIGENCE SUMMARY.
(Erase heading not required)

Hour, Date, Place 1915	Summary of Events and Information	Remarks and references to Appendices
1st	2 Sections of East Riding Coy working in Front Line trenches repairing and revetting, laying tram lines, 3 Coys 4th S. Lancs laying tram lines and revetting C.T's	APPENDIX I on condition of trenches attached.
2nd	As above. Lt GATTENS 56th Coy wounded also 2 Officers 4th S Lancs.	
3rd	As above. Companies making specimen gun emplacements in trenches	
4th	4th S. Lancs making road through new R.E. dump.	
5th	As above	
6th	" " E. Riding Coys erecting new Saw mill	
7th	" " Lt HOLMES joins 56th Coy.	
8th	" " Capt FRANCIS joins to command 56th Coy,	
9th-11th	" " making special M.G. emplacements near Front Line.	
12th	" " Cheshire Coy & 4th S. Lancs work on tunnelling out machine gun emplacements at BUS HOUSE St ELOI	

WAR DIARY

INTELLIGENCE SUMMARY.

Army Form C. 2118.

Hour, Date, Place	Summary of Events and Information	Remarks and references to Appendices
13ʰ-18ʰ	Work as usual	
19ʰ	Germans made gas attack on 6th Corps, Division stand by from 6.15 am till 11.40 am. Work then proceeds as usual	
20ʰ - 31ˢᵗ	Work as usual	

H S Syne
W Capple.
Adjt R.E. 3rd Divn

1-1-16.

{APPENDIX I}   SECRET.

3rd Division   By Lt Col C.S. WILSON R.E

The present condition of the trenches in the 3rd Div: area more particularly S. of the Canal which are in many places little more than mounds of mud and bits of rotten sand bags with no proper traverses, parados or splinter proofs calls for a very large amount of good revetting material if they are to be made tenable and capable of being maintained against an attack accompanied by a bombardment. They are at present neither, and afford very little protection to the garrison.

In addition practically all the support and reserve line trenches and their communications with the front line are in ruins in the sector S. of the Canal as is also the portion of the VOORMEZEELE switch from P. to VOORMEZEELE whilst from there to BELLEGOED though tenable at a pinch, it is in very bad repair.

The supply of revetting material is at present extremely bad, corrugated iron is unobtainable, hardly any expanded metal is to be got and we are reduced to wire netting and sand bags which cannot compete with the existing condition and necessitates eternal rebuilding to keep what we have in order. Consequently very little progress can be made with the urgent work of re-claiming the ruined defence works.

Ample supplies of corrugated iron or stout Expanded metal and timber in scantling are required, or failing these timber in planking which is already very short for hutting purposes, or brushwood must be supplied. The latter however to obtain an adequate supply would require a very considerable amount of labour which can very ill be spared from the troops and should be prepared and made up into hurdles and gabions by Civil or other labour behind the fighting area.

I should be glad if very urgent re-presentations could be made on this subject as the front line is at present not safe and the necessity of having the whole garrison in the front line owing to lack of support trenches must lead to heavy casualties in the event of bombardment; and the condition of the trenches if material is not available to put them in proper order must lead to a very serious wastage of men through sickness.

In short we are rapidly drifting into the same bad condition as prevailed last winter although this one has barely begun, with additional disadvantage of that the division is in an area which

is stripped of all material and it is forbidden to get anything for itself from outside its own area.

(Sd). C. S. Wilson
Lt Col RE
CRE 3rd Div

7-12-15

3RD DIVISION

COMMANDING ROY. ENGR.

AUG 1914-DEC 1918 1919 OCT

3rd Division
War Diaries
C. R. E.

January to December
1916

3rd Divisional Engineers.

C. R. E.

3RD DIVISION.

JANUARY 1 9 1 6.

Army Form C. 2118.

WAR DIARY
or
INTELLIGENCE SUMMARY.
(Erase heading not required)

C.R.E. III D.W.

Instructions regarding War Diaries and Intelligence Summaries are contained in F. S. Regs., Part II. and the Staff Manual respectively. Title pages will be prepared in manuscript.

Hour, Date, Place		Summary of Events and Information	Remarks and references to Appendices
RENINGHELST	1.1.16 to 4.1.16	2 Section took Coy in forward billets, two at Bock billets resting and making material for use of forward section. Three companies formed in forward billets, H.Q. and one company Camp E. Work of R.E. and Pioneers - repairing main buildings and constructing benches, laying tram lines vic. Hallsby Chateau, building old Ruinin constructing camps horse standings, R.E. and repairing	H.S.
"	5.1.16	erecting + fitting saw mill, making roofs and obtaining gravel. Pioneer Bn H.E.R. since came to relieve this place of 13th Bn. P King's Liverpool Regt.	H.S. Appendix I/II
"	6.1.16 to 22.1.16	Work as above	H.S.
"	23.1.16	" " . Germans exploded large mine post in front of BLUFF trenches, demolish	H.S.
"	24.1.16	" followed completely destroying trenches & burying occupants, far edge of BLUFF 4? crater	H.S.
"	25.1.16 & 27.1.16	Work as above, 2/Lt. HUDSON, W.E. Riding Coy. wounded	H.S.
"	28.1.16	Work as above. We exploded mine created German trench opposite R.s and destroyed German advanced trench.	H.S.
"	29.1.16	Work as above. 2/Lt. STEDHAM, H.E. joins 1/1 E Riding Coy R.E.	
"	30.1.16	" "	
"	31.1.16	" " . 2/Lt. CRANSWICK, P. joins 1/1 E Riding Coy R.E.	

APPENDICES	Subject
I	Recommendation
II	"
III	"
IV	Foot Plates for boots
V	Disinfectors

H.Sy.ure Capt. Adj R.E.
for C.R.E. 3rd Div.

Appendix I

3rd Division.

Now that the 4th Batt. SOUTH LANCASHIRE Regiment are leaving the division, I have the honour to bring to notice the good work they have done during the period they have acted as Divisional Pioneer Battalion, from July 25 to this date.

All ranks took up their duties with keenness and alacrity, and worked hard to make themselves efficient. I have always found them ready to take on any job that offered, and on several occasions they have done notably good work, especially in Sanctuary Wood when the trenches had been destroyed, and at St Eloi, under similar circumstances. Lt Col FAIRCLOUGH and all ranks of his battalion have worked hard and with excellent results.

Sd. C.S. WILSON
Lt Col RE
C.R.E. 3rd Div.

1-1-16.

Appendix II

3rd Division

I have the honour to bring forward the name of the undermentioned officer for a mention in despatches.

Lieut- Col BRERETON-FAIRCLOUGH
commanding 4/ South Lancashire Regt (T.F.)

Since July 25 the Battalion has been acting as a Pioneer Battalion and it is mainly due to his keenness and initiative, and the good spirit he has instilled into all ranks, that they have rapidly become efficient at their new duties, and done very good and valuable work.

(Sd) C.S. WILSON
Lt Col RE
CRE 3rd Div

1-1-16.

Appendix III

3rd Division

I have the honour to bring forward the undermentioned man, recommended by O.C. 172nd Tunnelling Coy R.E. for a mention in despatches.

172nd C.R.E. No. 112848 Sapper SIDDONS. T.

On 11th December 1915 displayed coolness and gallantry in rescuing a Sergeant who had been overcome by the fumes when exploring a mine gallery after the explosion of a charge, in his first effort he got the Sergeant along some distance but had to leave him, recovering a little though still suffering from the fumes, he again descended the mine and got the Sergeant to the foot of the shaft when he was got up.

(Sd) O.S. WILSON
Lt Col R.E.
C.R.E. 3rd Div.

1-1-16

Appendix IV

3rd Division

The foot plates for strapping round the foot when digging have been under trial by the Pioneer Battalion. They have been used both with ankle boots and with gum boots. The men like them and find them comfortable. They will also save the boots very much especially the gum boots. I would recommend that 1000 be issued to each division, these should be kept in the R.E. Park and issued to units as required, in the same way as entrenching tools.

(Sd.) C.S. WILSON
Lt. Col. R.E.
C.R.E. 3rd Divn.

5-4-16

Appendix V

3rd Division

The E. RIDING Field company is in need of a draft, so far it has received none — I am informed there are plenty of men ready to come out at their depôt. May the despatch of reinforcements be hastened please.

Sd. C.S. WILSON
Lt Col RE.
CRE 3rd Div.

3-1-16.

G.

I have seen O/C 172 Cy. RE & C.RE
3rd Division — & have discussed the
question with them.

I also saw A.A.General Spedan &
informed him what I considered
the proper procedure to be followed
& in this he concurs.

H.H.Tuson Bg

2-2-16

URGENT.   3rd Div   S.79   SECRET.

V Corps.

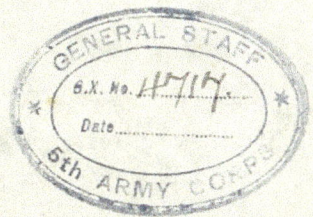

I forward a copy of correspondence between my C.R.E. and the C.E., V Corps on the subject of orders which have been given to the O.C. 172nd Tunnelling Company R.E. by the Controller of Mines, altering the orders for the execution of a defensive mine at the BLUFF, which had been given to him by my C.R.E. on my instructions. I also forward a copy of a letter from my C.R.E. from which it would appear that orders have also been given by the Controller of Mines altering the instructions I had given for the execution of a defensive gallery in front of ST ELOI, again without my being consulted.

2.   At present I am responsible for all defensive mining operations, and this must be the case if I am to be responsible for the safety of the front.

Whilst I welcome all expert advice in connection with mining operations, I request that you will cause instructions to be issued to the Controller of Mines that he is not to issue orders affecting defensive mining operations to the O.C. 172nd Tunnelling Company R.E., but that all such orders must be issued by the Division.

31st January, 1916.   Major General,
                                Commanding 3rd Division.

SECRET.

3rd Division.
———

The question of responsibility for mining operations on the Divisional front appears to be no longer clear. V Corps GX.3272 of 29/10/1915 laid down very clearly that Divisions were to be responsible for defensive mines, and the Tunnelling Company allotted to their Sector were to carry out the work.

In compliance with this I arranged how to start a new gallery south of the BLUFF, where it is important to get out as quickly as possible, with the O.C. 172nd Company R.E. and on account of the urgency we were both in agreement that the best method was to drive an adit. I found the Assistant Controller of Mines had been round and ordered a shaft to be sunk instead, without consulting the Division which is responsible for the front. I wrote on the subject to C.E. V. Corps, correspondence attached. The O.C. 172nd Company is on leave and his locum tenens was the officer referred to as quite agreeing by C.E. V Corps. This same officer has since informed me that he only meant that a shaft was the best way if water was met with, but taking into consideration the site, water was not probable; and if met with could be dealt with by a bore hole or small gallery to the Canal Bank.

I further found yesterday that the defensive work I had settled to be done with the O.C.172nd Co R.E. in front of Q.1 where the enemy was suspected of trying to get below our defensive galleries had been stopped under instructions of, I believe, the Controller of Mines G.H.Q., again without referring to or consulting the Division which is responsible for the safety of its front.

I submit that this state of affairs is more than likely to lead to serious disaster. While we are glad to have expert technical advice, the question of which course to follow must necessarily depend on the tactical considerations on the spot, and should be decided by the Division holding the front.

I have told the O.C. 172nd Co R.E. that he is not to carry out these instructions from outside authority or to stop work considered necessary by the Division without reference to the Division.

I think a ruling on this subject should be obtained as early as possible, as if the Division is to be responsible for the safety of its front, it must have control over the measures taken to secure it, also the Os.C. Tunnelling Companies want to know whose orders they are to carry out.

31/1/1916.   (sd) C.S.WILSON, Colonel,
              C.R.E., 3rd Division.

SECRET.

C. E., V Corps.
———

With reference to V Corps GX.3272 of 29/10/15. The O.C. 172nd Company R.E. has just informed me that the Assistant Controller of Mines, 2nd Army, has given him orders to alter the arrangements I had made for a new defensive mine south of the BLUFF on the north bank of the Canal, and has told him to sink a shaft instead of driving an adit. It is of the utmost importance from a tactical point of view that a gallery should be driven at this point with the least possible delay, and an adit is far the quickest, though it may of course be dished by water.

I think in case of defensive work of this nature orders should not be given over the heads of the Division holding the line, who are responsible for its safety, without consulting them, as the Assistant Controller of Mines cannot be expected to know the tactical situation, though his advice on technical points will be welcomed. Might in these cases, before the scheme of work is altered, the Controller or Assistant Controller see the G.S. or C.R.E. of the Division concerned, and explain his reasons, because the tactical reasons must often over-ride the technical.

29/1/16.   (sd) C.S. WILSON, Colonel,
                                        C.R.E., 3rd Division.

SECRET

C.R.E.,
    3rd Division.
    ———

Reference yours of 29/1/16 regarding mines.

I have seen the O.C. Company 172 this morning regarding the defensive gallery south of the BLUFF.

The proposed adit would have been impracticable. This arrangement has been tried in several cases with 175 and 177 Companies on the front, and has led to endless trouble and delay. Of course if there are no water troubles it is the quickest way- but in nearly every case where we have tried it, it has been a failure.

I feel sure that the shaft is the only possible way of ensuring success, and in this O.C. 172 Company quite agrees.

I have told the Acting O.C. Company that alterations are not to be made without keeping you informed and consulting you and I will speak to Captain Syme on this subject as soon as he comes back from leave.

I think in this case the Controller of mines was giving advice on a technical matter, but I will see him at the first available opportunity and see that no changes are made without consulting you. I missed him today.

30/1/1916.   (sd)   R.D.PETRIE, Brig-General,
                                     C.E., V Corps.

3rd Divisional Engineers.

C. R. E.

3RD DIVISION.

FEBRUARY 1916.

Confidential

WAR DIARY
of
H.Q., R.E. 3rd Division.

from 1-2-16
to   29-2-16

Vol XIX

3-3-16

VS Eyre Capt & Adj RE
for CRE 3rd Div

Army Form C. 2118.

WAR DIARY
-of-
INTELLIGENCE SUMMARY.
(Erase heading not required.)

Instructions regarding War Diaries and Intelligence Summaries are contained in F. S. Regs., Part II. and the Staff Manual respectively. Title pages will be prepared in manuscript.

Place	Date	Hour	Summary of Events and Information	Remarks and references to Appendices
	Feb 16			
RENINGHELST	1st to 3rd	-	} Work as usual	W.S.
"	4th	-	Orders for relief of Div. by 17th Divi: received.	W.S.
"	5th	-	Work as usual, except that all wiring sections of Field Companies work in Front Line.	W.S.
"	6.7.8.	-	Move & relief in progress	W.S.
MORDAUSQUE	9-17th	-	Training	W.S.
"	18th	-	ditto. E. Riding Coy. move to join 76th I.B. at the BLUFF. Entrain St OMER	W.S.
"	19, 20th	-	Training	W.S.
"	21st	-	56th Coy. leave for 17th Divi: area. Entrain St OMER.	
"	22nd	-	Training	
"	23rd	-	" 13th KINGS, who have been acting as Pioneer Battalion, rejoin 8th I.B. vice 4th GORDONS.	
"	24th 29th	-	Training	

H.S.pt Capt R.E.
for C.R.E. 3rd Div.

3/3/16.

3rd Divisional Engineers.

C. R. E.

3RD DIVISION.

MARCH 1916.

WAR DIARY
INTELLIGENCE SUMMARY.
(Erase heading not required.)

Army Form C. 2118.

Instructions regarding War Diaries and Intelligence Summaries are contained in F. S. Regs., Part II. and the Staff Manual respectively. Title pages will be prepared in manuscript.

Place	Date	Hour	Summary of Events and Information	Remarks and references to Appendices
NORDAUSQUE	1st		Unit training in close proximity to billet. Under orders to be entrained at 9 hours notice.	H.S.
"	2nd		as above	H.S.
"	3rd		Col. C.S. WILSON now Brig. General WILSON Comds. to take up duties J.C.E. 14th Corps.	H.S.
"	4th		Lt. Col. C.A. ELLIOTT joins from 81st Coy. as C.R.E. division. Orders for relief of 17th Div. by 3rd Div. received.	H.S.
"	5th		Transport parties of Cheshire and E. Riding Coys move by road to positions they occupy when in line.	H.S.
"	6		C.R.E. moves up to RENINGHELST. Cheshire Coy. dismounted, by rail to POPERINGHE and then march to billets.	H.S.
RENINGHELST	7th		Take over from 17th Div. The 78th & 7.Coy, 93rd 7.Coy, 105th 7.Coy, 106th 7.Coy, 7th Y.L. Pioneers and 6th S.W.B. Pioneers are all attached for work and administration.	H.S.
"	8th		Work on reclaiming trenches and strengthening positions on BLUFF	H.S.
"	9th		2 Sections of 56th 7.Coy relieve forward sections of 93rd Coy and take on their work.	H.S.
"	10th		Work	H.S.
"	11th		Work as above 93rd Coy. leave for 17th Div. Area.	H.S.
"	12th		Work as above	H.S.
"	13th		78th Coy, 105th Coy, 106th Coy and 6th S.W.B. Pioneers leave the Divisional and return POPERINGHE.	H.S.
"	14th		Work. No. 2 Coy. R.A.R.E. attached for work.	H.S.
"	15-16th		Reclaiming work well in progress.	H.S.

Army Form C. 2118.

WAR DIARY
~~INTELLIGENCE SUMMARY.~~
(Erase heading not required.)

Instructions regarding War Diaries and Intelligence Summaries are contained in F. S. Regs., Part II. and the Staff Manual respectively. Title pages will be prepared in manuscript.

Place	Date	Hour	Summary of Events and Information	Remarks and references to Appendices
RENINGHELST	17/3		Work at very high pressure, preparing for attack on part of Front. No 2 Coy R. MONMOUTH R.E. attached for work.	H.S.
"	18-25/3		ditto	
"	26/3		No 2 Coy R. Anglesey R.E. came by train from POPERINGHE to join 4th Army. By night all available men shutting front line trenches to withstand shock of mine.	H.S.
"	27/3	4:15am	6 Mines fired by 172 Tunnelling Coy round St ELOI. 9th I.B. assault German trenches. By night all three Field Companies and No 4 R. MONMOUTH Coy. go up to consolidate position and get communications through. Little work done owing to relief of Infantry and to heavy German shelling.	H.S.
"	28/3-31st		Work on reclaiming trenches damaged by enemy's artillery and in opening of communication with new front line.	H.S.

H.S.V. Copple
adj. R.E. 3rd Div.

1-4-16.

3rd Divisional Engineers.

C. R. E.

3RD DIVISION.

APRIL 1916.

WAR DIARY
INTELLIGENCE SUMMARY

C.R.E. 3rd Division — APRIL 1916

Army Form C. 2118.

Place	Date	Hour	Summary of Events and Information	Remarks and references to Appendices
RENINGHELST	1st–2nd		Work as usual.	
"	3rd		Forward and back dumps handed over to CRE 2nd Canadian Div.	
"	4th		Div. HQ move to FLETRE. CRE remaining behind.	
"	5th		Cheshire Co. move into rest billets. CRE's office to FLETRE. Lt. Col. ELLIOTT (CRE) on leave.	
FLETRE	6th		56th Co. move into rest billets.	
"	7th		1st Riding Co. move into rest billets.	
"	8th		2nd Riding Co. to LA CLYTTE for work on VIERSTRAAT Switch.	
"	9th		Water Board meeting. Lt Gordon leave.	
"	11th–12th		56th Co. LA CLYTTE	
"	13th		Div. went up to zone at Glenn notices. Capt. HOLDEN, 2Lts ROBERTSHAW & WARD join Cheshire Co.	
"	15th		Capt. P.K. BOUNOIS attached for instruction in latest fieldworks.	
"	16th		CRE and Adjt. to 50th Div. dumps, workshops etc. & to Vth Corps CRE	
"	18th		Lt. ISPLAYFAIR arrives from 12th F.Co. 6th Div. as Adjt.	
"	19th		Takes on duties. 56th into rest. 2 Ridings to LA CLYTTE	
"	20th		Capt HG. PYNE to 56th Co. as O.C. Capt. BOUNOIS leaves.	
"	21st		CRE visits centre & left section of 50th Div line with GOC & GSO1 3 Div.	

Army Form C. 2118.

WAR DIARY
or
INTELLIGENCE SUMMARY.
(Erase heading not required.)

April 1916

Instructions regarding War Diaries and Intelligence Summaries are contained in F. S. Regs., Part II. and the Staff Manual respectively. Title pages will be prepared in manuscript.

Place	Date	Hour	Summary of Events and Information	Remarks and references to Appendices
FLETRE	22nd		Whiting Co. relieve Cheshire Co. Cheshire Co. into line with 8th Bde.	
"	23rd		Work as usual.	
"	24th			
"	25th		Move to WESTOUTRE. Whitings take to rest billets. Took over workshops & dumps. CRE takes over from CRE 50th Div. 56th Co. into line with 9th Bde.	
"	26th		Leave re-opens. CRE's Conference every evening re movements.	
"	27th		CRE recd. round works. (26th) Orders issued for working parties to begin work by 1/4 past 2 a.m. and precautions to be taken against gas when wind is from E to S E.	
"	28th		L. Riding Co. to LOCREHOF Farm. Lt. Chalkener (Cheshire) on leave.	
"	29th		Gas Attack 1.25 am on right of Div. line. Field Co. stood to till 4 a.m. CRE & GOC Ra round sites for OP's. CRE 50th Div. called at 6 pm	
"	30th		Gas Attack 10.4 p.m. till 10.55 p.m. Field Co. Stood to.	
All "	26th		11th Labour Bn. 1st Entrenching Bn. U & 250th Co. attached for administration	
"	28th		136th A.T. Co. arrives & is attached for administration.	

7/5/16

B.P. Lanfear TRE
for CRE 3 Div.

3rd Divisional Engineers.

C. R. E.

3RD DIVISION.

MAY 1916.

MAR3

WAR DIARY
C.R.E. - 3rd - Division. May 1916
INTELLIGENCE SUMMARY.

VM 22

Army Form C. 2118.

Place	Date	Hour	Summary of Events and Information	Remarks and references to Appendices
WESTOUTRE	1st		CRE to CCVK Corps re Kemmel Water Supply. 1st Battn during Battn attached to Q for administration	
"	2		CRE & GOC RA annual Observing Posts a.m. and p.m.	
	3-4		Work as usual	
	5		2nd L.t. O. Forsyth joined 136th A.T. Co.	
	6		Work as usual	
	7		Capt. Pkr. M. Hall (E Riding) leave to England	
	8		Work as usual. OC's Cheshire & E Riding Co. met CRE	
	9		I/OC Fielding CRE 6th Div attached for instruction. 2nd Lt Riggall (E Riding) wounded	
	10		Major Harper (Cheshire) leave to England	
	11-12		Work as usual	
	13		I/OC Fielding back to England. Capt Hy Price posted & on instruction to CHATHAM (56th)	
	14		Major J.H. Henderson joins 56th Co as O.C. from Field Engineer II Corps	
	15		Major E.H. Taverton RE(TF) attached Cheshire Co. from England for instruction	
	16-17		Work as usual	
	18		Gas reported 12.33 a.m. Stand by 12.40 a.m., cancelled 1.5 a.m.	
	19		20th Battn K.R.R.C. from 3rd Div from 6th Div area & are camped at SCHERPENBERG	

Army Form C. 2118.

WAR DIARY
C.R.E. 3rd or Division
INTELLIGENCE SUMMARY.
(Erase heading not required.)

May 1916

Instructions regarding War Diaries and Intelligence Summaries are contained in F.S. Regs., Part II. and the Staff Manual respectively. Title pages will be prepared in manuscript.

Place	Date	Hour	Summary of Events and Information	Remarks and references to Appendices
WESTOUTRE	19th and		CO and 2nd in Command visit CRE to discuss work, employment &c	
	20		2nd Lt. Pickersgill joined E. Riding Co TF	
	21-23		Work as usual, particularly in fixing up front line fire in centre section	
	24		56th Co. to LA CLYTTE for work in VIERSTRAAT SWITCH	
	25-26		work as usual	
	27		2.50 p.m. Div RE Park handed over to 50th Div. 36th & "A" (act army Bn RE) detached from establishment of 3rd Div & attached to 50th Div. HQ & ONE to FLETRE, into rest	
	27	p.m.	Clothing and Refitting Cos to not billets	
FLETRE	28th		Cos. training, except 2 sections 56th Co "working" at VIERSTRAAT	
	29		Temp 2nd Lt. C.P. Williamson joined 56th Co for duty	
			2nd Lt. Bayes RE (TF) joined E. Riding &c	
	30		Cos. Training	
	31st			
AdD	29th		Orders received for Div to be held in readiness to move at 4 hrs notice after midnight May 31/June 1st	

BSPlayfair LWB
3/6/16

fr CW 3 Div

3rd Divisional Engineers.

C. R. E.

3RD DIVISION.

JUNE 1916.

Army Form C.2118.
SHEET. 1

WAR DIARY
C.R.E. – 3rd Division – Month of June 1916.
INTELLIGENCE SUMMARY.
(Erase heading not required.)

WO 95 / 23

Instructions regarding War Diaries and Intelligence Summaries are contained in F. S. Regs., Part II. and the Staff Manual respectively. Title pages will be prepared in manuscript.

Place	Date	Hour	Summary of Events and Information	Remarks and references to Appendices
FLETRE	1st	12 noon.	Orders to send 1 Field Co. to 24/5 and 1 to 50th Div. areas for Artillery Observing Post work.	
"		4 pm.	Ordered Cheshire Co. to 50th Div. and E. Riding to 24th Div. area.	
"	2nd	am.	CRE visited E. Ridings (S. of NEUVE EGLISE); Adjt. visited Cheshire Co. (LA CLYTTE) Cheshire move to SCHERPENBERG huts.	
"	3	11 am.	Orders for Divn. to be ready to move at 4 hrs. notice. Cos. told to continue work & be ready to recall working parties at once.	
"	4	–	Order for modified Strategic line issued. (Dismounted Portion only)	
"	5	–	2nd Suffolk Regt. at LOCRE at CRE's disposal for VIERSTRAAT line work & Artillery Observing Posts.	
"	7	1 pm.	Ordered 56th Co. to send 2 sections to work with 9th Bde. in ST ELOI sector.	
"	8	–	CRE visited Bg. G.S. Vth Corps re VIERSTRAAT work.	
"	9	–	CRE & GSO1 round VIERSTRAAT line.	
"	10–11	–	work as usual.	
"	12	–	1 Co. Pioneer Batn (20/KRRC) placed under orders of 50th Divn.	
"	15	–	Orders received to concentrate Field Co. in THIEUSHOEK area on 17th June.	
"		–	Orders received to march from Vth Corps Rest area on June 18th.	
"	18	9 am.	March to ZERMEZEELE area with CRE in command of following troops:–	

WAR DIARY

(CRE 2nd Division) Sheet 2

INTELLIGENCE SUMMARY
June 1916

Army Form C. 2118.

(Erase heading not required.)

Place	Date	Hour	Summary of Events and Information	Remarks and references to Appendices
FLETRE	18	(contd)	56th, Cheshire, & E.Riding Field Cos; 8th and 142nd Fd. Ambulances. 9th Bde. M.G. Cy. 2nd XI Mob. Vet. Section: 3rd Brit. Sanit. Section;	
WEMAERS CAPPEL	19	9 a.m.	Same. HQRE & Column to march to LEDERZEELE area. CRE's billet WEMAERS CAPPEL	
SAMANE	20	9 a.m.	HQ RE & same column march to Second Army Training Area. CRE's billet SAMANE. 56th Co. POLINCOVE: Cheshire Co. LEULINGHEM: E.Riding Co. SALPERWICK.	
TILQUES	21	—	Cos. ready to move at 9 hrs notice. Orders in event of mov. by train issued.	
—	22·23		Co. training — marching — patrolling etc. — defence of village & woods.	
—	24		Lt. A.W. Gordon rejoins 56 Co. from HQ. Second Army. Co. Training.	
—	25		2Lt. A.H. Clegg joins E.Riding Co. Co. Training.	
—	26	6 p.m.	CRE & GSO2 to VIERSTRAAT & DICKEBUSCH. Co. Training.	
—	27		Training.	
—	28		Lt. D.K. Finnimore RE rep. 56 Co. for 2nd Protein Park. Lt. D. Cosyns joins 56 Co. Div. to be at 6 hours notice to move from noon 29th June. Co. Training	
—	29	—	Div. to be at 6 hours notice to move from noon 1 July. Co. Training.	
—	30		Co. Training.	

Mayfair CRE
for CRE 3rd Divn.

1.7.16.

3rd Divisional Engineers.

C. R. E.

3RD DIVISION.

JULY 1916.

Army Form C. 2118.

WAR DIARY

C.R.E. 3rd Division — on Month of **JULY 1916**.

Sheet 1.

INTELLIGENCE SUMMARY
(Erase heading not required.)

Instructions regarding War Diaries and Intelligence Summaries are contained in F. S. Regs., Part II. and the Staff Manual respectively. Title pages will be prepared in manuscript.

CE 24

Place	Date	Hour	Summary of Events and Information	Remarks and references to Appendices
TILQUES	1	1.20am	Orders received to move by train; orders sent to Fd Coys.	
"	2	4am	HQ RE march from TILQUES. Train leaves ST OMER 8am; detain DOULLENS 5pm	
			march to and billet at LE MEILLARD, a stay at 2 hrs notice to move.	
LE MEILLARD	3	2pm	HQRE march to OLINCOURT, near FLESSELLES. CRE to trenches near FRICOURT with CE IInd Corps.	
OLINCOURT	4	8pm	HQRE march to CORBIE independently, via AMIENS.	
CORBIE	5	3am	Arrive & billet pm CRE & adjt visit CRE 18th Div. in BRAY dugouts re stores, water etc.	
"	6	am	CRE & adjt. to 18th Div. Trenches & to RE Park MERICOURT to see material & store arrangement.	
			2nd Lies commence to relieve 1/1cos of 18th Div. East Riding relieves 92nd Co. in CARNOY dugouts.	
			56th Cheshire Co. move to BRAY & bivouac.	
"	7	am	CRE & adjt. to MONTAUBAN & trenches. 51st relieves 80th Co. & Cheshire Co. relieves 79th at CARNOY.	
"	8	pm	HQ RE move to BRAY dugouts with Div. HQ. Major H.M. HENDERSON 56th Co. slightly wounded.	
BRAY	9		Preparations for attack. Stores sent forward; road CARNOY–MONTAUBAN repaired as far as	
			possible under OC 238 AT. Co RE. 18th Div. continue to run water supply with 1 section	
	10–13		Preparations continued.	
"	14	3.25am	Assault by 3rd Div. on German 3rd Line. RE allotted as follows:— 1 section Cheshire Co. to	
			8th Inf Bde. (& 1 Co. Pioneers). 1 section Cheshire Fd Co. to 9th Bde. Special party with 9th	

WAR DIARY

C.R.E. 3rd Division — JULY - 1916.

INTELLIGENCE SUMMARY

Army Form C. 2118.
Sheet 2.

Place	Date	Hour	Summary of Events and Information	Remarks and references to Appendices
BRAY	14 (cont)		Pate. for fortifying BAZENTIN-LE-GRAND :- 56th Co. RE less 2 sections & 1½ Co. Pioneers - 20th KRRC In Bat. Reserve - Cheshire Field Co. (less 2 sections) + 2 sections 56th F. Co.	
			With Reserve Bde. (76th) East Riding Field Co.	
			56th Co. assisted to clear BAZENTIN-LE-GRAND of snipers & proceeded with fortifying the "Keep". Lt GORDON. A.W. R.E. recommended for Military Cross in this connection.	
			Cheshire Co. assisted with consolidation. Reserve sections made 2 bridges to carry 6"	
			Runlags across MONTAUBAN ALLEY trench. East Riding Field Co. worked at	
"	15-17th		bridge & clearing of road CARNOY - MONTAUBAN - BAZENTIN with 2nd Suffolk Regt.	
"	16 -		Consolidation, carting of stores, road repair continued. 15th Major Hudherdson required 56th Co. Field Co. back to their affiliated Brigades.	for hospital.
"	18	3.45am	76th Bde. attack at LONGUEVAL + DELVILLE Wood. 2 sections East Riding Co. assist in consolidation. 2 Lts. S. CARLIN & J. M. JAMES (E. Riding Co.) wounded.	
BRAY	19	-	Orders to relieve 9th Bn. Div HQ move to Copse 'B' - HQRE to a wallah at A.20.d.7.7	
A.20.d.7.7 (Sheet b2c)	20		CRE a (left) ahead to see accommodation + take on dumps etc.	
			56th Co. on CARNOY - MONTAUBAN road. 2 Lts G. STONE and H. HATHWAITE join E. Riding F. Co.	

Army Form C. 2118.

WAR DIARY
CRE 3rd Division
INTELLIGENCE SUMMARY
(Erase heading not required.)

Place	Date	Hour	Summary of Events and Information	Remarks and references to Appendices
A 20 d 7.7	22		56th & Chesh. Co. on CARNOY - MONTAUBAN road. E.Riding "standing by".	3rd Div. OO 88
"			put Chesh Co at disposal of 8th Bde & E.Riding Co. 9th Bde —	
"	23	8pm	CRE sent to report on trenches in vicinity of N end of TRÔNES wood.	
			Road work continued. 1.35 pm. All working parties recalled ready for night work.	
		night	56th wiring in LONGUEVAL. Improving communication & traversing main N. road.	
			E.Riding wiring in DELVILLE wood, Cheshire Co. on a new trench.	
"	24	night	Worked by all 3 Co. wiring in DELVILLE wood & clearing LONGUEVAL alley Trench.	
"	25	1am	Orders for relief of Cos. issued. 56th relieved by East Anglian Co; Cheshire by 226th Co +	
			East Riding Co. by 5th F.d. Co. HQ.RE marched to BRAY August. 56th Co. to SANDPIT, Cheshires	
			HAPPY VALLEY, E.Riding Co & Pioneers MORLANCOURT.	
BRAY	26"		Cheshire Co. march to MEAULTE.	
	27		HQ RE with Div. HQ to TREUX. 56th Co. to VILLE sur ANCRE.	
TREUX	28		E.Riding Co. to MERICOURT.	
	29-31		Cos. clearing up & training.	
	31		Cheshire Co. (Nos 1 Section) move to WELCOME WOOD for building	
			section canvases dismantled huts at CHIPILLY.	

White HoRE
CRE 3rd Div.

1/8/16

3rd Divisional Engineers

C. R. E.

3rd DIVISION

AUGUST 1916

Army Form C. 2118.

Sheet Vol 25

WAR DIARY

C.R.E. 3rd Division — Month of August 1916.

INTELLIGENCE SUMMARY.

(Erase heading not required.)

Place	Date	Hour	Summary of Events and Information	Remarks and references to Appendices
TREUX	1-2-3	—	Companies training. Cheshire Co. at WELLCOME WOOD taking down huts & re-erecting them at the CITADEL. Also moving huts here from CHIPILLY to MEAULTE.	
"	4th	noon	Orders recd for 1FdCo, 800 Infantry & ½ Battn Pioneers to be ready to move next day. CRE & Adjt visit BGGS XIIIth Corps re work to be done :— 'C' and 'D' rear lines of defence	
"	5th		East Riding Coy moved to camp near the CITADEL	
		8:15am	CRE, Lt-Col NEWELL (OC E. Riding FdCo) & Major MARTIN (Cmdg detachment 20/KRRC Pioneers) motor up to CARNOY to see work to be done.	
"	7th		Adjt to Cheshire Co. CRE to advanced detachment & work on rear lines. Orders recd that Div will probably have another 10 days in Rest Area.	
"	8th		CRE & Adjt to VILLE and MEAULTE to see road repairs under 56th Co. Supervision with infantry party from 8th & 9th Bdes. Wagons from RA and Train. Also to Bath lines at MEAULTE. Work on C &D lines cancelled owing to shell fire (10.30pm)	
"	9th	4am	CRE & GSO1 to 'C&D' lines to see progress of work.	
"	10th		2nd Lt J.M.MORGAN joins 56th Co. for 2nd Labour Battalion. Orders to move next day. Work on roads cancelled.	
"	11th	11:20pm	56th Co. move to SANDPITS area. Cheshire Co. move to CITADEL, leaving an NCO	

Army Form C. 2118.

Sheet 2.

WAR DIARY

CR.E. 3rd Division — August 1916.

INTELLIGENCE SUMMARY.
(Erase heading not required.)

Instructions regarding War Diaries and Intelligence Summaries are contained in F. S. Regs., Part II. and the Staff Manual respectively. Title pages will be prepared in manuscript.

Place	Date	Hour	Summary of Events and Information	Remarks and references to Appendices
TREUX	1916 11		at WELLCOME WOOD and an Officer of NEAVITTE to hand over work in hand to 55th Div.	
			Officers of Cheshire Co. go round C & D lines to hand over work. CRE & Adjt. met CRE 55th Div. re taking over.	
	12	pm.	Div. HQ. move to FORKED TREE Camp. Cheshire Co. take over C & D line work. E. Riding Co. working. 2 Lt. H. A. BRADDOCK joins Cheshire Co.	
FORKED TREE	13th	-	Dumps of RE stores near CITADEL taken over. CRE & Adjt. to CRE 55th Div. re mixed dump for Bde. & Batt. HQ. 15 men from Inf. Btns. arrive at RE dump for unloading stores. Conference of Div. HQ. 9 pm. Conference of Field Co. Commanders & OC Pioneers 10:30 pm. Stores Cut & over dumps for Bde. HQ. to be started at once.	
"	14th	-	OC. 183 Tunnelling Co. called re expediting work on mined dugouts. 142 & 1 Officer & 20 /KRRC Pioneers join him for work with Tunnelling Co. 56th Co. move to near CITADEL. RE stores carted forward by I.Co. transport.	
"	15th		HQ RE move to Battle HQ near CONTOUR WOOD. 56th & E. Riding Co. work Camps near MINDEN POST. Work on dugouts & carting of stores continued. O.O. for attack next day allotted 1 section East Riding Co. to 76th Bde. and 1 section 56th Co. to 9/16 Bde. Remainder Div. Reserve.	

WAR DIARY
C.R.E. — 2nd Division — August 1916.
INTELLIGENCE SUMMARY.

Army Form C. 2118
Sheet 3.

(Erase heading not required.)

Summary of Events and Information

Work on Bde. dugouts stopped 2 p.m. Tramway completed. 1 required went out to work. One inf. relief failed to turn up. Carrying work late rather slower than anticipated. Assault by 9th & 7th Bdes. 4 Decd. Bde. R.E. Dump moved to MINDEN POST. 56th & E.Riding impart. coys & Bde. HQ dugouts & 4 put out tape for assembly of attack on LONELY TRENCH. MINDEN dump shelled, and some timber destroyed. No casualties at the Dump.

Attacks at 2.45 pm & 4.45 pm. 2 Lt. STONE (E.Riding Co) reported missing. Orders for relief of Div. by 55th Div. took on communication trenches to the captured positions. HQ R.E. moved back to FORKED TREE (5.30 pm)

E.Riding Co. to HAPPY VALLEY, 56th Co. to SANDPITS

Orders for relief by 20th Div.

HQ R.E. to TREUX, 56th Co. to VILLE, E.Riding Co. to MEAULTE.
CRE & Adjt. by car to BERNAVILLE. Transport & mounted men to FLESSELLES.
Div. HQ to BERNAVILLE. Dismounted men of field Co. entrain at MERICOURT for CANDAS. 56th Co. to LANCHES; Cheshire Co. EPECAMPS; Earl Riding Co. MONPLAISIR. Resting

Army Form C. 2118.

C.R.E. 3rd Division WAR DIARY August 1916. Sheet 4.

INTELLIGENCE SUMMARY

(Erase heading not required.)

Place	Date	Hour	Summary of Events and Information	Remarks and references to Appendices
	1916.			
BERNAVILLE	25th	8am	HQ to FROHEN-le-GRAND. 56th Co. to MEZEROLLES. Cheshire Co. WAZANS. E. Riding Co. BOUBERS.	
FROHEN-le-GRAND	26th	8am	HQ to FLERS. 56th Co. to NEUVILLE au CORNET. Cheshire Co. to BLANGERMONT. E.Riding Co. GRAND RIEZ.	
FLERS	27th	8am	HQ to MONCHY CAYEUX. CRE to CRE 16th Div. re taking over – (RAIMBERT)	
			56th Co. to PETIT ANVIN, Cheshire Co. TANGRY, E.Riding Co. FONTAINE les BOULANS.	
MONCHY-CAYEUX	28th	7.30 am	CRE & Adjt. by car to 1st Corps HQ to see C.E. Visited MINE Park, 31st AT. Co. RE & Div. workshops. Turned into billets at NOEUX les MINES. Capt. LEE, 31st AT. Co. RE came to hand over maps & plans of the area to CRE. Cheshire Co. to nr BRUAY.	
NOEUX les MINES	29th	–	CRE & Adjt. to PHILOSOPHE to see billets for Co. Also to FOSSE 3, MAZINGARBE.	
			CRE 8th Div. & 253rd Tunnelling Co. RE. Cheshire Co. to PHILOSOPHE home line MAZINGARBE	
"	30th	–	CRE to village line. Officers of Cheshire & E.Riding Co. shewn round the line by Capt STRONG, 15th Co RE, & Capt. L. of 152nd Co. of Officer. E.Riding Co. to PHILOSOPHE and units.	
			time lines at MAZINGARBE. 56th Co. to MARLES les MINES.	
	31st	–	56th Co. less 1 section to VILLA ARNOULD. 1 section building at LAPEUVRIERE.	
			CRE to line with OC. 20/KRRC Pineau. Adjt. to MNX. MAZINGARBE with Antoine re	
			batt.; LES BREBIS re electric current for Batt. pm. CRE & Adjt. to all avct. Co.	

1/9/16

M. Lewis
CRE 3rd Div RE

3rd Divisional Engineers.

C. R. E.

3RD DIVISION.

SEPTEMBER 1916.

WAR DIARY / INTELLIGENCE SUMMARY

Army Form C. 2118

C.R.E. 3rd Division — September 1916.

HQ RE 3D SHEET-1.

Place	Date	Hour	Summary of Events and Information	Remarks and references to Appendices
NOEUX-les-MINES	1	am	CRE to Line. Adjt. to PHILOSOPHE & FOSSE 3 Dump. Pioneer Officers reconnoitre Trench Tramway System with view to better traffic control. Lieut. VAN NESS appointed O/C Tramways and O/C Advanced RE Park, FOSSE 3, with his JHQ at FOSSE 3 (PHILOSOPHE). 3 men of 56th Co. to Divl. Workshop, NOEUX-LES-MINES, (Engine driver, carpenter & sawyer)	20/KRRC (Pioneers)
"	2	"	2/Lt. PARRY (20/KRRC) put i/c tramway construction under Lieut. VAN NESS. Cheshire Co. begin work on dugouts in LONE TRENCH and on Medium Trench Mortar Emplacements. Intended to BEUVRY re. electric current to huts at the Alouëtte MAZINGARBE	
"	3	"	6 men 20/KRRC to Divl. Workshop. CRE to Line. Adjt. to MAZINGARBE RE dump and to CRE 40th Div. re. plans & information about an sector. 2/Lt. SINCLAIR (Cheshire Co) Spotted to England	
"	4	"	OC 283rd Co. called re. work on tramways, & necessity for 16 lb. rail with new points tractor. Section of 56th Co. working at LABEUVRIERE again. 56th Co.	
"	5	am	CRE to Line. pm. CRE & Adjt. to CE I Corps re tramway extension & repairs	
"	6	"	56th & 100 KRRC Pioneers start continuous shifts on mined dugouts in Reserve Trench. CRE visited trench tramway system by trolley. New siding made at the terminus "KINGSBRIDGE STATION." 2/Lt HAITHWAITE (East Riding) joins HQ RE as Field Engineer (relieving) and takes over hutting work.	
"	7	"	CRE and Adjt. to MINX re. making of 'RAT BOXES'.	
"	8	"	Wate supply to fort Line temporarily out of action owing to the plungers rod at FOSSE 7 breaking. East Riding Co. draft with Kiva. 200 RAT BOXES sent to FOSSE 7. 720 Forest Poles drawn for Horse Standings.	
"	9	"	180 RAT BOXES sent to FOSSE 3. Cheshire & E.Riding Co. begin to put them in position.	
"	10	"	ditto. Conference at Divl. HQ; Brigadier, CRA & CRE attend.	
"	11	"	173	
			3 men sent to Rest Camp BOULOGNE. Unsuccessful attempt to get Civilian Carpenters & Bricklayer locally.	

Army Form C. 2118

Sheet 2

WAR DIARY
or
INTELLIGENCE SUMMARY

C.R.E. 3rd Division   September 1916. contd.

Place	Date	Hour	Summary of Events and Information	Remarks and references to Appendices
NOEUX les MINES	12	-	Current turned on to Electric huts at MAZINGARBE by the Gaz Société de Force et Lumière, BEUVRY. Huts supply reported not working to Right Battalion.	
	13	-	Major F.L.N. GILES, R.E. arriving to command Cheshire Field Co. (Temporarily) Lieut A.W. GORDON. (S.Co) arranged Initiation Conference to RE henceforward 1 per day given to Companies in turn.	
	14	-		
	15	-	Adj. to MINX re shortage of corrugated iron. Supply arrives; work on horse standings greatly assisted.	
	16	am	Huts supply alright again. CRE round line with Gor 9th Bde & OC Cheshire Co. from 3 slightly shelled, no damage. Adj. to Brining & Cheshire Co. 6 have run of 20/KRRC to Bde Workshop for hutting work. OC 253rd Tunnelling Co. called re work in listening galleries. Adj. with Field Engineer to huts of 76th Bde, & to POSTS 3. Capt. P.P. HENRIQUES joins Cheshire Field Co.	
	17	-	Lt. Col. SEWELL, RE from GHQ, inspects Brig RE Workshop. GOC 8th Bde. called re Torpedoes, wire-mowing mats, trench ladders & bridges, & RE party to accompany a raid for destroying a trench hostn emplacement. Adj. to Div School with GSO2, & to First Army workshop, BETHUNE.	
	18	-	Adj. to Army Workshops re Torpedoes, & mobile armoural charges. Field Engineer with Staff Capt RA round RA line lines & camps to suggest improvements.	
	19	-	Field Engineer instructs a squad from Brigades & Artillery in hutting, so that they will be able to carry out tuck of work themselves. CRE visits FLAMMEN-WERFER display. 2nd Lt GOURLEY (Cheshire Co) detailed to command RE party to accompany 8th Bde Raid. Adj. 6 to & RE Park	/Sgd/

1875 Wt. W5p3/826 1,000,000 4/15 J.B.C. & A. A.D.S.S./Forms/C. 2118.

Army Form C. 2118
Sheet 3.

WAR DIARY

C.R.E. 3rd Division   September 1916 contd

INTELLIGENCE SUMMARY
(Erase heading not required.)

Place	Date	Hour	Summary of Events and Information	Remarks and references to Appendices
NOEUX les MINES.	20	12:30 am	Warning that Div. is to be relieved & moved to training area. CRE & Adj. 8th Div. called & looking over different sectors - work CRE visits CRE 40th Div. for same reason for right sector. 1 to 8th Bde. at FOSSE 3 sent back to their battalion.	
"	21	am	56th Co. march with 8th Bde. Group to ALLOUAGNE Area.	
"	22	-	HQ RE to BOMY. 56th Co. to CUHEM, Cheshire Co. to AUCHEL	
BOMY	23	am	Cheshire Co. to MATRINGHEM., E. Riding to AUCHEL.	
"	24	-	E. Riding Co. to LIGNY-lez-AIRE.	
"	25	-	All companies training - Programme contain marching, drilling, rapid wiring, bridging (pontoon & trestle) use of explosives extended order drill schemes for Officers and NCOs, branching & knotting parties etc. CRE to E. Riding Co. 3 Envios. Conference at Div. Htd - Army Commander present. CRE attends. fetching stone for training purposes from MINX and 20 to RE Park.	
"	26	-	CRE to Conference on the Ground at 3.45 pm. Army Commander present.	
"	27	-	Adj. to BETHUNE to purchase material for signalling sheets. CRE to 56th Co., E. Riding Co. and 20/KRRC Pioneers.	MS [?]
"	28	-	Lt. S. CARLIN, E. Riding Co. awarded Military Cross. CRE to Cheshire & E. Riding Co. Adj. to WANDONNE RE Park, MINX, CEI Corps & BETHUNE re stores	
"	29	-	CRE visited 20/KRRC Pioneers & selected site for specimen M.G. Emplacement.	
"	30	-	Adj. to BETHUNE and RE Park, LILLERS, re stores. CRE visited 56th Co. at work.	

M Quist
LtColRE
CRE 3rd Division.

3rd Divisional Engineers.

C. R. E.

3RD DIVISION.

OCTOBER 1916.

Army Form C. 2118.

WAR DIARY
C.R.E. — 3rd Division.
INTELLIGENCE SUMMARY
Month of October 1916.

(Erase heading not required.)

Instructions regarding War Diaries and Intelligence Summaries are contained in F.S. Regs., Part II. and the Staff Manual respectively. Title pages will be prepared in manuscript.

Place	Date	Hour	Summary of Events and Information	Remarks and references to Appendices
	1916			
BONY	1st.	—	Holiday from training ordered by G.O.C. CRE to Conference on new Practice Ground 2.45 pm	
"	2nd–3rd		Training	
"	4		Divl. Attack Practice & Stokes Mortar Bombardment demonstration.	
"	5	am	HQ to MONCHY CAYEUX, 56th Co. to HERNICOURT, Chaline Co. to PREDEFIN, E. Riding Co. to BERGUENEUSE	
MONCHY CAYEUX	6	8.45 am	RSM with horses & transport, marched with Div. HQ to join Artillery Column. CRE Adj. by car to ACHEUX & return.	
"	7	am	CRE & Adj. by car to new Div HQ at BERTRANCOURT – Interpreter & Officer follow by lorry.	
			RSM and transport join up with HQ after marching from ETREE WAMIN. Field Companies told to entrain St POL 11.55 pm. Train started about 8 hours late.	
BERTRANCOURT	8	—	Field Cos. arrive ACHEUX 8.30 pm. 56th Co. to 5th Co. West (2nd Div); Chaline Co. Rt & Riding to those of E. Anglian Co.	
"	9	9.45am	Conference as to work to be done; CRE & Coy. Commanders at MAILLY MAILLET.	
"	10		CRE to line. Adj. with our BEAUSSART dump. Capt. NEWMAN, 20/I.C.R.R.C. temp. in charge. Cos. working on preparation of material, formation of dumps, C.Ts, T.M. Emplacements, deep dugouts etc. CRE to BGC. Conference at 6.30pm.	
"	11		CRE to line. Offensive preparations continued.	
"	12		Preparations contd. CRE Regt. to Co. roleumps.	

Army Form C. 2118.

WAR DIARY

C.R.E. 3rd Div'n on Month of October 1916.

INTELLIGENCE SUMMARY

SHEET - 2.

(Erase heading not required.)

Instructions regarding War Diaries and Intelligence Summaries are contained in F.S. Regs., Part II. and the Staff Manual respectively. Title pages will be prepared in manuscript.

Place	Date	Hour	Summary of Events and Information	Remarks and references to Appendices
1916.				
BERTRANCOURT	13		CRE to Line. Adjt to Rebark. Major F.L.N. GILES leaves Charlwin G. for CRE Second Army	
"	14		Capt. P.B. HENRIQUES takes on Charlwin G.	
"	15		CRE to Line. Adjt to R.Park. Scarcity of timber. CRE + Adjt to CE. V Corps.	
"	16		A little timber received. CRE to Line. A.S. to BEAUSSART.	
"	17		Conference of Co. Commanders having order received for Div'n to move northwards, 5pm. E.Riding Co. ordered to COURCELLET. Town began not expecting V'th Corps troops, refuses their admission. They return to MAILLY MAILLET. XIII'th Corps S.O.I claim R.E. Dump at COURCELLET. Complete muddle all day. No tubes received.	
"	18		CRE tats, to COURCELLET and then to see CE V Corps re getting the R.E. Dump. Orders for 56th & E.Riding Co'ys to go to COURCELLET. E.Ridings move into billets. Charlwin Co. into a field. No room for 56th Co. who return to BEAUSSART. Hdqs. move to BUS-les-ARTOIS.	
BUS	19.		Timber arrives at BEAUSSART Siding. 223rd Co. RE (31st Div) ordered to vacate COURCELLET. 56th 2nd Co. take their billets. Lt. WALLACE (20/KRRc)	
"	20.		d his party tath on the R.E. Dump. CRE tats, visit Company billets. Lt HAITHWAITE (E.Riding Co.) admitted into Hospital Sick. CRE to Line. Adjt to Companies & R.Park. Lt. WALLACE attached to 56 Co. to be near his work	

Army Form C. 2118.

WAR DIARY

C.R.E. 3rd Div. or month of October 1916. Sheet 3.

INTELLIGENCE SUMMARY.

(Erase heading not required.)

Place	Date	Hour	Summary of Events and Information	Remarks and references to Appendices
BUS	21	—	CRE to line. Adj. to 56 Co., RE Dump, & BEAUSSART. 5pm CRE & GSO, LS Conference at V Corps. & 6.30 pm to Bde. Conference.	
"	22		CRE to Cos. Adj. to BEAUSSART. Afternoon Office.	
"	23		Very foggy there. Operations postponed 24 hrs. 2nd Lt. SINCLAIR (Cheshire J.C.) left to join RFC, GMB, as Acting Engineer Officer.	
"	24		Very wet. Postponement of 48 hrs. Div. HQ & 9IC Bde. HQ dugouts completed. 56th Co. & 100th Infantry start repairing road W of COLINCAMPS to EUSTON journal.	
"	25		Work as usual. Lt. P. CRANSWICK (E. Riding J.C.) admitted into Hospital sick.	
"	26		Very wet. With CRE to COURCELLES, BEAUSSART, LEAUVILLERS (RE Park) & CE V Corps.	
"	27		Fair. Work as usual. 48 hours postponement. Capt. R. de H. HALL joins HQ as AA&R adj¹. Lt. PLAYFAIR returned to HEBUTERNE on 31st for Junior Staff Course.	
"	28		Wet day. CRE to line. Adj¹ & Capt. HALL office. Work as usual.	
"	29		Shortage of timber. Wet. Postponement of 5 days.	
"	30			
"	31		Morning CRE to line. Lt. PLAYFAIR left to HESDIN to Junior Staff Course. Afternoon CRE to Engineers of Adj¹ & Interpreter to MAILLEUX arrange for setting Broughwood. Fine day.	

E.W. Watson
Captain
& Adj. RE 3rd Div.

3rd Divisional Engineers.

C.R.E.

3RD DIVISION.

NOVEMBER 1916.

WAR DIARY
C.R.E. – 3rd Division – November 1916
INTELLIGENCE SUMMARY

Army Form C. 2118.

SHEET 1. VOL 28

(Erase heading not required.)

Place	Date	Hour	Summary of Events and Information	Remarks and references to Appendices
	1916			
BUS-LES-ARTOIS	1st Nov		C.R.E. adj. & Interpreter to COURCELLES, & LOUVENCOURT. Then to MARIEUX and VAUCHELLES. Arranged agreement with M. Gosselin of latter place to cut brushwood price 360 francs per hectar. Afternoon C.R.E. to see huts in Bus. Adj. Office.	
"	2nd Nov		C.R.E. to line. Adj. Office.	
"	3rd Nov		C.R.E. to line. Adj. to MARIEUX & COURCELLES dumps. C.R.E. to companies.	
"	4th Nov		C.R.E. ISTCHEUX to see C.E. V.th Corps. Adj. KATIEUX watertrough.	
"	5th Nov		Capt HENRIQUES, Cheshire F.Cy evacuated shell shock. Capt CLOUGH 5th F.Cg to command Cheshire Co temporarily. C.R.E. to line & BEAUSSART. Adj to BEAUSSART & VAUCHELLES.	
"	6th Nov		C.R.E. to line. Adj. Office & to Conference at Div. H.Q.	
"	7th Nov		C.R.E. & Adj. to VAUCHELLES to see NISSEN huts with contractor, brushwood cutting.	
"	8th Nov		C.R.E. to line. Adj. to R.E. dumps COURCELLES & companies.	
"	9th Nov		C.R.E. to line. Adj. to BEAUSSART & COURCELLES. C.R.E. & Adj. to VAUCHELLES.	

Army Form C. 2118.

WAR DIARY

C.R.E. 3rd Division — November 1916, continued

INTELLIGENCE SUMMARY

SHEET 2

(Erase heading not required.)

Instructions regarding War Diaries and Intelligence Summaries are contained in F.S. Regs., Part II. and the Staff Manual respectively. Title pages will be prepared in manuscript.

Place	Date	Hour	Summary of Events and Information	Remarks and references to Appendices
	1916			
BUS-LES-ARTOIS	10th Nov.		C.R.E. & Companies. Adjt to LOUVENCOURT. C.R.E. to conference at Div. H.Q.	
"	11th	6 p.m.	Coy Commanders & C.O. Pioneers to conference with C.R.E. C.R.E. to Companies. Adj. Office. Operation Order for impending attack. 2 Sections E. Rid. Co. with 76th Inf. Bde. Cheshire 7th Co. & 1 Co Pioneers for consolidation of SERRE. 2 Sections E. Riding Co. & all 5th H.C. in Div. Reserve	
"	12th		C.R.E. & Adj. Office.	
"	13th	1.30 p.m.	C.R.E. moved to advanced Div. H.Q. Attack on Serre. C.R.E. at Adv. Div. H.Q. Attack not a success owing to mud. No R.E. work done.	
"	14th	4 p.m.	C.R.E. at Adv. Div. H.Q. Adj Office & COURCELLES. C.R.E. returned to BUS. Companies resumed normal work.	
"	15th		C.R.E. & Adj. & Companies. 2nd Lieut SAVAGE 58th Co. killed.	
"	16th		3rd Div. transferred to XIIIth Corps. C.R.E. & Lieut S.G. THOMPSON Cheshire Co. joined H.Q. R.E. for Hutting work.	
"	17th		C.R.E. & Lieut. Adj. & Lieut THOMPSON to ACHEUX & LEAVILLERS. Capt. J.K. BLAIKIE joined Cheshire 7th Co.	

T2134. Wt. W708-776. 500000. 4/15. Sir J. C. & S.

WAR DIARY

Army Form C. 2118.

C.R.E. 3rd Division — November 1916 (continued)

INTELLIGENCE SUMMARY.

(Erase heading not required.)

SHEET. 3

Place	Date	Hour	Summary of Events and Information	Remarks and references to Appendices
	1916			
BUS-LES-ARTOIS.	18th Nov.		C.R.E. to see XIIIth Corps. C.E., C.R.E. + Adj to Companies.	
	19th Nov.		C.R.E. to line, Adj to C.E. XIIIth Corps.	
"	20th Nov.		C.R.E. & Companies. Adj + Lieut THOMPSON with Staff Capt R.A. to select sites for Horse Standings.	
"	21st Nov.		C.R.E. to line with Div. Commander. Adj to DOULLENS.	
"	22nd Nov.		C.R.E. + Adj to C.E. XIIIth Corps. to see NISSEN Huts at J.19.d. C.R.E. + Adj to COURCELLES. to see Hutting Coys.	
"	23rd Nov.		C.R.E. to line. Adj Office + to C.E. XIIIth Corps. about Wiring YELLOW LINE. O.C. Pioneers to see C.R.E. re Wiring YELLOW LINE.	
"	24th Nov.		O.C. Pioneers to see C.R.E. C.R.E. + Adj to see Hut in & around BUS. C.R.E. to Coys + COURCELLES dumps.	
"	25th Nov.		C.R.E. to line. Adj Office.	
"	26th Nov.		C.R.E. to line. Lieut THOMPSON to VARENNES. Adj Office. Party of 48 men from Inf Battns under Lieut F.M. SMITH, 1st Royal Scots. arrived at BUS. to work on Hutting.	
"	27th Nov.		C.R.E. to line. Adj Office. moved Office to BILLET K.27.	
"	28th Nov.		C.R.E. + Adj to BEAUSSART, to COURCELLES. R.E. dump + Coys.	

WAR DIARY

C.R.E. 3rd Division — November 1916 (continued)

INTELLIGENCE SUMMARY

Army Form C. 2118.
SHEET 4.

Place	Date	Hour	Summary of Events and Information	Remarks and references to Appendices
	1916			
BUS LES - ARTOIS	29th Nov.		C.R.E. 3 Div. Adj. & Lieut THOMPSON were H.Q. at Courcelles & the Coll. Pionrs. Printed warning (China Series) YELLOW LINE	
"	30th Nov.		C.R.E. Officer 152nd Co. R.E. arrived for work on YELLOW LINE. C.R.E. & Lieut THOMPSON went round billets - Bus with Div Commander.	

Kirkham
Capt R.E.
for C.R.E. 3rd Div.

3rd Divisional Engineers.

C. R. E.

3RD DIVISION.

DECEMBER 1916.

3rd Divisional Engineers.

Army Form C. 2118.

C.R.E. 3rd Division Vol 29 Sheet. 1

WAR DIARY
INTELLIGENCE SUMMARY.
(Erase heading not required.)

Month of December - 1916

Place	Date	Hour	Summary of Events and Information	Remarks and references to Appendices
BUS-LES-ARTOIS	1916 1st		O.C. 157th & 72nd C.S R.E. & C.R.E. to YELLOW LINE. Adj to Billet inspection at COURCELLES by Div. Commander.	
"	2nd Dec		C.R.E to inspection of A.A. Horse Standings with Div. Commander, then to Coys at COURCELLES. Adj to Billet Inspection at LOUVENCOURT with Div. Commander.	
"	3rd		C.R.E to Line. Adj Office + to 157th 72 C.S R.E.	
"	4th		Conference at Div. H.Q. C.R.E attended. Adj to BERTRANCOURT Sidings, CRE to Coys	
"	5th		C.R.E to Line.	
"	6th		C.R.E to line. Adj to see newest standings. Shortage of timber. Visit by C.E 5th Army.	
"	7th		C.R.E went on leave. Temp. Col. E.M. NEWELL D.S.O. P. Anthony 72 Cy acting C.R.E.	
"	8th		Adj to VAUCHELLES to settle for Billeward. 8th Battn Cavalry Pioneers arrived. 1 Coy. to 3rd Div for work on YELLOW LINE. Weather very wet. FRANCE	
"	9th		Col Newell to line. Adj. Office.	
"	10th		Col Newell to COURCELLES + Adj to Coys.	
"	11th		Col Newell to see O.C. 157th 72 C.S R.E.	
"	12th		Col Newell to line. Adj. Office.	

Army Form C. 2118.
Sheet 2

WAR DIARY
C.R.E. of 3rd Division
INTELLIGENCE SUMMARY. Continued.
(Erase heading not required.)

Place	Date	Hour	Summary of Events and Information	Remarks and references to Appendices
BUS-LES	13th		153rd 74 C.E. R.E. left to rejoin 37th Div. Colonel & his Adj. to see Hutting & Staging.	
ARTOIS	14th		81st 74 C.E. R.E. arrived to replace 153rd C.E. for work on YELLOW LINE. Colonel to 15 COURCELLES. Adj. Office.	
	15th		Conference at Div. H.Q. Colonel attended. Adj. to Courcelles.	
	16th		Col. Incurell visits G.S.O.1 round area allotted to Div. for Spring Hutting etc. for Houtcourt.	
	17th		Col. Incurell takes Adj. & Lt. Thompson to Murray Hutted Camps, Wheeling of Bond on Provisional Billetting scheme for Spring. Major HENDERSON 325 C.E. to inspect new Brig. School VAUCHELLES for a week.	
	18th		Col. Incurell's Office. Adj. & Lt. Thompson to see Hutting & Staging. C.R.E. returned from leave.	
	19th		2nd R. Horse & Cavalry Pioniers Bat.y moves to replace them for work on YELLOW LINE. C.R.E. Office. Capt. A.B. CLOUGH 325 C.E. appointed O.C. 210th C.E. R.E.	
	20th		C.R.E. to 81st & 79 R.E. & to COURCELLES. Adj. to Allies with for Spring Billetting Scheme	
	21st		C.R.E. to him & to See C.E. 8th M. Corps. 82nd 74 C.E. R.E. left.	
	22nd		81st 74 C.E. R.E. arrived for work on YELLOW LINE. C.R.E. Office.	
	23rd		C.R.E. to see new Sector of line taken over from 7th Div. Very Good. O.C. 81st C.E. R.E. to see C.R.E.	

Army Form C. 2118

SHEET - 3

WAR DIARY
C.R.E. 2nd Division, continued
INTELLIGENCE SUMMARY
(Erase heading not required.)

Place	Date	Hour	Summary of Events and Information	Remarks and references to Appendices
	1916		DECEMBER.	
BUS- LES- ARTOIS	24th Dec.		Capt. A.B.CLOUGH left 56th C.E. Major HENDERSON 56th C.O to take command of 210th C.O.R.E.	
	25th		CHRISTMAS DAY. By order of Corps Commander as far as possible all work suspended.	
"	26th		C.R.E. to line. Adj to sit on G.C.M.	
"	27th		C.R.E. to Coys at COURCELLES. Adj at G.C.M.	
"	28th		C.R.E. & G.S.O.1. round line.	
"	29th		C.R.E. office. Adj & Lt. Thompson to select sites for camps near SOUASTRE-AU-BOIS.	
"	30th		C.R.E. to line. Adj office.	
"	31st		C.R.E. to line. Lieut Thompson to see Div. School VAUCHELLES.	

Matthews
Captain.
for C.R.E. 3rd Div.

3nd Division

War Diaries

C.R.E's.

January To December

1917

Army Form C. 2118.

SHEET 1.

WAR DIARY

C.R.E. 3rd Division - Month of January 1917.

INTELLIGENCE SUMMARY.

(Erase heading not required.)

Vol 30

Instructions regarding War Diaries and Intelligence Summaries are contained in F.S. Regs, Part II. and the Staff Manual respectively. Title pages will be prepared in manuscript.

Place	Date	Hour	Summary of Events and Information	Remarks and references to Appendices
BUS-LES-ARTOIS	1917 1st Jany	3:am	C.R.E. to line. C.R.E. 32nd Div. came to make arrangements about taking over.	
	2nd		C.R.E. Office. Adj. to TOURCELLES.	
"	3rd		Advance parties of 1 Off. & 6 O.R. each from Chatham & Medway F.C. of 1st CANAPLES area.	
"	4th		C.R.E. to line. Adj. to CANAPLES. Infantry Working party detailed.	
"	5th		2 Sections Chatham F.Co. in relief by 1 Sec. 218th Co. 32nd Div. to STOUEN by lorry. Wagon by road.	
"	6th		C.R.E. to line. Adj. Office.	
"	7th		C.R.E. to visit G.O.C. 32nd Div. Adj. visit Adj. 32nd D.W.R.E. to TOURCELLES. Wings & Coys. Relie[f].	
"	8th		C.R.E. TOURCELLES. Lieut. THOMPSON 15 Ammns. to Ency Stores.	
"	9th		82nd Co. marched to BEAUSSART for work under E.in.C. Corps. Remainder of Chatham F.Co. to PUSCHEVILLERS. R. & J. Co. to PUSCHEVILLERS. H.Q. R.E. moved by road to CANAPLES.	
CANAPLES	10th		C.R.E. round area with Q.A.A. & R.M.G. C. SKERREN went on Corse. Lieut. THOMPSON of adj.	
"	10th		Chatham Co. marched to LANCHES. R.B.d.Co. to PERNOIS.	
	11th		C.R.E. & Adj. 15 F.A.d.Co. at PERNOIS. Coys. training & Hutting. Draftly Little.	
	12th		C.R.E. with D.W. Mickity. Office to Rifle Ranger. Lieut. THOMPSON to STOUEN.	
	13th		C.R.E. to Chatham F.Co. LANCHES.	
	14th		C.R.E. to lecture by D.W. Commander. C.E. Mrs. Corps. calls re Office.	

Army Form C. 2118

SHEET 2

WAR DIARY

INTELLIGENCE SUMMARY

C.R.E. 3rd Division, January 1917, contd

(Erase heading not required.)

Place	Date	Hour	Summary of Events and Information	Remarks and references to Appendices
CANAPLES	1917 15th Jan.		C.R.E. to ROUEN. Lieut. THOMPSON to CANDAS. Capt. A. H. ERNST. R.A.M.C. attached 156 Coy to ship.	
"	16th		C.R.E. R.E. H.Q.	
"	17th		C.R.E. to CANDAS.	
"	18th	(A.M)	C.R.E. to Chaulnes Reg. (P.M) to Div. School VACHELLES with G.O.C.	
"	19th		Lieut. THOMPSON to AMIENS to buy linoleum for Div. School. Major H.M. HENDERSON	
"			O.C. 56th C.R.E. appointed C.R.E. 18th Div.	
"	20th		C.R.E. to ROUEN.	
"	21st		C.R.E. to FIEFFES. Lt. THOMPSON to ROUEN.	
"	22nd		C.R.E. Office. Capt. HALL returned from leave.	
"	23rd		C.R.E. to HALLOY. Lt. THOMPSON went on leave. Adj. Office moved always	
"	24th	(P.M)	C.R.E. to ROUEN. (P.M) C.R.E. + adj. to FIEFFES	
"	25th		C.R.E. adj. + Interpreter to Chateau de LANCHES	
"	26th		C.R.E. to ROUEN. Orders received for Div. to move north. Daylight unknown	
"	27th		C.R.E. + adj. Office. Handing over with etc. to C.R.E. 31st Div.	
"	28th		56 Coy marched from BEAUVART to SARTON. Chr/hat to LANCHES to AUTIEULLE	
"			S. Ruly + Co. PERNOIS to PRESCHVILLERS.	
FLERS	29th		Division transferred to Third Army. Coys entrained & marched under Brigade arrangements. H.Q. R.E. moved to FLERS.	

1875 Wt. W293/826 1,000,000 4/15 J.B.C. & A.   A.D.S.S./Forms/C. 2118.

Army Form C. 2118

SHEET 3.

WAR DIARY

C.R.E. 3rd Division — January 1917 — contd

INTELLIGENCE SUMMARY

(Erase heading not required.)

Place	Date	Hour	Summary of Events and Information	Remarks and references to Appendices
	1917			
FLERS	30th Jan		Division came under XVIIth Corps. Corps continued march. Div H.Q. moved to VILLERS-CHATEL.	
VILLERS-CHATEL	31st Jan		Corps continued march. 58th Coy to DIEVAL, Chinh. Co. 15. MARQUAY, S. Reilly's. LCAUCOURT. CRE & adj to AUBIGNY. E.C.E. XVII. Hqtrs. to L & 8 RE Park. SAVY.	
		P.M.	C.R.E. & adj to C & E Corps. NOYELLES-VION. Received orders for 2 Fd Coys & Pioneer Batt. to be transferred to VI Corps to work.	

Blackburn
Capt R.E. (T).
for C.R.E. 3rd Div.

WAR DIARY

Army Form C. 2118

C.R.E. - 3rd Division.
Month of February, 1917.
INTELLIGENCE SUMMARY
(Erase heading not required.)

Sheet 1.
Vol 31

Place	Date	Hour	Summary of Events and Information	Remarks and references to Appendices
	1917.			
VILLERS-CHATEL	1st Feb.		C.R.E. & A.A. + Q.M.G. to 17th Corps. + to WARLUS. 438th (Cheshire) F.I. Co. moved to VILLERS-SIRE-SIMON. 329th (F. Riding) Co. to AMBRINES	
— do —	2nd Feb.		2 Sections 58th Co. to A.C.Q. for Hutting work under XVII Corps. C.R.E. + adj. visit Camp Commandant to WARLUS to see about new Divl. H.Q. + to C.O. 67 Corps + AMBRINES.	
— do —	3rd Feb.		H.Q. + 2 Sections 329 Co. to WARLUS. 2 Sections 329 Co. + 2 Coys Pioneers remain at AMBRINES, Bunking Barns. 438 Co. to ARRAS. Transport to Divisions. Work with 12th Div. 2 Co. H.Q. + 2 Coys Pioneer. C.R.E. + adj. 67 Corps Park Divisions + to AGNEZ to C.R.E. 12th Div.	
— do —	4th Feb.		C.R.E. + adj. to WARLUS + to 17th Corps.	
— do —	5th Feb.		Lieut THOMPSON returned from leave. C.R.E. to bed with bad cold.	
— do —	6th Feb.		Adj. + Lieut THOMPSON to ARRAS to 438 Co. Dugouts & Girls School. Lock up WARLUS	
— do —	7th Feb.		C.R.E. sees Lieut P. BLACK, R.A.M.C. joined 58 Co. as M.O. ½ Divl. R.E. Adj. + Camp Comm. visit to LIGNEREUIL + WARLUS.	
LIGNEREUIL	8th Feb.		Divl. H.Q. moved to LIGNEREUIL. Div transferred 6 to 17 Corps. H.Q. + 2 Sects. 58 Co. to HOUVIN-HOUVIGNEUL. C.R.E. ready to assist at NOYELLE-VION on "Offensive Use Appces".	
— do —	9th Feb.		C.R.E. to line with F.S.O.1. Lieut THOMPSON to AMBRINES + 128 Co. LE-HAMEAU. To Bunking.	
— do —	10th Feb.		C.R.E. + adj. to WARLUS WARRAS to 438 Co. Pioneers. 330 Co. Conference at Divl. H.Q.	
WARLUS	11th Feb.		Divl. H.Q. moved to WARLUS at midday. H.Q. + 2 Sections 58 Co. from HOUVIN-HOUVIGNEUL + 2 Sections 56 Co. from ACQ to ARRAS.	
— do —	12th Feb.		C.R.E. to line with F.S.O.1. Adj. 67 Corps. Dump Street C.E. 17 Corps Wyte Foot. 58 Co. returned from LE PARC & School of Instruction.	

Army Form C. 2118
Sheet 2

WAR DIARY
INTELLIGENCE SUMMARY

C.R.E. 3rd Division. February, 1917 continued

(Erase heading not required.)

Place	Date	Hour	Summary of Events and Information	Remarks and references to Appendices
	1917			
WARLUS	13th Feb.		C.R.E. & Adj. adj. with AA & QMG. 6th Corps re. Hutting schemes.	
–do–	14–		C.R.E. & Adj. with O.C. 529 C.E. Adj. LAMBRINES & LIENCOURT. Eminence from water to advanced Divl. R.E. dump, near Girls' School, Rue de TEMPLE. ARRAS.	
–do–	15th Feb.		C.R.E. & Adj. with G.O.C. 9th Bde. Adj. WANQUETIN. 1 Sec 529 C.E. from AMBRINES to WANQUETIN for Hutting.	
–do–	16th Feb.		1 Sec 529 C.E. from AMBRINES to LIENCOURT for Hutting. C.R.E. 6th Divn. C.E. 6th Corps called. Notice received, not send to LIENCOURT, & hence halt without other work. Sent to WANQUETIN. Frozen slow.	
–do–	17th Feb.		C.R.E. & Adj. WANQUETIN. HQ & 2 Sections 529 C.E. less transport moved to ARRAS.	
–do–	18th Feb.		C.R.E. & Adj. with G.S.O.1. Adj. to DUISANS & LIENCOURT. Road precautions in force. On account of Thaw. No lorries available.	
–do–	19th Feb.		C.R.E. & Adj. daily. All conferences working on hurried elements for Brigades & Batt. HQ & F.T.M. Emplacements.	
–do– /S	22 Feb.		Pioneers recalumning C.T.S.	
–do–	23rd Feb.		C.R.E. & conference with C.E. XVIII Corps. Transport of 508 C.E. & 1 Sec 30 C.E. moved to AMBRES	
–do–	24 Feb.		C.R.E. & Adj. G.O.C. 37th Div. inspected Field Co. horses. Adj. & Telephoned to ISPOL.	
–do–	25th Feb.		1 Day canvas & paper for Targets & to 248 R.E. Park.	
–do–	26th Feb.		C.R.E. & Divn. to see O.C. C.R.E. & Corps.	
–do–	27th Feb.		Road precaution withdrawn at 7 a.m. C.R.E. & Divn.	
			Road precautions in force again. Only Field Co. transport getting out. No le C.	
–do–	28th Feb.		Forward dumps. C.R.E. & Divn. Adj. to WARLUS.	

Blomer
Captain
For C.R.E. 3rd Divn

3 Div
April 1917

APPENDIX "A".

Report on R.E. Preparations during February, March & April for Offensive Operations on 9th April, 1917.

1. The 3rd Divisional Headquarters arrived at WARLUS on 11th February and from two days after that date the R.E. preparations may be said to have commenced.

The situation of R.E. and Pioneer Personnel then was :-

56th Fd. Co. R.E. just arrived in ARRAS.

438th (Cheshire) Fd. Co. R.E. and 20th K.R.R.C. (Pioneers) (less 100 men employed on bunking barns) had been in ARRAS a few days working under 12th Division; all this work was wasted as it was not what the 3rd Division wanted.

529th (E.Riding) Fd.Co.R.E. - 2 Sections at WARLUS erecting Divisional Headquarters.
    1 Section at WANQUETIN with 50 Pioneers erecting NISSEN Huts.
    1 Section at LIENCOURT with 50 Pioneers bunking barns.

Hutting. 2. The hutting may be dealt with in a few words. The scheme was to increase the accommodation in the back area by erecting NISSEN Huts and Bunking barns.
Shortness of material, largely due to Thaw precautions being in force delayed this considerably.
Roughly speaking - 2 Sections of the 529th (E. Riding) Fd. Co. R.E. and 100 Pioneers were employed on it continuously from about 12th February to 5th April and during that period erected

    84 NISSEN Huts at   WANQUETIN.
    12   "   "   "   LIENCOURT.
    15   "   "   "   WARLUS.

while 1,500 bunks were constructed and 500 repaired in various Villages.

Preparations for the Offensive.
3. These may really be said to have started on 15th February some two or three days being spent in finding out what was actually required as the ideas of the 3rd Division did not agree altogether with those of their predecessor.

Two excellent systems of tunnels made by the New Zealand Tunnelling Company joining up various caves were approaching completion and full advantage was taken of the safe communication they afforded, the Brigade and Battalion Headquarters being made off the tunnels, and thus provided with safe communications.

The main items of work then decided on were roughly :-

(a)   4 Main C.T's. - IMPERIAL, 20th STREET, ICELAND and 15th STREET.

/(b)

Appdx A. cont'd

(b)   3 Brigade Headquarters.

(c)   4 Battalion Headquarters for the 76th (front) Brigade.
         3 Battalion Headquarters for the 9th Brigade.

(d)   T.M.Emplacements for 5 Batteries of 2" Trench Mortars.

(e)   CIRCULAR TRENCH & CABLE TRENCH to give lateral communication.

The above works (a) and (e) - C.Ts. and lateral communication were entrusted to the 20th K.R.R.C. (Pioneers).
Each Field Company constructed the Headquarters of its affiliated Brigade.

2 Battalion Headquarters were constructed by each of the 56th and 438th Field Companies R.E.

The 3 Field Companies had nominally about 600 infantry working with them up to about the middle of March; when this number was gradually reduced.

Other items taken in hand later on were :-

In the RONVILLE System of Caves (to be used for assembling the 8th Infantry Brigade) the Pioneers constructed deep latrines, urinals and ablution benches, water being laid on by the VII Corps.

ALADDIN'S CAVE, found by accident by the Pioneers when digging the CIRCULAR TRENCH, was cleared and 3 entrances made into it, so that it could be used as a "Q" Dump and some 60 Pack animals were stabled in it.

3 Bridges were made under roads by the 56th Field Co. R.E. where CABLE TRENCH cut across them, fit to carry any traffic.

Advanced Divisional HdQrs. A suitable site for these had to be found and gave some trouble. Eventually it was decided to utilise RUSSELL CAVE. This when cleared by the New Zealand Tunnelling Co. was found to provide very little accommodation. The same Company then constructed a new dug-out close by, which took all the advanced Divisional Headquarters except signals, Orderlies, and Officers Mess who were placed in the old cave. The fitting up of this of this Headquarters was carried out by the 56th Field Co. R.E.

Trench Mortar Emplacements. One section of the 438th (Cheshire) Fd. Co. R.E. was detailed for this as soon as they arrived in the area, and remained continuously at it, with working parties of R.A., T.Ms., and Infantry.
2 Sections of the 56th Field Co. R.E. were also employed later on for a short period.

Appdx. A. Cont'd.

Originally 5 Batteries of M.T.Ms. were to have been constructed, but owing to the retirement of the enemy from the front of our right, most of these became useless and eventually only 5 2" T.Ms. were used Besides Heavies.

4. **R.E. Dumps & Stores.**

An old workshop alongside the GIRL'S SCHOOL was selected as the main R.E. Dump. The accommodation it afforded was limited and later on as material came in, another Dump called the 'Reserve Dump' was formed on the RUE DE RIETZ.

The Pioneers established a dump of their own in a house in the RUE DU TEMPLE.

2 Advanced Dumps were formed, well forward, just before operations commenced, one close to the original front line by 15th STREET; the other just West of STRAFE WOOD.

The supply of materials at first was slow and scanty, partly on account of deficiency of transport as "Thaw precautions" prevented lorries running for a considerable period and partly due to a scarcity of materials, particularly of sawn timber and tools.

It can hardly be said however that work was ever appreciably held up for want of materials, (this does not apply to hutting) - something which could be made to do, was usually obtainable.

By Zero Day, difficulties had been overcome, and the dumps could be considered as fairly well stocked.

Trench Foot Bridges and Trench Ladders. 600 of each were obtained from the Army Park. This number appears to have sufficed.

Artillery Bridges. 24 were obtained, - which sufficed.

The tools issued for the assault to the different Brigades were as follows:-

	Picks.	Shovels.
8th Infy. Brigade.	300	500
9th Infy. Brigade.	490	980
76th Infy. Brigade.	-	1000

5. **'Q' and Brigade Dumps.**

The Divisional Advanced 'Q' Dump was in ALADDIN'S CAVE, into which three entrances had been made, one of them was large enough to admit pack animals which were stabled in the cave till required.

2 or 3 of the old shafts were also fitted up with windlasses, for hoisting or lowering stores.

Appdx A. Cont'd

Water was laid on into this cave for filling Petrol Tins.

Brigade Dumps for S.A.A. grenades etc. were made off the tunnels, mostly by the Brigades themselves, with R.E. supervision and assistance.

6. Roads.
(a) The main road in the area was the ARRAS - CAMBRAI Road, a first class pavé road, but cut about in our area by several trenches, - 3 Barricades, shell holes etc.

(b) Along the Southern Boundary ran a track, metalled for the first 500 yards to a very limited extent. Beyond that it was only a mud track.

The XVIII Corps undertook to make good the CAMBRAI Road up to our front line, which they did except that our Pioneers did the final filling in of trenches and demolition of Barricades.

They also undertook to make it good on the day of battle up to just by the first German trench. Beyond this point up to the BOIS DES BOEUFS had to be made passable for transport as quickly as possible.

The Intelligence regarding this portion gathered from aeroplane photographs showed that 9 trenches crossed it, and that certainly one large pit, probably 25 ft. wide and 8 ft. deep had been dug right across it; possibly also two others; 2 Barricades also existed at TILLOY. This intelligence proved fairly correct, but the 2 Barricades were destroyed by Artillery fire, only one pit was found and this was more of the nature of a very wide trench with a barricade of agricultural implements, and it was not so wide as anticipated.

To deal with this road 1 section 529th (E.Riding) Field Co. R.E. and the 20th K.R.R.C. Pioneers (less 1½ Platoons) were detailed with Pioneer Battalion of the 37th Division as 2nd relief and N.Z. Tunnelling Coy. and one A.T. Coy. R.E. as 3rd relief.

The scheme was briefly - for the section of the R.E. to erect a trestle bridge over the Pit - using one of their WELDON Trestles and superstructure for the purpose; this was carried out by hand.

All other trenches to be filled in and corduroyed with sleepers: a single track for horsed transport to be got through first, and then widened, made fit for lorries &c.

Tools were collected, about 2,500 sleepers supplied by C.E. VI Corps and disposed of in dumps by the Pioneers.

All parties of the 20th K.R.R.C. Pioneers were very carefully organised, told off to a definite task, tools and material allotted beforehand.

Appdx A. Contd

On the 9th April - at 9-15 a.m. the Liaison Officer of the XVIII Corps was ordered to commence work on his portion. At 9.25 a.m., the first Coy. of the 20th K.R.R.C. Pioneers was ordered to move up, but on reaching the spot found it too hot to work for another two hours, and suffered 10 casualties. The remainder of the Battalion and section of 529th (E.Riding) Fd. Co. R.E. were ordered up at 1.35 p.m. and got on alright with the work.

A track 10 ft. wide and fit for lorries (it is doubtful if this was the case at the trestle bridge) was reported through about 10-0 p.m. on the 9th.

On the 10th, C.E., VI Corps assumed charge of the road.

(c) The track along the Southern Divisional Boundary was wanted to enable Field Guns to get forward. 1½ Platoons of the 20th K.R.R.C. Pioneers were allotted to this. Trenches were prepared for bridging, bridges and material collected.

This party under Lt. THOMAS was ordered up at 9-15 a.m. and the track was ready by the time the guns arrived.

Continued heavy traffic, coupled with wet weather destroyed it, and it became hopeless unless corduroyed throughout: no more sleepers were available for it after the 12th. A good deal of work was done on it by Field Companies in the meantime, but it dropped out of use.

Two level crossings were made just N and S of ARRAS Railway Station in case either of the bridges was destroyed and in order to provide additional road facilities.

Their value was fully proved when the bridge North of the Station blew up.

7. Allotment of R.E. and Pioneers for the Offensive

The 3 Field Companies were allotted for work on 9th April as follows:-

76th Infantry Brigade.

2 Sections 529th (E.Riding) Fd. Co. R.E. with 2 Platoons 2nd Suffolks.

Half a section R.E. and one Platoon of the Suffolks were employed on improving the Push Pipe Crater just South of the CAMBRAI Road to use as a C.T. and digging through the lip into the German Sap W.12. The Push Pipe was exploded at 5-30 a.m. and formed a crater about 15 ft. deep. At first there was a considerable amount of shell fire here, and the casualties amounted to 5 R.E. (20 per cent) and 5 Infantry.

At 9-5 a.m. this section moved forward to join the other 1½ sections on constructing Strong Points in the German First Line System.

The Platoon of Infantry finished the C.T. at 1 p.m.

The 2 sections altogether constructed 3 Strong Points on 9th and another on 10th.

Appendix 'A' Continued.

9th Infantry Brigade.

56th Field Co. R.E. and 2 Platoons of Infantry attached.

Three sections and Infantry party constructed 3 Strong Points in the HARP - East of TILLOY and West of QUARRY.

The 4th section erected a screen on the CAMBRAI Road on the night 8th/9th to cover the Brigades advancing from view from the North and afterwards examined German dugouts and got a Well in TILLOY into working order.

Casualties - 1 Officer and 2 men wounded.

The Strong Points were completed by 4.30 p.m. On 10th April the Company was employed on "wiring" the BLUE Line.

8th Infantry Brigade.

2 sections 438th (Cheshire) Fd. Co. R.E. and 2 Platoons of the 1st R.S.F.

These were moved up at noon on 9th but as the "BROWN" Line had not been captured, they were sent back again.

On the 10th they were again sent forward and after the capture of the "BROWN" Line, constructed 2 Strong Points in it. Later on, they cut gaps in the wire for Cavalry to pass through.

Casualties - 3 wounded.

Of the remaining R.E., 1 Section of the 529th (E.Riding) Fd. Co. R.E. was employed to erect a trestle bridge in the pit on the CAMBRAI Road, as has already been mentioned under "Roads".

The remaining section of this Company and one section of the 438th (Cheshire) Fd. Co. R.E. were employed in the evening of the 9th on the South Artillery Track, the remaining section of the 438th (Cheshire) Fd. Co. R.E. being detailed for fire duty in ARRAS.

On the 10th these three sections were employed on on the South Artillery Track.

On the 11th, 12th, and 13th all three Field Companies were employed on the South Artillery Track except that on the 11th and 12th the 529th (E.Riding) Fd. Co. R.E. stood by for 48 hours in BOIS DES BOEUFS ready to consolidate GUEMAPPE when taken and on 13th 2 sections of the 56th Field Co. R.E. acted similarly.
In neither case were they used.

When not at work the Companies lived in their cellars in ARRAS.

Appendix 'A' Continued.

The employment of the Pioneers was entirely on Roads and has been already des-cribed. In addition on the night 8th/9th, 100 of them were sent off to dig out 5 Tanks which had stuck near the CITADEL. They succeeded in freeing three of them.

8. Lessons learnt.

No particular new lessons are apparent, but the value of thorough careful preparations which worked without a hitch on the day must be recognised.

Army Form C. 2118.

WAR DIARY
— or —
INTELLIGENCE SUMMARY.
(Erase heading not required.)

C.R.E. 3rd Division. Month of March, 1917.

SHEET - 1.

WO/33

Instructions regarding War Diaries and Intelligence Summaries are contained in F.S. Regs., Part II. and the Staff Manual respectively. Title pages will be prepared in manuscript.

Place	Date	Hour	Summary of Events and Information	Remarks and references to Appendices
WARLUS	1917. March 1st		C.R.E. & adj. to WANQUETIN & LIENCOURT. Afternoon to ARRAS presentation of D.C.M ribbon to C.S.M. QUIGLEY 438th (Cheshire) Fd. Co. R.E.	
	2nd		C.R.E. to line. Adjutant office.	
	3rd		C.R.E. to ARRAS with Divl. Commander. Adjutant to see Pioneers & Corps.	
	4th		C.R.E. to line. Adjutant office.	
	5th		C.R.E. Office. C.E. VIth Corps called in afternoon.	
	6th		C.R.E. to line. Visit B Commander in Chief to Divl. H.Q. C.R.E. present.	
	7th		C.R.E. & Adjutant to WANQUETIN & LIENCOURT. 2/Lt THOMPSON returned from LIENCOURT.	
	8th		C.R.E. & 2/Lt THOMPSON to the line. Adjutant to ARRAS to present at Court Martial.	
	9th		C.R.E. & adjutant to line & to R.E. dumps in ARRAS.	
	10th		C.R.E. to line with C.E. VIth Corps. C.R.E., adjutant & 2/Lt THOMPSON to lecture on Tanks.	
	11th		C.R.E. to line. Adjutant to ARRAS. 2/Lt THOMPSON office.	
	12th		C.R.E. to line. Captain HALL left to command 529th (E. Riding) Fd. Co. R.E.(T.F.), Lt. Col. E.M. NEWELL left to become C.R.E. 58th Division. 2/Lt THOMPSON becomes acting adjutant. Lt. C.P. WILLIAMSON 56th Fd. Co. killed in action.	
	13th		C.R.E. to line. Adjutant to MONDICOURT and DOULLENS.	
	14th		C.R.E. to line. Adjutant office.	
	15th		C.R.E. to line. Adjutant to DUISANS to see VIth Corps R.E Park	
	16th		C.R.E. office.	
	17th		C.R.E. to line with Divl. Commander. Adjutant office.	
	18th		C.R.E. to line at dawn to make a reconnaissance. Adjutant to select	

Army Form C. 2118.

WAR DIARY
or
INTELLIGENCE SUMMARY.

(Erase heading not required.)

C.R.E. 3rd Division   March 1917, continued
SHEET 2.

Place	Date	Hour	Summary of Events and Information	Remarks and references to Appendices
WARLUS	1917. March 18th		Site for "pipe pushing" demonstration. C.R.E to line in evening. Germans retiring to HINDENBURG line.	
	19th		C.R.E to line. Adjutant office.	
	20th		C.R.E & adj conference at Divl. H.Q at 9.30 a.m. Conference at C.R.E's office in afternoon. O.C. Corps Pioneers present.	
	21st		C.R.E to line. Adj to C.E VIIth Corps office & No 8 R.E Park re tools. / Section B 529 d (3 Riding) td. Co. R.E arrived in ARRAS at 9.0am from LIENCOURT	
	22nd		C.R.E to line. Adjutant office.	
	23rd		C.R.E. to line. Adjutant to ARRAS re dumps.	
	24th		C.R.E to line. Adjutant to WANQUETIN re hutting.	
	25th		C.R.E to line. Adj. office. 2/LT CRANE H.E. joined 56th td G. R.E.	
	26th		C.R.E to see C.E VIIth Corps. Adjutant to NANQUETIN about huts for dumping surplus stores (Adjutant R.E 3rd Div)	
	27th		C.R.E to line. Adj office. Captain PLAYFAIR. I.S.O, assumed duties of S.M 76th Inf Bde.	
	28th		C.R.E to line. Adjutant office.	
	29th		C.R.E to line. Adjutant office.	
	30th		C.R.E & adjutant to line.	
	31st		C.R.E to ARRAS in afternoon. Adjutant office.	

S.G. Humphreys Lt. R.E. (T)
for C.R.E 3rd Div.

Headquarters R.E. 3rd Division

WAR DIARY or INTELLIGENCE SUMMARY

Month of April 1917   Army Form C. 2118.

MO R & 3 D Sheet 2
WO 95 33

Place	Date	Hour	Summary of Events and Information	Remarks and references to Appendices
ARRAS	April 10th		C.R.E. went round all roads that thing. Adjutant to reconnoitre NEUVILLE VITASSE road in 14th Division area. 2 Sections Cheshire Fd Coy on South Artillery track. Ordered 2 Riding Fd Coys Transport East of ARRAS & other Field Coys & Pioneers West of ARRAS.	
"	"	1.10 am	Orders received for 2 Riding F. Coy to move forward to assembly position with 9th Inf Bde. This Fd Coy is now under orders P.C.R.E.	
"	"	4. am	O.C. 2 Ridings called to get Written orders that he is now under C.R.E.'s orders. G.S.O.I gave this.	
"	"	6.0 am	Ordered up tool carts of 2 Ridings to N.2.a. (BOIS DES BOEUFS) Cheshires 50th Fd Coy & 50 T.M.B. working on roads. C.R.E. inspected "Office" & horses ordered up from WARLUS to advanced Divl. H.Q. roads.	
"	12th		C.R.E. to South Artillery track advanced repair centre & 2 Ridings. Adjutant to R.E. dump, 5o companies & Pioneers are ordered back to ARRAS. Adjutant to move forward if GUEMAPPE 2 Sections to be ordered to stand by ready to move forward if GUEMAPPE is taken.	
"	13th		C.R.E. to road in morning. Adj to TILLOY in afternoon. Division to be relieved to-night.	
"	14th		C.R.E. & adj rode over South Artillery track & back down 12th Divl road then to companies in ARRAS & on to old quarters in WARLUS. Field Coys & transport moved back to WARLUS.	
WARLUS	15th		C.R.E. & adj office. Companies resting.	
"	16th		C.R.E. to companies in morning. Adj in afternoon.	
"	17th		C.R.E. to ARRAS to companies. Adj to PREVENT. Companies testing pontoons.	
"	18th		C.R.E. to companies in ARRAS. Adj to C.R.E. 29th Divn & to 8th & 76th Inf Bdes.	
"	19th		C.R.E. to ARRAS in morning to conference at Divl H.Q. at 4 pm. Adj to ARRAS	
"	20th		C.R.E. & adj. to 17th & 29th Division in ARRAS. To C.E. VI Corps in afternoon.	

Headquarters R.E. 3rd Division   WAR DIARY   Month of April 1917   Army Form C. 2118.

Instructions regarding War Diaries and Intelligence Summaries are contained in F. S. Regs., Part II. and the Staff Manual respectively. Title pages will be prepared in manuscript.

INTELLIGENCE SUMMARY
(Erase heading not required.)

Sheet 1.

Place	Date	Hour	Summary of Events and Information	Remarks and references to Appendices
WARLUS	April 1st		C.R.E. to line at dawn. Adj. office. C.E. IIIrd Corps called in afternoon to discuss operations.	
"	April 2nd		C.R.E. to line. Adj. to WANQUETIN re barn for dumping supplies stores which are ordered to be dumped. 2 C.B. H.J.F. GOURLEY rejoined 436th (Cheshire) Field Coy from hospital (wounded).	
"	3rd		C.R.E. to line. Adjutant office. Orders received to board floor of hut of ST SAUVEUR tunnel.	
"	4th		'V' day. 3mo projectors used. Section 3 529th (E. Riding) Fd Co. moved from WANQUETIN to ARRAS.	
"	5th		C.R.E. to ARRAS. C.E. VIth Corps called in afternoon 'W' day.	
"	6th		'X' day. Adj office. In afternoon C.R.E. to watering point West BARRAS	
"	7th		'Q' day. C.R.E's adj office. C.R.E. adj. moved at 10pm to advanced Divisional H.Q. in RUSSEL CAVE.	
ARRAS	8th		'Y' day. C.R.E's adj to companies & Pioneers	
"	9th		Z day. 5.30am Zero hour. 7.0am Lt THOMAS' party of KRRC (Pioneers) ordered up to AUCKLAND CAVE. 7.40am warned Pioneers about mining of CAMBRAI road. 8.0am Lt THOMAS' party passed advanced H.Q. en route for AUCKLAND cave. 8.40am Lt DIXON reported section of Cavalry wagons at Cavalry barracks. He went on to report to C.E. IIIrd Corps, leaving orderly Rest. 9.15am 18th Corps assistant field Engineer liaison officer ordered to move up. 9.35am that CAMBRAI ROAD party of KRRC ordered to move up so far as first 3 trenches. 10.0am Report received from Pioneers that South Attrely track ground soft & cut up by shell fire.	
		1.35 pm	Rest of Pioneer battalion ordered to move up.	
		1.45 pm	2nd in command 9th N.Staff Batt" (Pioneers) reported arrival.	
		6.25 pm	1 section each Cheshire & E. Riding Fd Coys ordered to work on South Attley track.	
		9.05 pm	C.E. VIth Corps 2d division received as to Pioneers continuing work on 10th	
		10.5 pm	Orders issued to Pioneers for work on 10th	

Headquarters R.E. 3rd Div.
WAR DIARY *or* **INTELLIGENCE SUMMARY**
(Erase heading not required)
Army Form C. 2118.
Month of April 1917 Sheet 3

Place	Date	Hour	Summary of Events and Information	Remarks and references to Appendices
WARLUS	April 21st		C.R.E. to 17th Div. area. Enrolled ARRAS. Adj. to conferences in ARRAS	
"	22nd		C.R.E. & adj. to companies in ARRAS. Adj. to 8 & 17 & 76th Bdes. In evening to Pioneers	
"	23rd		C.R.E. 2nd & 1st Div in reserve. C.R.E. adj. & officer moved at 8.30 p.m. to HOTEL DE L'UNIVERS	
ARRAS	24th		C.R.E. to conference at 10 a.m. Conference 9 Coy commander 10.30 a.m. Corps ordered to move to positions near TILLOY. H.Q. transport arrived at area West of ARRAS from WARLUS	
"	25th		C.R.E. to conferences at 2 p.m. Coys reported new positions by 4.0 p.m. C.R.E. to companies in morning, adj. in afternoon. 2nd Lt. E.H. LOAM joined 56th Fd Coy R.E.	
"	26th		C.R.E. & adj. moved in afternoon via BEAURAINS, during to ammunition dump on RUE DE RIETZ. Being on fire to advanced Divl. H.Q. 2 at B BOIS DES BOEUFS	
Advanced Divl. H.Q.	27th		C.R.E. to companies. Adj. to RIETZ GIRLS SCHOOL dumps. C.R.E. to MONCHY at night with Col. INGLIS (Pioneers). 2nd Lt. A. PICKERSGILL 529th (2nd Riding) Fd Coy wounded.	
"	28th		C.R.E. to mud road. Adj. to dumps in ARRAS. Arranged that 56th Div. can draw up to Rly RIETZ dump & after form a dump of their own. 2nd Lt. J.H. ALDEN 529 (2nd Riding) Fd Coy wounded.	
"	29th		C.R.E. to ARRAS to meet C.E. VI th Corps. Adj. to dumps in afternoon. 2nd Lt. J.W.G. WHITEHOUSE joined 56th Field Coy R.E.	
"	30th		Adj. to C.R.E. 56th Div & to dumps. C.R.E. Road conference at advanced H.Q. with Coy commanders at 2.15 p.m. C.R.E. to MONCHY at night.	

May 2nd 1917.

S.G. Thompson
Lt.-R.E.
for Lieut. Colonel R.E.
C.R.E. 3rd Division

May 1914. Sheet No 1.

Army Form C. 2118.

WAR DIARY
or
INTELLIGENCE SUMMARY.
(Erase heading not required.)

Headquarters C.R.E. 3rd Division

Instructions regarding War Diaries and Intelligence Summaries are contained in F. S. Regs., Part II. and the Staff Manual respectively. Title pages will be prepared in manuscript.

Place	Date	Hour	Summary of Events and Information	Remarks and references to Appendices
Advanced Divl H.Q.	May 1st		C.R.E. to Coys in morning. Adj. to R.E. dumps in afternoon.	
"	2nd		C.R.E. to Coys & presented M.M. to 2 sergeants of 56th Fd. Coy. Adj. to dumps. 438th & 529th Coys Pioneers moved to North of CAMBRAI Road.	
"	3rd		Z day Zero hour 3.45am. Situation obscure.	
"	4th		Conference of Coy commanders at 4.0 pm. Orders sent to 3 Coys & Pioneers for digging trench N.E. of MONCHY & wiring wood etc. C.R.E. to MONCHY at night.	
"	5th		C.R.E. to Coys. Adj. to dumps in afternoon. C.R.E. to line at night.	
"	6th		C.R.E. to Coys in morning. Adj. office.	
"	7th		C.R.E. to Coys. Adj. to weave up German M.G. emplacement E. of Brown line & to Coys in afternoon. C.R.E. to line at night.	
"	8th		C.R.E. to Coys. Adj. office. C.R.E. to line at night.	
"	9th		C.R.E. to line at dawn. Adj. to dumps in ARRAS. 2nd Lt M.J. WADSLEY 529th Fd Coy admitted Fd. Amb. Shellshock.	
"	10th		C.R.E. to communication trench at dawn. Adj. office.	
"	11th		C.R.E. to Coys in morning. Adj. in afternoon.	
"	12th		C.R.E. to C.Y. in morning & to Coys. Adj. to ARRAS to dumps. Adj. to dumps. 1 Coy Pioneers & 1 section 529th Fd Coy under orders of G.B.C. 76th Inf Bde for attack on DEVIL'S TRENCH. Attack failed.	
"	13th		C.R.E. to communication trench at dawn. The C.R.E. & Adj. 729th Div called in afternoon to discuss taking over C.R.E. to Coys.	
"	14th		Adj. to ARRAS to arrange for lorries & to Coys. 56th Fd Coy moved to SIMENCOURT 438th to DAINVILLE 529th to DUISANS. Pioneers ordered to stand by at 8.0 pm but they had already moved to AGNEZ LES. DUISANS.	

May 1917. Sheet No 2.

Army Form C. 2118.

Headquarters C.R.E. 3rd Division

WAR DIARY
or
INTELLIGENCE SUMMARY.
(Erase heading not required.)

Place	Date	Hour	Summary of Events and Information	Remarks and references to Appendices
WARLUS	May 15th		C.R.E. & adj. leave advanced Divl. H.Q at 9.0 am. C.R.E. to see C.E. VIth Corps. Adj. to 488th Fd Coy & Warlus.	
"	16th		C.R.E. to 56th in morning. C.R.E. & adj. to AVESNES LE COMTE in afternoon Ammunition dump at WANQUETIN blew up as we were passing it.	
"	17th		C.R.E. moved to NOYELLETTE. C.R.E. & adj. to see C.E. XVIIIth Corps. 529th Fd Coy moved. 2nd Lt. R.C.W. PICKLES joined 529th Fd Coy.	
"	18th		C.R.E. to WANQUETIN. 488th Fd Coy & 529th Fd Coy joined. C.R.E. to WANQUETIN for work in adjoining villages. 56th Fd Coy moved from VIth Corps to XVIIIth Corps to LIENCOURT.	
LIGNEREUIL	19th		receiving orders from VIth Corps, 56th Fd Coy moved to LIGNEREUIL. C.R.E. went on leave. 2nd Lt. GIBBS left H.Q.R.E. moved at 9 am. F.M. DEAN joined H.Q.R.E. 56th Fd Coy moved to 18th Corps school ST POL for work. Adj. & Lt Dean rode to WANQUETIN to see Corps. Adj. to 56th Fd Coy in afternoon.	
"	20th		Adj. to ST POL with D.C. Signals. Lt DEAN to LIENCOURT. Adj. to rifle range at DENIER	
"	21st		Adj. to 56th Fd Coy. To Sawmills BOIS DE FAYE to arrange about timber & to LIENCOURT & see Pioneers who arrived there from ARRAS at 4.0 pm.	
"	22nd		Adj. & rifle range DENIER. Lt DEAN to IZEL-LEZ-HAMEAU about bricks.	
"	23rd		Adj. office in morning. To WANQUETIN to see Corps in afternoon	
"	24th		Adj. office in morning. To arrange for afternoon party on rifle range.	
"	25th		To Pioneers in afternoon. To rifle range in afternoon	
"	26th		Adj. & Lt DEAN to 8th & 9th Bnd Rides in morning. Adj. with Major CONDER to 56th in afternoon. 2nd Lt D.P. MORGAN joined 56th Fd Coy R.E. 2nd Lt J.H. PARKIN and H.J. COOK joined 529th (2. Riding) Fd Coy R.E.	
"	27th		Adj. office in morning. In afternoon went to WANQUETIN with Lt. Col. NEWELL C.R.E. 58th Div. 2nd Lt. J.A. RIGGALL left 529th Fd Coy to become adj. R.E. 58th Division	

May 1917   Sheet No 3
Army Form C 2118.

WAR DIARY
or
INTELLIGENCE SUMMARY.   Headquarters C.R.E. 3rd Division

(Erase heading not required.)

Place	Date	Hour	Summary of Events and Information	Remarks and references to Appendices
LIGNEREUIL	May 28th		Adj to prosecute at Driver CRAIG's trial at MANIN. Lt. Bean to lecture by G.O.C. XVIII Corps.	
	May 29th		Adj. office.	
	30th		Adj & Lt. Bean to 76th M.G. Coy in morning. To lecture by G.O.C. 3rd Div. in afternoon. C.R.E. returned from leave.	
	31st		C.R.E. adj & Lt. Bean to ARRAS to arrange for taking over from 29th Div. To Hd. Coy at WANQUETIN & to Pioneers at LIENCOURT.	

S.G. Thompson
Lt & adj. R.E.
for C.R.E. 3rd Division.

Army Form C. 2118.

Month of June 1917. SHEET 1

WAR DIARY or INTELLIGENCE SUMMARY.
(Erase heading not required.)

Headquarters R.E. 3rd Division

Vol 35

Instructions regarding War Diaries and Intelligence Summaries are contained in F.S. Regs., Part II. and the Staff Manual respectively. Title pages will be prepared in manuscript.

Place	Date	Hour	Summary of Events and Information	Remarks and references to Appendices
LIGNEREUIL	June 1st		C.R.E. adj. & Lt Dean to DENIER & BOIS DE FAYE.	
ARRAS	2nd		H.Q. R.E. moved at 8.15 am to 4 Boulevard CARNOT ARRAS. C.R.E. to left sector of front. Adj to dumps. 56th Fd Coy moved from ST POL to camp by WATERY WOOD. 438th Fd Coy moved to H. 32. 529th Fd Coy moved to HOULETTE WORK.	
"	3rd		C.R.E. to line at dawn. Adj. to dumps. Divl HQ moved to 2 PLACE ST CROIX ARRAS. 2nd Lt. G.A. PALETHORPE joined 529th Fd Coy.	
"	4th		Adj & Lt Dean to Companies & Pioneers. C.R.E. in afternoon to see C.E. VIth Corps. Coys working on deep dugouts. Pioneers digging & wiring.	
"	5th		C.R.E. to line at dawn. Lt Dean to 438th Fd Coy. Adj. to dumps.	
"	6th		C.R.E. to line. Adj. to 438th & 529th Fd Coys.	
"	7th		C.R.E & adj. to No 3 Tramway Coy R.E. In afternoon to C.R.E. 9th Division re taking over from 3rd Div. IVORY & FEUCHY dumps.	
"	8th		C.R.E. to line. C.R.E & adj. 9 4th Div. called to arrange taking over dumps & work in Northern sector.	
"	9th		Adj. went on leave. 2/Lt Dean a/adj. C.R.E & a/adj to R.E Workshop.	
"	10th		C.R.E. to line. a/adj. to 56th Fd Coy & to make trench frames for C.E. VI Corps.	
"	11th		C.R.E. to line at 5.0 am. a/adj. to R.E. Workshops. C.R.E & a/adj. to RITZ dumps.	
"	12th		C.R.E to line at 5.0 am. a/adj. to RONVILLE, RITZ dumps & R.E Workshops. ARRAS shelled.	
"	13th		Major E.H.W. FOOT 56th Fd Coy R.E. wounded. C.R.E. to 56th Fd Coy R.E. a/adj. to Corps dressing station. Q. & RITZ dumps & R.E. Workshop.	
"	14th		"Z" day. Zero hour 7.20am. Attack complete success. C.R.E & a/adj. to Corps Pioneers. 2/Lts H. HAITHWAITE, C.G. FUNNELL & J. BRODIE joined 529th Fd Coy R.E.	

Army Form C. 2118.

SHEET. 2.

Month of June 1917.

WAR DIARY
or
INTELLIGENCE SUMMARY

(Erase heading not required.)

Headquarters R.E. 3rd Division.

Place	Date	Hour	Summary of Events and Information	Remarks and references to Appendices
ARRAS	June 15th		Adj. R.E. 12th Div called re taking over. Adj. to RITZ dump. C.R.E. Office.	
"	" 16th		C.R.E. took C.R.E. 12th Div to line at 6.0 a.m. Adj. to workshop & dumps.	
"	" 17th		ARRAS shelled in morning. Adj. to workshop. C.R.E. & Adj. to Roadlines.	
"	" 18th		German counter-attack at 1.20 a.m. 2/Lt. PARKIN killed. 2/Lt. R.C.W. PICKLES wounded. both 529th Fd Coy R.E. C.R.E. to line. Adj. to dumps. 56th Fd Coy arrived in ARRAS. 438th Fd Coy moved with 8th Inf Bde.	
"	" 19th		529th Fd Coy arrived in ARRAS. Adj. to RITZ dump to hand over. 2nd Lt. J.J. FISHER joined 436th Fd Coy.	
LE CAUROY	" 20th		H.Q. R.E. moved to LE CAUROY. 56th Fd Coy moved with 9th Inf. Bde. 529th Fd Coy moved in buses with 76th Inf. Bde. Adj. returned from leave.	
"	" 21st		C.R.E. Adj. & Lt. Dean to 438th Fd Coy R.E. at BERLENCOURT. C.R.E. in afternoon to 529th Fd Coy at CAUMESNIL in afternoon.	
"	" 22nd		C.R.E. to FREVENT. Adj. to AVESNES. 56th Fd Coy supplying 40 sappers at FOSSEUX constructing ammunition dump.	
"	" 23rd		C.R.E. & Adj. to see 56th Fd Coy at GOUY-EN-ARTOIS. 2/Lt. G.T. COTTERELL joined 438th Fd Coy.	
"	" 24th		C.R.E. left at 10.30 a.m. to go to new area. Lt DEAN left H.Q. R.E. to be 2nd in command of 56th Fd Coy.	
"	" 25th		Adj. to see 529th Fd Coy. C.R.E. returned. Adj. to see Pioneers.	

WAR DIARY
or
INTELLIGENCE SUMMARY.
(Erase heading not required.)

Month of June 1917 SHEET 3
Army Form C. 2118.
Headquarters R.E. 3rd Division.

Place	Date	Hour	Summary of Events and Information	Remarks and references to Appendices
LE CAUROY	June 26th		C.R.E. & adj. to see bridge being built by 438th Fd Coy R.E. at WAMIN.	
"	27th		C.R.E & adj. to see 529th Fd. Coy. In afternoon rode over to see Pioneers.	
"	28th		C.R.E & adj. to LIENCOURT to see 438th Fd Coy march past en route for MILLY. By car to 46th Divl. H.Q. to arrange relief of Field Companies.	
"	29th		Office in morning. Afternoon C.R.E & adj. rode to MAGNICOURT.	
"	30th		Office. Preparing for move.	

S.G. Thompson Lt. R.E.
Adj. R.E. 3rd Div.
For C.R.E. 3rd Div.

SECRET.

~~O.C. 56th Field Co. R.E.~~
O.C. 438th (Cheshire) Fd. Co. R.E.
O.C. 529th (E.Riding) Fd. Co. R.E.
3rd Division "G".
~~3rd Division "Q".~~
8th Infantry Brigade
~~9th Infantry Brigade.~~
76th Infantry Brigade.
C.R.E., 12th Division.

Relief of 3rd Divl. Engineers by 12th Divl. Engineers.

438th (Cheshire) Fd. Co. R.E. will hand over its work to 529th (E.Riding) Fd. Co. R.E. on 16th June, sufficiently for the East Ridings to pass it on to the 70th Field Co. R.E. when it arrives.

On 16th June, the 438th (Cheshire) Fd. Co. R.E. will move to ARRAS in its own time, and join the 8th Infantry Brigade Group in readiness to march under its orders on 17th : on 16th the Sappers employed at the RITZ and Girls School Dumps will be withdrawn. Pioneers to take their places are being arranged.

The 529th (E.Riding) Fd. Co. R.E. will put a caretaking party in the billets of the 438th (Cheshire) Fd. Co. R.E. until the arrival of the 69th Field Co. R.E.

69th Field Co. R.E. - arrives in ARRAS on 17th - moves forward to billets vacated by the Cheshire Fd. Co. R.E. on 18th and takes over the work of the 56th Field Co. R.E. on 18th in the Left Sector.

56th Field Co. R.E. - Will hand over work to 69th Field Co. R.E. on 18th June, will move to ARRAS on 18th, join the 9th Infantry Brigade Group and marches with it on the 20th June.

It will leave a caretaking party in its billets till the arrival of the 70th Field Co. R.E. on 19th. Any sappers employed in dumps will be withdrawn by arrangements with 69th Fd. Co. R.E. in time to march with the Company.

70th Field Co. R.E. - Arrives at ARRAS on 18th. Moves on 19th to billets vacated by the 56th Field Co. R.E. and takes over work of Cheshire and E.Riding Fd. Cos. R.E. on 19th.

529th (E.Riding) Fd. Co. R.E. - will hand over its own and Cheshire Co's work to 70th Field Co. R.E. on 19th : move to ARRAS on 19th : joins 76th Infantry Brigade Group and moves with it on 20th by Busses.

Any Sappers employed in dumps to be withdrawn by arrangement with 70th Field Co. R.E. in time to accompany the Company.

87th Field Co. R.E. - Arrives in ARRAS on 19th, and may possibly remain there.

Sappers employed at Divl. Workshops are to rejoin their unit in ARRAS in the evening of the 19th.

Lt. Colonel, R.E.

15/6/1917.   C.R.E., 3rd Division.

Vol 36.

WAR DIARY
For Month ending 31st July 1917.

Headquarters R.E. 3rd Division.

Army Form C. 2118.
SHEET 1.

C.R.E. 3rd Division WAR DIARY JULY - 1917
INTELLIGENCE SUMMARY.
(Erase heading not required.)

Place	Date	Hour	Summary of Events and Information	Remarks and references to Appendices
LIENCOURT	1st		H.Q. R.E. moved to 48th Inf. H.Q. (I.34.a.3.5. Sheet 57c) H.Q. Transport stayed the night at ACHIET-LE-PETIT. 438th Fd Co. R.E. moved to LEBUCQUIERE. C.R.E. & adj. visited them	
			56th & 599th Fd Cos moved to ACHIET-LE-PETIT.	
I.34.a.3.5	2nd		56th & 599th Fd Cos moved to LEBUCQUIERE. Gas alarm at night.	
"	3rd		C.R.E. to line at dawn. Adj. to HUN dump BAPAUME. Gas alarm at night.	
"	4th		3rd Fwg. H.Q. arrived at I.34.a.3.5. 2nd Lt M.J. WADSLEY joined H.Q. as Intelligence Officer.	
"	5th		C.R.E. to line. Adj. to Companies & VELU dump.	
"	6th		C.R.E. to line. Adj. Office	
"	7th		C.E. IV Corps & Staff officer called. Adj. to 60th VELU dump.	
"	8th		C.R.E. to line. Adj. to 76th Inf Bde.	
"	9th		C.R.E. to line. Adj. to HUN dump & 3rd Div. Rest Camp.	
"	10th		C.R.E. to Pioneers & Companies. Adj. to Companies.	
"	11th		C.R.E. & 2/Lt Wadsley to HERMIES. 2/Lt Wadsley fell & broke his arm. Adj. to SELIGNY FREMICOURT.	
"	12th		C.R.E. to line & Pioneers. Adj. to Dumps & Cos. 2/Lt A.J.F. GOURLEY arrived in place of Wadsley	
"	13th		C.R.E. to line. Adj. to 258th Tunnelling Co & to SLAG HEAP at night with Nissen huts.	
"	14th		C.R.E. to line. Adj. to BEAULENCOURT.	
"	15th		C.R.E. to line. To 42nd Divl RE's in afternoon to give lecture. Adj. to Companies.	
"	16th		C.R.E. to line. Adj. office.	
"	17th		C.R.E. to line. Adj. VELU dump & Corps.	
"	18th		C.R.E. to line. Adj. to Corps. C.E. IV Corps & C.R.E. IV Corps Troops called	

Army Form C. 2118.

WAR DIARY

C.R.E. 3rd Division JULY 1917 continued

INTELLIGENCE SUMMARY.

SHEET 2.

(Erase heading not required.)

Place	Date	Hour	Summary of Events and Information	Remarks and references to Appendices
T.34.a.3.5	19th		C.R.E. to conference at IX Corps H.Q. Adjt to FREMICOURT, LEBUCQUIERE & BAPAUME.	
	20th		C.R.E. to line & Coys. Adjt to 8th Inf Bde.	
	21st		C.R.E. to intermediate line with G.S.O.1. Adjt to select hutting site with A.A.T.Q.M.G. & to C.E. IV Corps re hutting.	
"	22nd		C.R.E. to line. Adjt to VELU dump & Coys.	
"	23rd		C.R.E. to line. Adjt. office.	
"	24th		C.R.E. to line. Adjt. to Companies.	
"	25th		C.R.E. to line. Adjt. to dump.	
"	26th		C.R.E. Adjt. to C.E. IV Corps & to O.C. Light Rly BAPAUME	
"	27th		C.R.E. to FREMICOURT & to Coys. Adjt to BEUGNY.	
"	28th		C.R.E. to line. Adjt to Coys & dumps.	
"	29th		C.R.E. office. Adjt. to BEAULENCOURT	
"	30th		C.R.E. to line. Adjt to dump. Lt. Col. A.G.T. CUSINS R.E. arrived for attachment.	
"	31st		C.R.E. to line. Col. CUSINS & adjt to dump & Coys.	

S.G. Thompson
Lt. Adjt. R.E.
for C.R.E. 3rd Division

Army Form C. 2118.

WAR DIARY

C.R.E. 3rd Division.

INTELLIGENCE SUMMARY.

Month of (Erase heading not required.) AUGUST - 1917.

Vol 37 Sheet 1.

Place	Date	Hour	Summary of Events and Information	Remarks and references to Appendices
I 34.a.3.7	1917 August 1st		C.R.E. Col. CUSINS & MAJOR HALL to line in morning. C.R.E. Col. CUSINS & Adjt to C.R.E 62nd Div. re taking over Northern sector. C.R.E 9th Div. called re taking over Southern sector.	
"	2nd		C.R.E. to Corps. Col Cusins & Adjt to MEAULTE & HUN Dumps BAPAUME.	
"	3rd		C.R.E to line. Adjutant to hutting site.	
"	4th		C.R.E. Col Cusins & adjt. to FREMICOURT re new Northern sector.	
"	5th		C.R.E to Corps & Pioneers. Adjt. to Corps & Div. H.Q. C.R.E. to new Northern sector.	
"	6th		C.R.E & Col. Cusins to LAGNICOURT sector. Adjt. to HUN dump & Div. H.Q. FREMICOURT.	
"	7th		C.R.E & Col Cusins to line. Adjt to FREMICOURT.	
"	8th		C.R.E & Col Cusins to line. Adjt to HUN dump BAPAUME. C.E IV Corps called.	
"	9th		C.R.E & Adjt to FREMICOURT. Adjt to Corps & dumps	
"	10th		C.R.E & Col. Cusins to line. Adjt to FREMICOURT.	
"	11th		C.R.E. to line. Adjt to dumps & Corps.	
"	12th		C.R.E & Col Cusins to line. Adjt to FREMICOURT.	
"	13th		C.R.E & adjt to VELU & Corps. C.R.E & Col Cusins to line Adjt to HUN dump.	
"	14th		C.R.E to line at night with Major WARD Adjt to dumps & Corps.	
"	15th		C.R.E to line at night with Major HALL. Adjt to FREMICOURT.	
"	16th		C.R.E to line. Adjt to BEUGNY & FREMICOURT.	
"	17th		C.R.E to 'A' Coy Pioneers. Adjt to IV Corps Rest Station BEAULENCOURT.	
"	18th		C.R.E & Col. Cusins to LAGNICOURT at dawn. Adjt. to BEUGNY, FREMICOURT & HUN dumps.	

Army Form C. 2118.
SHEET 2

WAR DIARY
C.R.E. 3rd Division
INTELLIGENCE SUMMARY
(Erase heading not required.)

Month of AUGUST - 1917. continued

Place	Date	Hour	Summary of Events and Information	Remarks and references to Appendices
I.34.a.3.7.	Aug.19th		C.R.E. to FREMICOURT. Adjt to dumps & Corps. 2nd Lt. H.J.F. GOURLEY went on leave.	
"	20th		C.R.E. to Corps & 9th Inf Bde. Adjt to FREMICOURT	
"	21st		C.R.E. & Col Cairns to line. Adjt to dumps & Corps.	
"	22nd		Adjt to HAPLINCOURT. In afternoon to FREMICOURT & BAPAUME, C.R.E. office.	
"	23rd		C.R.E. to line. Adjt to FREMICOURT. C.R.E. to Pioneers	
"	24th		C.R.E to 8th Inf Bde. Adjt to dumps & Corps	
"	25th		C.R.E & Col Cairns to line. Adjt to BEUGNY.	
"	26th		C.R.E & adjt to FREMICOURT. Adjt to dumps & Corps.	
"	27th		C.R.E & Col Cairns to line. Adjt to YTRES. R.E dump.	
"	28th		C.R.E & Adjt to C.E. IV Corps. Adjt to FREMICOURT. C.R.E. to 56th Fd Co. R.E	
"	29th		C.R.E to line. Adjt to dumps & Corps.	
"	30th		C.R.E & Col Cairns to LAGNICOURT. Adjt to PERONNE. No 3 Reinforcement Coy. R.E at LA FLAQUE. Capt. BLACK R.A.M.C. left 438th Fd Co. R.E to report to IV Corps Reinforcement Camp ROCQUIGNY.	
"	31st		Adjt to dumps & Corps. C.R.E & Col Cairns to 76th Brigade area.	

September 1st 1917.

S.G. Thompson
Capt. R.E
for C.R.E. 3rd Division

Sheet 1.

Army Form C. 2118.

WAR DIARY

INTELLIGENCE SUMMARY

C.R.E. 3rd DIVISION.   MONTH OF SEPTEMBER 1917.

HQ R.E. 3rd D.

Vol 38

(Erase heading not required.)

Instructions regarding War Diaries and Intelligence Summaries are contained in F. S. Regs., Part II. and the Staff Manual respectively. Title pages will be prepared in manuscript.

Place	Date	Hour	Summary of Events and Information	Remarks and references to Appendices
	1917			
I.39a.3.4 (Sheet 57c)	1st		C.R.E 56th Division & adjt called re details of relief. C.R.E 56th Div & C.R.E 3rd Div went round LOUVERVAL sector. Adjt 3rd & 56th Div to No 7 R.E. Park BAPAUME.	
"	2nd		C.R.E's 3rd & 56th Division went round LAGNICOURT sector. Adjt to BEUGNY & LEBUCQUIERE hutting.	
"	3rd		C.R.E in car to new area. Adjt to COMBLES	
"	4th		56th Fd Co. moved to BEAULENCOURT	
"	5th		438th Fd Co. moved to YPRES. C.R.E & Col Cuvier to C.R.E 36th Div. C.R.E Col Cuvier & adjt to C.R.E 16th Division at MORENVILLE	
"	6th		529th Fd Co.R.E. moved to BARASTRE. C.R.E. to see drain dug by Pioneers. Adjt to Corps.	
"	7th		C.R.E. to see rifle range at LETRANSLOY. Adjt to 438th Field Co.	
"	8th		C.R.E to 56th & 529th Field Corps.	
"	9th		C.R.E to rifle range. Adjt to Corps.	
"	10th		C.R.E. Col Cuvier & adjt to 56th & 529th Fd Corps.	
"	11th		C.R.E. to Corps.	
"	12th		C.R.E & Col Cuvier to IV Corps. Adjt to 529th Fd Coy R.E.	
"	13th		C.R.E to 529th & 56th Fd Corps. Adjt to 438th Fd Coy.	
"	14th		C.R.E to Corps. Adjt to 56th Fd Coy.	
"	15th		C.R.E & adjt in Camp.	
"	16th		C.R.E & adjt left at 2.0 pm for new area. Arrived at ST OMER.	
WATOU	17th		C.R.E & adjt to WATOU & then to C.E. V. Corps	
	18th		C.R.E. adjt to C.R.E 9th Division at BRANDHOEK.	
	19th		C.R.E & adjt to Corps at VLAMERTINGHE. H.Q. R.E. arrived at WATOU.	

Sheet 2
Army Form C. 2118.

WAR DIARY

C.R.E. 3rd DIVISION   SEPTEMBER 1917 continued
INTELLIGENCE SUMMARY.

(Erase heading not required.)

Place	Date	Hour	Summary of Events and Information	Remarks and references to Appendices
	1917			
WATOU	Sep.20		Col Cairns left to take charge of hutting at VLAMERTINGHE. C.R.E. & adjt to Pioneers	
"	21st		C.R.E. & adjt to conference with Corps at 4:30 p.m. & to C.E. V Corps	
POPERINGHE	22nd		C.R.E. & adjt to line with C.R.E. 9th Division. H.Q. R.E. moved to POPERINGHE. 529th Fd Co. moved to YPRES	
"	23rd		C.R.E. to line. Adjt to R.E. dump & C.R.E. 9th Div. also Corps Dump. 56th & 438th Fd Coy moved from VLAMERTINGHE to YPRES.	
RAMPARTS YPRES.	24th		C.R.E. & adjt to advanced Divl. H.Q. in RAMPARTS YPRES. Rear H.Q. at BRANDHOEK	
"	25th		C.R.E. to POTIJZE road. Didn's sent to Corps for work on 26th	
"	26		2 day. Zero hour 5·50am. Corps & Pioneers on consolidation, duckboard tracks & road. 2nd Lt. G.A. MANNING 438th Fd Co. R.E. killed.	
"	27th		C.R.E. to road at 6.0 am. 56th Fd Co. work on road to gun positions	
"	28th		Adjt to MILL COT with Col HUGHES 3rd D.A.C. re ammunition dump. C.R.E. 3rd Australian Div. called to arrange about relief.	
"	29th		C.R.E. to road in morning. Adjt to 529th Fd Co. 529th move from YPRES to BRANDHOEK area.	
"	30th		529th Fd Co. R.E. move from BRANDHOEK to WINNEZEELE area. Adjt to Rear H.Q. 56th Fd Co. move from YPRES to BRANDHOEK area.	

Oct 2nd 1917.

S.G. Thompson
Capt R.E.
for C.R.E. 3rd Division

SHEET 1.

Army Form C. 2118.

WAR DIARY

C.R.E. - 3d. Division - Month of OCTOBER - 1917

INTELLIGENCE SUMMARY.

(Erase heading not required.)

Instructions regarding War Diaries and Intelligence Summaries are contained in F.S. Regs., Part II. and the Staff Manual respectively. Title pages will be prepared in manuscript.

Place	Date 1917	Hour	Summary of Events and Information	Remarks and references to Appendices
YPRES	Oct 1st		C.R.E. & adjt left RAMPARTS YPRES and proceeded to WINNEZEELE. 56th Fd Coy left BRANDHOEK area & proceeded to WINNEZEELE area. 438th Fd Coy left YPRES & went to BRANDHOEK.	
WINNEZEELE	2nd		C.R.E. & adjt to 56th Fd Coy. 438th Fd Coy left BRANDHOEK & marched to WINNEZEELE.	
"	3		C.R.E. & adjt to Coys.	
"	4		H.Q. R.E. marched from WINNEZEELE to RENESCURE. Fd Coys move with Bdes	
RENESCURE	5.		H.Q. R.E. left RENESCURE at 11.30 pm & marched to WIZERNES & entrained for BAPAUME.	
HAPLINCOURT	6.		H.Q. R.E. arrived at I.34.a near HAPLINCOURT at 4.0 p.m.	
"	7		C.R.E. Col Cruins & Adjt to BAPAUME to see C.R.E. 62nd Division.	
"	8.		Adjt to YPRES to see 56th Fd Coy R.E.	
"	9.		56th Fd Coy marched from YPRES to FAVREUIL. C.R.E. & Col Cruins went round new line. Adjt & Major WARD round back areas with adjt 62nd Division	
"	10.		529th Fd Coy marched from BARASTRE to FAVREUIL. C.R.E. & Col Cruins to ECOUST	
"	11		438th Fd Coy marched from BEAULENCOURT to BEUGNATRE.	
MONUMENT H.15.c.	12.		H.Q. R.E. moved to MONUMENT H.15.c. & took over from 62nd Division.	
"	13.		C.R.E. to line. Adjt to Coys.	
"	14.		C.R.E. & Col Cruins to line. Adjt to ACHIET-LE-GRAND to VI Corps dumps	
"	15.		C.R.E. office. Adjt to R.E. dumps.	
"	16.		C.R.E. to line. Adjt to VAULX.	
"	17.		C.R.E. to line. Adjt to office.	

SHEET. 2. Army Form C. 2118.

WAR DIARY

C.R.E. 3rd Division — October 1917 – continued

INTELLIGENCE SUMMARY.

(Erase heading not required.)

Place	Date 1917	Hour	Summary of Events and Information	Remarks and references to Appendices
MONUMENT H.15.c.	Oct.18th		C.R.E. & Col Cruins to line. Adjt to ACHIET-LEGRAND	
"	19th		C.R.E. & Col. Cruins to VAULX. Adjt Office	
"	20th		C.R.E. left on leave to United Kingdom. Col Cruins & Adjt to Corps.	
"	21st		Adjt to 3rd Division Depot Battalion at ACHIET-LE-PETIT. Col Cruins to SAPIGNIES	
"	22nd		Col. Cruins to line. Adjt to NOREUIL to see 56th Coy.	
"	23rd		Col Cruins & Adjt to BULLECOURT to inspect work on tencles	
"	24th		Col Cruins & Adjt to AMIENS to purchase R.E. stores. Lt W.A.N.SMITH joined 56th Coy R.E.	
"	25th		Col Cruins to 76th Inf Bde. Adjt to MORY re hutting.	
"	26th		Col. Cruins to line. Adjt to Corps dump	
"	27th		Col Cruins & Adjt to 352nd E+M Coy at ARRAS re engine & blower for gumboot store.	
"	28th		Col Cruins & Adjt to MORY & SUCRERIE re hutting & road. C.E. VI Corps called.	
"	29th		Col Cruins to line to see new T.M. emplacement. Adjt to BOYELLES R.E. dumps.	
"	30th		Col Cruins to 438th Fd Coy. Adjt to meeting of Winter Sports.	
"	31st		Col. Cruins to line. Adjt to MORY re hutting. C.R.E. returned from leave to U.K.	

S.G. Thompson
Capt R.E.
for C.R.E. 3rd Division

November 1st 1917.

Army Form C. 2118.

SHEET 1

WAR DIARY
or
INTELLIGENCE SUMMARY.
(Erase heading not required.)

C.R.E. 3rd Division. Month of November 1917.

Place	Date	Hour	Summary of Events and Information	Remarks and references to Appendices
MONUMENT COMMEMORATIF HIS C.	1st		C.R.E & adjt office.	
	2nd		C.R.E. to conference at Divl. H.Q. Adjt to 3rd Division Defct Batts camps at ACHIET-LE-PETIT.	
	3rd		C.R.E & Col Cravino to line. Adjt to Corps.	
	4th		C.R.E + Col Cravino to line. C.R.E + adjt to MORY in afternoon.	
	5th		C.R.E to 8th Inf Bde + 438th Field Coy. Adjt to BOYELLES re camouflage figures.	
	6th		C.R.E to line. Adjt to Corps.	
	7th		C.R.E. to line. Adjt office.	
	8th		C.R.E + Col Cravino to line. Adjt to 56th Field Coy R.E.	
	9th		C.R.E to line. Adjt to MORY.	
	10th		C.R.E to line. Adjt to Corps.	
	11th		C.R.E + Col Cravino to line. Adjt to MORY.	
	12th		C.R.E to line. Col Cravino left to be C.R.E Third Army troops.	
	13th		C.R.E to line. Adjt to ECOUST to see 529th Fd Coy re tracks.	
	14th		C.R.E & C.R.A to line; Adjt to FAVREUIL + St Foley + winter sports meeting.	
	15th		C.R.E. to FAVREUIL workshops. Adjt to Pioneers.	
	16th		C.R.E. Lt. A.W. DAVIES 438 Fd Coy to England. Authority A.G. A/345..01	
			Major WARD + Lt COOK wired to rejoin their units.	
	17th		C.R.E. to line. Adjt to NOREUIL to see 438th Fd Coy	
	18th		C.R.E + Lt Gourlay to ECOUST + NOREUIL. C.R.E. to MORY. Lt G.R. PHILLIPS R.A.M.C. to 45.C.C.S.	

Army Form C. 2118.
SHEET - 2

WAR DIARY
INTELLIGENCE SUMMARY
(Erase heading not required.)

CRE 3rd Division November 1917.

Place	Date	Hour	Summary of Events and Information	Remarks and references to Appendices
MONUMENT COMMEMORATIF H.15.C.	19th		C.R.E. to Corps & 8th Inf Bde. Adjt to 9th Labour Coy & No 7 R.E. Park. O.t. Beverley fixing water troughs at SUCRERIE. 2nd Lt. G.W.L. DAY rejoined 56th Fd Coy from Rest Station.	
	20th		Z day Zero Hour 6.20 a.m. Good progress made. Division took its objectives. 3 Field Coys each 600 a section & Pioneers working in 2 shifts on ECOUST-BULLECOURT road. 3 sections 252nd Tunnelling Coy withdrawn from 3rd Div. 1 section 174th T.C. allotted in lieu.	
	21st		C.R.E. & adjt office. Adjt to No 7 R.E. Park.	
	22nd		C.R.E. to ECOUST - BULLECOURT road. C.R.E. & adjt to 529th Field Coy R.E.	
	23rd		C.R.E. & adjt office.	
	24th		C.R.E. & adjt to BULLECOURT road at dawn. In afternoon to gumboot store & dump.	
	25th		C.R.E. to Pioneers & 529th Fd Coy. Adjt office & to FREMICOURT.	
	26th		C.R.E. & adjt to Pioneers, 529th, 438th Fd Coys & VAULX dump.	
	27th		C.R.E. to new line in morning. Adjt to ACHIET-LE-PETIT to rifle range of 3rd Div Sigt Batt.n	
	28th		C.R.E. to VAULX, NOREUIL road & MORY. Adjt to MORY.	
	29th		C.R.E. & adjt to 56th Division re taking over new line. To 9th Bde in afternoon.	
	30th		C.R.E. & Lt Beverley to LAGNICOURT section taken over by 3rd Div Adjt office.	

30-11-17.

S.G. Maufaan
Capt & Adjt
for C.R.E. 3rd Division

Army Form C. 2118.

SHEET 1.

Month of December 1917. WAR DIARY
or
~~INTELLIGENCE~~ SUMMARY. Headquarters R.E. 3rd Division

Vol 41

Place	Date	Hour	Summary of Events and Information	Remarks and references to Appendices
MONUMENT COMMEMORATIF BAPAUME	1st		C.R.E. to line. Adjt to VAULX dump.	
"	2nd		C.R.E. & adjt to Corps.	
"	3rd		C.R.E. to line. Adjt to BOYELLES. Capt McGILL 438th Y&Ly to ROUEN as instructor. 2nd Lt E.H. ELCOCK joined 438 Y&Ly Coy RE	
"	4th		C.R.E. & Adjt to MORY in morning. To No 1 RE Park in afternoon.	
"	5th		C.R.E. to NOREUIL wood. Adjt to AMIENS to purchase stores.	
"	6th		C.R.E. Adjt office	
"	7th		C.R.E. to line. Adjt to VAULX	
"	8th		C.R.E. to rec 105th Y&Coy 28th Division. CRE & Adjt to 56th Y&Coy & FAVREUIL	
"	9th		C.R.E. to line to inspect mining. Adjt to dumps & store	5.9"Y
"	10th		Raid standing to Adjt to MORY to select new dump.	
"	11th		Enemy attacked at 6.40am & captured APEX.	
"	12th		C.R.E. & adjt office. Ct G.W. PALETHORPE M.C. 529th Y&Coy wounded	
"	13th		C.R.E. office. Adjt to NOREUIL to 9th & 2nd Bde to arrange working for 26th Division Pioneers	
BEHAGNIES	14th		H.Q. 3rd Division moved to BEHAGNIES. Pioneers digging new tunnel	
"	15th		C.R.E. & 2nd Bde. Adjt to MORY & Corps. 56 & 529th Y&Coys moved their new H.Q. from FAVREUIL to MORY. 438th Y&Coy from H12 central to ERVILLERS.	
"	16th		C.R.E. to Line. Adjt to Corps.	

WAR DIARY or INTELLIGENCE SUMMARY

(Erase heading not required.)

Army Form C. 2118.
SHEET 2.

Place	Date	Hour	Summary of Events and Information	Remarks and references to Appendices
BEHAGNIES	17th		C.R.E. to line. Adjt to Camp MORY Dump.	
	18th		C.R.E. to line. Adjt to 438th Fld. Coy.	
	19th		C.R.E. to line. Adjt to MORY Dump and Camp. Lt J. BRODIE 529 Fld. Coy. wounded	
	20th		2nd Lt. H.F. MILLER joined 529 Fld. Coy. and 2nd Lt. T.C. FAGG joined 56th Fld. Coy for duty.	
	21st		C.R.E. with G.S.O.I. to site new hurdles, etc. Adjt to GOMIECOURT to inspect hutting.	
	22nd		C.R.E. with G.S.O.I. to site new hurdles etc. Adjt to Camp and MORY Dump.	
	23rd		C.R.E. with G.S.O.I. to site new hurdles. Adjt to MORY Dump.	
	24th		C.R.E. to line with G.S.O.I. Adjt office.	
	25th		C.R.E. to line to inspect wiring. Adjt to Dump.	
			C.R.E. to Pioneer and 56th Fld. Coy. Adjt to HENDECOURT to inspect camps for 76th Inf. Brigade. 2nd Lt F.W. CHAPMAN joined 529 Fld. Coy.	
	26th		C.R.E. to forward Camps & Bdes. Adjt to 529 Fld. Coy.	
	27th		C.R.E. and Col. GOODWIN 40th Division to line. 529 Fld. Coy. moved to HAMELINCOURT	
	28th		C.R.E. and Adjt to MORY to see 438 Fld. Coy's new Camp. Adjt in afternoon to HENDECOURT	
	29th		C.R.E. to see 56th Fld. Coy.	
	30th		C.R.E. and A/Adjt to 438 Fld. Coy in morning and to 529 Fld. Coy. in afternoon. Adjt went on leave. Lt. H.J.F. GOURLEY a/Adjt. Div. Claim no. 9 in line.	
	31st		C.R.E. and a/Adjt to Camps and HQs. of 76th Inf. Bde at BLAIRVILLE & HENDECOURT and to 529 Fld. Coy.	

3rd Division

War Diaries

R.E. H.Q.

~~January to 31st December 1918~~

1918 JAN — 1919 OCT

Headquarters R.E. 3rd Division.

WAR DIARY
or
INTELLIGENCE SUMMARY.
(Erase heading not required.)

JANUARY 1918. Army Form C.2118. Sheet 1.

Place	Date	Hour	Summary of Events and Information	Remarks and references to Appendices
BEHAGNIES	Jan 1st		C.R.E. & 56th 438th La Cop & Pioneers. A/Adjt to ACHIET-LE-GRAND.	
"	Jan 2nd		C.R.E. office. A/Adjt to BOYELLES. R.E. dump 529, 56th La Coy & Pioneers	
"	3rd		C.R.E. & A/adjt to BOYELLES, No 8 R.E. Park ARRAS & 76th M.G. Camp HENDECOURT.	
"	4th		C.R.E. & O.C. 438th La Coy round 2nd line in 34th Div area. A/Adjt to 438th La Coy.	
"	5th		C.R.E. & G.S.O.1 round front area 34th Div. A/Adjt to 438th La Coy & Pioneers	
"	6th		C.R.E. & A/adjt to GOMIECOURT. C.R.E. to 438th La Coy to present ribbons to MAJOR WARD M.C. & Cpl SHARROCK M.M. A/adjt to 438th Coy horse lines.	
GOMIECOURT	7th		Div H.Q. moved to GOMIECOURT. C.R.E. & G.S.O.1 round 34th Div area.	
"	8th		C.R.E., C.R.A. & G.S.O.1 to proposed intermediate line.	
"	9th		C.R.E. to proposed intermediate line. A/adjt to MEAULTE R.E. Workshops	
"	10th		C.R.E. & A/adjt to BOYELLES. 8th & 9th Inf Bde H.Q. Junctions 56th Falco & HENIN. I Sec 438th to ST LEGER	
"	11th		C.R.E. to 1st Battle Zone 56th & 438th La Cop. A/adjt to BOYELLES & 529th Field Coy.	
"	12th		C.R.E. to La Coy horse lines. A/adjt to BOYELLES, No 8 R.E. Park.	
"	13th		C.R.E. to new line. A/adjt to BOYELLES.	
"	14th		C.R.E. & A/adjt to Pioneers in morning. To C.R.E. 34th Div & VII Corps Lgt Rly Offices	
"	15th		C.R.E. to 1st Battle zone. A/adjt to BOYELLES & BEAURAINS. Adjt returned from leave	
"	16		C.R.E. & G.S.O.1 to 34th Div area. Adjt office.	

WAR DIARY
INTELLIGENCE SUMMARY.
(Erase heading not required.)

JANUARY, 1918. Army Form C.2118.
Sheet 2.

Place	Date	Hour	Summary of Events and Information	Remarks and references to Appendices
GOMIECOURT	Feb 1st		C.R.E. to site new line with O.C. 56th & 438th Tel. Coys. Adjt to C.R.E. 34th Division	
	Jan 18th		C.R.E. to site new division of line. Adjt to Pioneers	
	19th		C.R.E. to new area to inspect work. Adjt to BOYELLES. Major GORDON 56th Tel Coy returned from Course at BLENDECQUES	
	20th		C.R.E. G.S.O.1. Adjt to take out Reserve line. In afternoon to C.R.E. 34th Division	
	21st		C.R.E. office. Adjt + G.S.O.2. to WAILLY to select target positions. C.E. VI Corps called	
	22nd		C.R.E. to 438th Tel Coy. C.R.E. + G.S.O.1 to battle zone to see arrival of working parties. Adjt office.	
	23rd		At Gouzley went on leave. C.R.E. + adjt office.	
	24th		C.R.E. + Adjt to HENIN HILL + 438th Tel Coy. To BELFAST Camp in afternoon	
	25th		C.R.E. + G.S.O.1 to GUEMAPPE. Adjt to BELFAST Camp. C.R.E. to conference at Bde. H.Q. 4.0 p.m.	
	26th		C.R.E. to line. Afternoon to C.R.E. 34th Division. Adjt to BELFAST Camp.	
	27th		C.R.E. office. Adjt to No.6 R.E. Park ARRAS + HENIN R.E. Dump.	
	28th		Lt Co. + Pioneers moved to BOIRY-BECQUERELLE + took over from 34th Division	
BOISLEUX-AU-MONT	29th		Divl. H.Q. moved at 10.0 am to BOISLEUX-AU-MONT C.R.E. to line. Adjt. office.	
	30th		C.R.E. to line. Adjt to HENIN	
	31st		C.R.E. to line. Adjt to HENIN + Corps at BOIRY-BECQUERELLE. C.E. VI Corps called	

S.S. Thompson
Capt R.E.
For C.R.E. 3rd Division
4-2-18.

Army Form C.2118.

Sheet 1.

HQ R.E.
3rd. Division.
February 1918.
Vol 43

WAR DIARY
INTELLIGENCE SUMMARY
(Erase heading not required.)

C.R.E.

Instructions regarding War Diaries and Intelligence Summaries are contained in F.S. Regs., Part II. and the Staff Manual respectively. Title pages will be prepared in manuscript.

Place	Date	Hour	Summary of Events and Information	Remarks and references to Appendices
BOISLEUX AU MONT	1918. Feb 1st		C.R.E. to line. Adjt office.	
	2nd		C.R.E to line. Adjt to BOYELLES dump.	
	3rd		C.R.E. & adjt to 529th Y & Coy, 9th Inf Bde & HENIN.	
	4th		C.R.E. to line. Adjt office.	
	5th		C.R.E. to line. Adjt to Train H.Q. C.E. VI Corps called.	
	6th		C.R.E & Adjt to 9"/76" Transport lines, also Coy horse lines. Lt Gourley returned from leave.	
	7th		C.R.E. to line. Adjt & Lt Gourley to 25th Division.	
	8th		C.R.E to line. Adjt to Corps.	
	9th		C.R.E. to line. Adjt to Corps and HENIN.	
	10th		C.R.E. to line. Adjt to Northern section by special Light Rly car.	
	11th		C.R.E to new proposed Rds H.Q. C.E. VI Corps called. Adjt to No 5 R.E Park. R.S.M. Jeffrey joined as relief for T/R.S.M. PALMER.	
	12th		C.R.E & Adjt to Corps & Pioneers.	
	13th		Col. C.A ELLIOTT CRE left to become C.E. XIII Corps. Lt Col. W.C. COOPER arrived as C.R.E.	
	14th		C.R.E & Major HALL to left section of line. Adjt to No 5 R.E Park.	
	15th		C.R.E & Major HALL to line. Adjt to HENIN & Corps.	
	16th		C.R.E & Major HALL to COJEUL valley. Adjt office.	
	17th		C.R.E office. Adjt to Corps dump.	
	18th		C.R.E to Pioneers. Adjt to No 4 R.E Park re much trials.	
	19th		C.R.E & Lt Gourley to reconnoitre Blue line. Adjt to dump & Corps & 9th/76" Transport lines.	
	20th		C.R.E & Capt Bean to new Rds H.Q. Adjt to Corps.	

Army Form C. 2118.
Sheet 2.

WAR DIARY

C.R.E. - 3rd Division February 1918.
INTELLIGENCE SUMMARY. Continued.

(Erase heading not required.)

Instructions regarding War Diaries and Intelligence Summaries are contained in F. S. Regs., Part II. and the Staff Manual respectively. Title pages will be prepared in manuscript.

Place	Date	Hour	Summary of Events and Information	Remarks and references to Appendices
BOISLEUX AU MONT	1918. Feb 21st		C.R.E. to see 257th Tunnelling Coy. Adjt to No 8 R.E. Park & VI Corps	
"	" 22nd		C.R.E. to Corps. Adjt to Third Army H.Q. & 25th Division	
"	" 23		C.R.E. to Coy. horse lines to meet G.O.C. Adjt office.	
"	" 24		C.R.E. & Cl. Gourley to roads in forward area. Adjt to new Bde H.Q. in SHAFT tunnel	
"	" 25		C.R.E. with Major HALL to COJEUL valley. Adjt to Corps.	
"	" 26		C.R.E. to line. Adjt to No 8 R.E. Park.	
"	" 27		C in C. visited Divl H.Q. & met Divl staff. C.R.E. to inspect MERCATEL - BEAURAINS road Adjt to ERVILLERS & lecture on economy at BEHAGNIES.	
"	" 28		C.R.E. & Adjt office.	

S.G. Thompson
Capt R.E.
3-3-18. for C.R.E. 3rd Division

3rd Divisional Engineers

C. R. E.

3rd DIVISION

MARCH 1918

Headqrs. R.E. 3rd Division

WAR DIARY
or
INTELLIGENCE SUMMARY

Army Form C. 2118.

MARCH, 1918.

Place	Date	Hour	Summary of Events and Information	Remarks and references to Appendices
BOISLEUX AU-MONT	March 1st		C.R.E. to see Coy. Commanders. Adjt to No 7 R.E. Park	
"	2nd		C.R.E. + G.S.O.1 to line. Adjt to Barnley to HENIN and FICHEUX. 8th Inf Bde front taken over by 34th Division.	
"	3rd		C.R.E. to Pioneers. Adjt to No 8 R.E. Park Corps dump.	
"	4th		C.R.E., Lt Ganley to COJEUL valley. Adjt office.	
"	5th		C.R.E. to Pioneers. Adjt to No 8 R.E. Park	
"	6th		C.R.E. office. Adjt to dumps and Field Corps	
"	7th		C.R.E. to line with C.E. VI Corps. Adjt office	
"	8th		C.R.E. to Corps. Adjt to No 7 R.E. Park	
"	9th		C.R.E. to Cojeul valley with C.E. VI Corps. Adjt to Corps	
"	10th		C.R.E. + G.S.O.1 to AVELUY. Adjt to No 8 R.E Park. C.E. XII Corps called	
"	11th		C.R.E. to conference at 8th Inf. Bde H.Q. Adjt to No 8 R.E. Park	
"	12th		C.R.E. to Corps. Adjt to No 8 R.E. Park. HENIN + Corps.	
"	13th		C.R.E. to Corps + Pioneers. Adjt to No 8 R.E. Park + Victoria dump. Reconnoitred track	
"	14th		C.R.E + G.S.O.1 to inspect minefields. Adjt to No 7 R.E. Park.	
"	15th		C.R.E. to Corps. Adjt to HENIN dumps.	
"	16th		C.R.E. to inspect destruction of MESSU. Adjt to No 8 R.E Park	
"	17th		C.R.E. reconnaissance of bridges over the COJEUL. Adjt to Corps	
"	18th		C.R.E. to Pioneers + new trench. Adjt to Third Army workshops.	
"	19th		C.R.E. office. Adjt to Corps	

Headqrs. R.E. 3rd Division

MARCH 1918.

Sheet 2.
Army Form C. 2118.

WAR DIARY
or
INTELLIGENCE SUMMARY
(Erase heading not required.)

Place	Date	Hour	Summary of Events and Information	Remarks and references to Appendices
BOISLEUX AU-MONT	March 20th		CRE + adjt of 40th Division came over to arrange details of relief.	
"	21st		German offensive started. 3rd Div front intact. Corps Pioneers standing by.	
"	22nd		Div Corps moved to area H. WAILLY. Pioneers to BEETZACOURT. 3rd Divl. HQ moved from BOISLEUX-AU-MONT to BRETENCOURT.	
BRETENCOURT	23rd		CRE + G.S.O.2. to see Corps + Bdes. Adjt to Corps. All Lacrops Pioneers working on PURPLE line.	
"	24th		CRE to FICHEUX to new line. Adjt to Pioneers. Work centred on PURPLE line.	
"	25th		CRE + Lt. Gourley to PURPLE line.	
"	26th		C.R.E. + Lt. Gourley to PURPLE line. Adjt to Corps at WAILLY + PURPLE line.	
"	27th		C.R.E + Lt. Gourley to PURPLE line. Adjt to new Corps dump at SAVINCOURT + Pioneers.	
"	28th		Germans attack 3rd Divl front. 11.5 a.m. 3rd Corps + Pioneers all under command of Lt. Col. MARTIN ordered to hold PURPLE LINE. Relieved at night by two Bdes of 2nd Canadian Division.	
"	29th		CRE + adjt 2nd Canadian Division came to arrange taking over Division. Relieved at 11.0 pm. CRE + adjt to LUCHEUX. CRE returns to BRETEN-COURT to issue orders for move to Hd. Corps. La Corps move to GOUY.	
LUCHEUX	30th		Hd. Corps move to IVERNY. 35th + 235th, 529th to OPPY.	
"	31st		CRE + Adjt to Corps.	

S.G. Thompson
Capt. R.E.
for C.R.E. 3rd Division

31-3-18.

3rd Divisional Engineers

WAR DIARY

C. R. E.

3rd DIVISION

APRIL 1918

War Diary
C.R.E. 3rd Division
APRIL 1918.

WAR DIARY

Hdqrs R.E. 3rd Division

APRIL 1918. Sheet 1. Army Form C.2118.

Place	Date	Hour	Summary of Events and Information	Remarks and references to Appendices
BRUAY	1-4-18		HQrs dismantled RE to BRUAY. Transport to AVERDOIGNT. Division in I Corps	
BRUAY	2-4-18		Transport to LABEUVRIERE. H.Q. to same place in afternoon.	
LABEUVRIERE	3rd		CRE & Gourlay to reconnoitre MAISTRE Line. Adjt office.	
"	4th		Adjt to Field Cashier and BRUAY Fd Corps moved with Brigade groups.	
"	5th		Div HQ moved from LABEUVRIERE to FOUQUIERES.	
FOUQUIERES	6th		CRE to see C.E. I Corps & 9th Inf Bde re working parties.	
"	7th		CRE & Lt Gourley to Army line. 56th Fd Coy moved to HERSIN, 529th to AIX-NOULETTE	
"	8th		Div HQ moved to LABEUVRIERE. CRE to Army line.	
LABEUVRIERE	9th		CRE & Gourlay to Army line. Adjt to I Corps to see Staff Officer	
"	10th		C.R.E. to Army line. Adjt to CHOCQUES to see RE dump.	
OBLINGHEM	11th		Div H.Q. moved to OBLINGHEM. Transport to BUSNETTES. Division under XI Corps 56th & 438th Fd Coys to OBLINGHEM area, 529th to HINGES-MI BERNENCHON area. 438th & 529th Fd Coys under 8th & 76th Inf Bdes. 56th in reserve.	
"	12th		Adjt to No.4 RE Park. C.R.E. to new line behind CANAL 56th Pioneers digging posts	
LABEUVRIERE	13th		Div. H.Q. moved at 1.0 am. Adjt to 56th Fd Coy, Pioneers FOUQUEREUIL dump. CRE & 4th Division called re relief of Pioneers & 56th. 56th Pioneers digging posts & wiring behind LA BASSEE CANAL.	
"	14th		CRE to Corps Pioneers. Adjt office	
"	15th		CRE & Adjt to Corps Pioneers Entrenching battalion. All Corps wiring at night	
"	16th		C.R.E. to Corps Pioneers. Adjt to 56th Fd Coy.	
"	17th		C.R.E. to Corps Pioneers. Adjt to 438th Fd Coy.	
"	18th		Adjt to Court Martial at ANNEZIN. C.R.E. office.	

Hqrs. R.E. 3rd Division APRIL 1918. Sheet 2.
Army Form C. 2118.

WAR DIARY
or
INTELLIGENCE SUMMARY.
(Erase heading not required.)

Place	Date	Hour	Summary of Events and Information	Remarks and references to Appendices
LABEUVRIERE	April 19th		C.R.E. to Corps & Pioneers. Adjt to FOUQUEREUIL dump.	
"	20th		C.R.E. office. Adjt to are alleged defective baths at LAPUGNOY.	
"	21st		C.R.E. to 56th Fd Coy & Pioneers. Adjt prosecutor in Court-Martial at ANNEZIN.	
"	22nd		C.R.E. to 9th Bde 5B Fd Coy & Pioneers & to bridge over CANAL DE LA LAWE. Adjt to No 4 R.E. Park.	
"	23rd		C.E. XIII Corps called also C.R.E. 46th Division re taking over right Bde front.	
"	24th		C.R.E. to No 4 R.E. Park. Adjt office.	
"	25th		C.R.E. to HINGES defences. Adjt to 529th Fd Coy.	
"	26th		C.R.E. & G.S.O.1. to HINGES defences. Adjt to dumps & Corps.	
"	27th		C.R.E. to Pioneers & Fd Coy. Adjt to LILLERS & FOUQUEREUIL dumps.	
"	28th		C.E. XIII Corps called re strengthening of CANAL bridge. C.R.E. to Pioneers. Adjt office.	
"	29th		C.R.E. to Pioneers & HINGES defences. Adjt to 438th Fd Coy.	
"	30th		C.R.E. & Lt Sowley to Pioneers & Fd Corps 76th Iny. Bde & reconnaissance of road bridges. Adjt office.	

S.G. Thompson
Capt & Adjt. R.E.
For C.R.E. 3rd Division

4-5-18.

Headquarters R.E. 3rd Division

MAY 1918

Sheet 1
Army Form C. 2118.

WAR DIARY
or
INTELLIGENCE SUMMARY.
(Erase heading not required.)

Instructions regarding War Diaries and Intelligence Summaries are contained in F.S. Regs., Part II. and the Staff Manual respectively. Title pages will be prepared in manuscript.

Place	Date	Hour	Summary of Events and Information	Remarks and references to Appendices
LABEUVRIERE	May 1st		C.R.E. to HINGES. In afternoon to C.E. XIII Corps. Adjt to CE 438th Fd Coy. Lt Stanley to AIRE.	
"	2nd		C.R.E. & B.S.O.I to line. Adjt office & to 438th Fd Coy. E.H. ELBECK 438th Fd Coy wounded.	
"	3rd		C.R.E. to line. Adjt to 529th Fd Coy & ANNEZIN dump.	
"	4th		C.R.E. to A.T. Coy at FOUQUEREUIL. Adjt to 3 Field Corps. Lt Stanley to ECLUSE D'ESSARS	
"	5th		C.R.E. to line. Adjt to dumps & Corps.	
"	6th		C.R.E. office. Adjt to 56th Fd Coy & dump.	
"	7th		C.R.E. to Pioneers. Adjt to ANNEZIN. 2nd Lt E.H. LOAM killed in action 56th Fd Coy.	
"	8th		C.R.E. to line. Adjt office.	
"	9th		C.R.E. office. Adjt to transport lines with Col Pragnell.	
"	10th		C.R.E. & O.C. Pioneers to line. Adjt to No 2 R.E. Park, FOUQUEREUIL & 529th Fd Coy. 2nd Lt. A.P. WEIR joined 438th Fd Coy.	
"	11th		C.R.E. office. Adjt to No 1 R.E. Park.	
"	12th		C.R.E. office. Adjt to dump & 438th Fd Coy.	
"	13th		C.R.E. to 529th Fd Coy & 76th Inf Bde. Adjt & Lt Stanley to dumps & budget at E.7.d.2.5	
"	14th		C.R.E. & O.C. Pioneers to line. Adjt to new dump. ANNEZIN dump closed.	
"	15th		C.R.E. office. Adjt to dumps & Coys. 2nd Lt A.W. CUNLIFFE joined 56th Fd Coy.	
"	16th		C.R.E. to line. Adjt to No 1 R.E. Park.	
"	17th		C.R.E. to line. Adjt to PERNES to purchase stores.	
"	18th		C.R.E. office. Adjt to No 1 R.E. Park.	
"	19th		C.R.E. to BETHUNE defences. Adjt to Water Supply depot at DIEVAL	
"	20th		C.R.E. to BETHUNE retrenchment with B.S.O.I. Adjt to 9th Inf Bde. dump. 56th Fd Coy, Pioneers & No 1 Coy A.S.C. Lt FISHER 438th Fd Coy wounded (gas)	

Headquarters R.E. 3rd Division

MAY 1918. Sheet 2.
Army Form C. 2118.

WAR DIARY
or
INTELLIGENCE SUMMARY.
(Erase heading not required.)

Instructions regarding War Diaries and Intelligence Summaries are contained in F.S. Regs, Part II. and the Staff Manual respectively. Title pages will be prepared in manuscript.

Place	Date	Hour	Summary of Events and Information	Remarks and references to Appendices
LABEUVRIÈRE	May 21st		C.R.E. to line. Adjt to dump & 438th F.Coy R.E.	
"	22nd		C.R.E. office. Adjt to No 1 R.E. Park.	
"	23rd		C.R.E. to line. Adjt to Corps.	
"	24th		C.R.E. to Corps. Adjt to dump.	
"	25th		C.R.E. to line. Adjt to PERNES to purchase saw too.	
"	26th		C.R.E. to Corps. Adjt to dump & 56th F.Coy R.E.	
"	27th		C.R.E. to Pioneers. Adjt with D.A.Q.M.G. to water point at GOSNAY & to 529th F. Coy.	
"	28th		C.R.E. office. Adjt to dump. Proceeded at Court Martial & to PERNES.	
"	29th		C.R.E. to line. Adjt to Corps. 2nd Lt. T.M. COTTRELL joined 438th F.Coy.	
"	30th		C.R.E. to Corps. Adjt to dump.	
"	31st		C.R.E. to line. Adjt to Corps.	

3-6-18.

S.G. Thompson
Capt & Adjt. R.E.
for C.R.E. 3rd Division

Headquarters, R.E. 3rd Division.

Month of JUNE, 1918.
Army Form C. 2118.
Sheet 1.

Vol 47

WAR DIARY
or
INTELLIGENCE SUMMARY.
(Erase heading not required.)

Instructions regarding War Diaries and Intelligence Summaries are contained in F. S. Regs., Part II. and the Staff Manual respectively. Title pages will be prepared in manuscript.

Place	Date	Hour	Summary of Events and Information	Remarks and references to Appendices
LABEUVRIER	June 1st		C.R.E. office. Adjutant to R.E. Park LILLERS	
"	2nd		C.R.E. to line in evening with G.S.O.2. Adjt to water points & 56th Tollery.	
"	3rd		C.R.E. to line. Adjt to AIRE to concrete factory.	
"	4th		C.R.E. to line with O.C. Pioneers. Adjt to ALLOUAGNE re timber	
"	5th		C.R.E. to new practice ground. C.E. XIII Corps called. Adjt office.	
"	6th		C.R.E. to practice ground. Adjt to No.1 R.E. Park.	
"	7th		C.R.E. to practice ground. Adjt to 529th & 56th Tel coys	
"	8th		C.R.E. to line. Adjt to 529th Fd coy & water point at GOSNAY	
"	9th		C.R.E. to conference at Div. H.Q. Adjt to 529th Fd Coy & to site of new batts.	
"	10th		C.R.E. & O.C. Pioneers to 9th Bde. Adjt to FOUQUEREUIL & CHOCQUES to value timber	
"			C.E. XIII Corps called	
"	11th		C.R.E. to line. Adjt to dump.	
"	12th		C.R.E. office. Adjt to 438th Tollery R.E.	
"	13th		C.R.E. to line. Adjt to MARLES-LES-MINES, gravel siding & ALLOUAGNE.	
"	14th		C.R.E. office. Adjt to dump & Pioneers. 3rd Div. attacked and advanced their front on frontage of 3,500 yds to average depth of 400 yds Zero 11.45pm	
"	15th		C.R.E. office. Adjt to 438th Tollery.	
"	16th		C.R.E. office. Adjt to dump	
"	17th		C.E. XIII Corps called. Adjt to 56th Tollery. C.R.E. to see wiring at night	

Headquarters R.E. 3rd Division	Month of JUNE 1918.
Army Form C. 2118.
Sheet 2.

WAR DIARY
or
INTELLIGENCE SUMMARY.
(Erase heading not required.)

Place	Date	Hour	Summary of Events and Information	Remarks and references to Appendices
LABEUVRIERE	June 18		C.R.E. office. Adjt to dump.	
"	19th		C.R.E. to 438th Fd Coy. Adjt to LAPUGNOY re gate & to 56th & 529th Fd Coys	
"	20th		C.R.E. office. Adjt to dump.	
"	21st		C.R.E. to MONDORE farm. Adjt to ST SAUVEUR.	
"	22nd		C.R.E. office. Adjt to Corps.	
"	23rd		C.R.E. office. Adjt to dump & 56th Field Coy.	
"	24th		C.R.E. left to go on leave Major HALL 529th Fd Coy arrived to be A/C.R.E.	
"	25th		Major HALL Adjt to see C.E. XIII Corps	
"	25th		A/C.R.E. to line at dawn & to concrete factory at AIRE in afternoon. Adjts dumps.	
"	26th		A/C.R.E. to 9th & 76th Bdes. Adjt to dump & to purchase lime & then to R.E. Park BURBURE.	
"	27th		A/C.R.E. to Pioneers. Adjt to dump.	
"	28th		A/C.R.E. to LE VERTANNOY. In afternoon with Adjt to PERNES & DIEVAL.	
"	29th		A/C.R.E. office. Adjt to Corps & enquiring re loss of mules.	
"	30th		A/C.R.E. to 76th Bde. Adjt to 56th & 529th Fd Coy re new billets & to baths at MARLES	
- LES- MINES				

2-7-18.

S.G.Rowntown
Capt & Adjt R.E.
For C.R.E. 3rd Division

Headquarters R.E. 3rd Division

Month of JULY, 1918.

Army Form C. 2118.

Sheet 1

WAR DIARY.
&
INTELLIGENCE SUMMARY.
(Erase heading not required.)

Instructions regarding War Diaries and Intelligence Summaries are contained in F. S. Regs., Part II. and the Staff Manual respectively. Title pages will be prepared in manuscript.

Place	Date	Hour	Summary of Events and Information	Remarks and references to Appendices
LABEUVRIERE	1-7-18		A/CRE Major Hall & Adjt to R.E dump in afternoon to PERNES, 251st Tunnelling Coy & Batts.	
"	2-7-18		A/CRE to Pioneers. Adjt to Batts at MARLES-LES-MINES.	
"	3-7-18		A/CRE to line. Adjt to CHOCQUES, 76th & 9th Inf Bde H.Q, 56th & 529th ta Coys forward.	
"	4-7-18		A/CRE & Adjt to C.E. XIII Corps & R.E Park BURBURE.	
"			A/CRE to line. Adjt to CHOCQUES also Batts, 56th & 529th ta Coys. To meeting at Div H.Q re War Savings.	
"	5-7-18		A/CRE to Pioneers. Adjt to dumps & in afternoon to AIRE	
"	6-7-18		A/CRE to line. Adjt to CHOCQUES & 438th ta Coy	
"	7-7-18		A/CRE to 56th ta Coy & 9th Inf Bde. In afternoon with Adjt to Batts at MARLES-LES-MINES 251st Tunnelling Coy, 56th & 529th ta Coys. Lt H.J.F.GOURLEY left H.Q.R.E to become 2nd in command 438th ta Coy vice Capt J.McGILL who left to command 7th ta Coy	
"	8-7-18		A/CRE ill. Adjt office.	
"	9-7-18		A/CRE to Hospital. Adjt to dump	
"	10-7-18		Adjt to dump with G.S.O.1 to inspect MOIR PILL BOX. Office.	
"	11-7-18		Adjt to Pioneers. To PERNES. Adjt to try & buy scythes.	
"	12-7-18		Adjt to 76th Bde, Batts at CHOCQUES, MARLES-LES-MINES & 3rd D.A.C with A.A & Q.M.G.	
"	13-7-18		Adjt to FRUGES to buy scythes & Batts & dump. Light Railway to R.E dump started	
"	14-7-18		Adjt to dump. Major HALL A/CRE returned from Hospital	
"	15-7-18		Adjt to dump. Lt Colonel R.P. PAKENHAM-WALSH, M.C. arrived as C.R.E.	

Sheet 2.

Headquarters R.E. 3rd Division.

Month of JULY, 1918.

Army Form C. 2118.

WAR DIARY.

INTELLIGENCE SUMMARY.

(Erase heading not required.)

Instructions regarding War Diaries and Intelligence Summaries are contained in F. S. Regs., Part II. and the Staff Manual respectively. Title pages will be prepared in manuscript.

Place	Date	Hour	Summary of Events and Information	Remarks and references to Appendices
LABEUVRIERE	16-7-18		C.R.E & Major Hall to Brigades & Corps. Adjt to R.E Park BURBURE. 2nd Lt H.J. COOK came to H.Q. R.E. as assistant adjt.	
"	17-7-18		C.R.E & Major Hall to line. Adjt to dump.	
"	18-7-18		C.R.E & Major Hall to see bridge prepared for demolition. Adjt to dump. CAUCHY A LATOUR & PERNES	
"	19-7-18		C.R.E & Lt. COOK to line, Major Hall to PARIS-PLAGE Adjt to dump 2nd Lt MADDY joined 56th Fd Coy	
"	20-7-18		C.R.E & Lt Cooke to line. Adjt to new A.R.P. and to R.E Park BURBURE	
"	21-7-18		C.R.E. to see C.R.E. 40th Division. Adjt to Corps.	
"	22-7-18		C.R.E. to Corps. Adjt to A.R.P. & dump.	
"	23-7-18		C.R.E & Lt. Cook to line. Adjt to XIII Corps & R.E Park BURBURE	
"	24-7-18		C.R.E & Lt. Cook to line, Adjt to XIII Corps & PERNES.	
"	25-7-18		C.R.E. to line. Adjt to dump & Pioneers.	
"	26-7-18		C.R.E. to line. Adjt to Corps.	
"	27-7-18		C.R.E. to HINGES with O.C. 251st Tunnelling Coy. Adjt to dump C.R.E. to 5th & 46th Divisions	
"	28-7-18		C.R.E. officer & judging Limbers for horse show. 2nd Lt D. LAW joined 529th Fd Coy	
"	29-7-18		C.R.E to conference at Fifth Army H.Q. Adjt to CAUCHY A LA TOUR & AUCHEL.	
"	30-7-18		C.R.E. to line. Adjt to judge mule race at AUCHEL. Major Hall 529th Fd Coy left to become C.R.E 50th bis	
"	31-7-18		C.R.E. to line with C.R.E 46th Div. Adjt to BURBURE Park & Corps.	

2-8-18.

S.G. Thompson
Capt & Adjt. R.E.
for C.R.E 3rd Division

Army Form C. 2118.
Sheet 1.

WAR DIARY
or
INTELLIGENCE SUMMARY.
(Erase heading not required.)

C.R.E. 3rd Division. Month of AUGUST, 1918.

Vol 49

Place	Date	Hour	Summary of Events and Information	Remarks and references to Appendices
	1918.			
LABEUVRIERE	1.8.18		CRE and Adjt to line. Elimination of Field Coy Transport for XIII Corps Horse Show.	
	2.8.18		CRE in office. Adjt and Elimination of Handle XIII Corps Horse Show.	
	3.8.18		CRE judging at 3rd Div Horse Show. Adjt in office.	
	4.8.18		CRE 3rd Div and CRE 19th Div visited 3rd Div Dump & arranged to hand over Adjt wind on one month's special leave. U.K. H/Cook RE A/Adjt RE Adjt RE 19th Div. Lieut INGS joined the 56th Field Coy RE for duty.	
	5.8.18		CRE to lunch with C.E. 5th Army & CRE 19th Div. Box Cm. attached to CRE for duty. Lieut A/Capt O'Sullivan took command of 56th Field Coy RE vice Major Hill CRE 56th Field.	
	6.8.18		CRE 3rd Div met CRE 19th Div & discussed handing over notes. Adjt 19th Div met A/Adjt 3rd Div & evacuated handing over notes & visited dumps. A/adjt med with 3rd Div Claim Officer & representative of French Mission to inspect alleged damage at FOUQUEREUIL. Major AW GORDON 56th Field Coy & Major EVANS of 82nd Fd Coy. killed on return from line after handing over.	
	7.8.18		CRE at office & to 56th Fd Coy. Adjt 19th Div visited 3rd Div HQ LABEUVRIERE. A/adjt 3rd Div handed over detachments and the Command of the 3rd Div handed to the G.O.C. 19th Div 10 a.m. A/adjt took over billets at AUCHEL at 9.30 a.m & retained LABEUVRIERE.	
AUCHEL	8.8.18		CRE to 438th Fd Coy & funeral Major GORDON & EVANS & HQ BOYS in Small Fd @ FOUQUEREUIL. Afternoon CRE & A/adjt to 20th KRRC materials.	
	9.8.18		CRE & 56th Field Coy RAIMBERT & 52nd Coy AMETTES. A/adjt NEDONCHELLE & AMETTES, CRE at A.C.9, machine, MON CUZON DU REST returning to CRE from heavy.	
	10.8.18		CRE to 438th Coy & Adjt in office o/adjt at AIRE. // Lieut McREA reported for duty with 438th Coy.	
	11.8.18		CRE with 6uds & Adjt visited AIRE. at Office in afternoon. Received warning movement order.	
	12.8.18		CRE at XIII Corps Horse Show & to 56th field Coy. A/adjt with HQ inspected visited XIII Corps Show, received warning movement order.	
	13.8.18		Received orders 4.15 a.m. Show closed CREs offices 12 noon AUCHEL & offices at BAVINCOURT 6 p.m.	
BAVINCOURT	14.8.18		CRE to 56th Fd Coy. A/adjt to Corps HQ & Dumps & undimals.	
	15.8.18		CRE to VI Corps HQ & 52nd Coy NIULY. Interview with C.E. A/adjt to Corps HQ & 3rd Div MT Column.	
	16.8.18		CRE to 56, 438 & 52nd Fds Coys. A/adjt at Corps HQ re materials.	
	17.8.18		CRE & 56 & 438 Fd Coys afternoon at office. A/adjt drew materials from RE Park.	

Army Form C.2118/13.

WAR DIARY / INTELLIGENCE SUMMARY

Army Form C. 2118.
Sheet 2.

C.R.E. 3rd Division
AUGUST 1918 continued

Place	Date	Hour	Summary of Events and Information	Remarks and references to Appendices
BAVINCOURT	18-8-18		CRE to Church Service to offices. Adapt office. CRE interview with G.O.C 3rd Div at 9pm.	
	19-8-18		CRE to 52nd, 43rd + Sqn 220 Cps tgms instruction in connexion of O.O.Cs interview. Called on C.E. VI Corps + at Corps in "Q" office. Adapt in office all day. Final instructions issued to field Cops in connexion with Operation on 21st inst.	
	20-8-18		CRE to Adapt: 5, 8, 9th + 76th Bttn. refuse materials required. + 56th + 438th field Cops. adapt saw individuals & ordering direct. 8, 9th Bttn. Div HQ closed at BAVINCOURT & opened at POMMIER at 7pm.	
POMMIER	21-8-18	2.30 am	CRE "W. Miller + 7 orderlies left POMMIER & took up Battle HQ. at forward Div HQ. Zero 4.55 am.	
	22-8-18		CRE visited offices POMMIER BELLE VUE aerodrome. Capt KENNY took command 56th Field Coy. CRE returned to Forward HQ.	
	23-8-18		CRE at Forward Div HQ. Adapt at offices threw materials from Cops Park.	
	24-8-18		CRE at Forward Div HQ. Adapt moved to Div HQ. CRE to POMMIER & returned to Div HQ. Adapt at offices at Div HQ. 3rd Div Westwick VI Corps onwards. Forward Div HQ moved to trench in front of MONCHY-AU-BOIS.	
	25-8-18		CRE at Forward Div HQ. Equip visited towards Div HQ.	
	26-8-18		CRE at Forward to the Adapt office all day.	
	27-8-18		CRE at Forward Div HQ. Major GREIG left 438th Field Coy to which he is Director of Works. Adapt at LA COUCHIE. for purpose of obtaining kits.	
	28-8-18		CE interviewed RSM JEFFERY at POMMIER also CSM ANDREWS & SERGT DAVIES. for commissions. Rear Div HQ. closed at POMMIER. 5pm. opened at BOIRY ST MARTIN. same hour. Met CRE at new Div HQ. 3rd Div. Welsh Gds.	
	29-8-18		CRE went to new Forward Div HQ near HAMLINCOURT. met CRE Guards Div. Adapt at HQ 3 RE Park + new 3 Div HQ. Inspected Guards Dumps at RANSART.	
	30-8-18		CRE at 3 Div HQ. Adapt visited 3 Div HQ. Inspected proposed site for dump HAMLINCOURT.	
	31-8-18		CRE at 3 Div HQ. Adapt visited 3 Div HQ. also Div Dump. took sample of water to HQ 3 Div Authur. received first consignment of RE Material from Cops Park.	

2/9/18

A.Cock Lt Col
S/d/C.R.E 3rd Div

Headqrs. R.E. 3rd Division

Month of SEPTEMBER 1918.

Army Form C. 2118.

Sheet 1.

WAR DIARY or INTELLIGENCE SUMMARY.
(Erase heading not required.)

Instructions regarding War Diaries and Intelligence Summaries are contained in F.S. Regs., Part II. and the Staff Manual respectively. Title pages will be prepared in manuscript.

Place	Date	Hour	Summary of Events and Information	Remarks and references to Appendices
HAMLINCOURT	Sept 1st		C.R.E. visited units repairing roads. Adjt clearing R.E. material from S.A.A. dump near BOIRY ST MARTIN.	
	2nd		C.R.E. visited units repairing roads. C.R.E. to inspect new Divl. H.Q at RANSART. 3rd Division relieved by Guards Division.	
RANSART	3rd		C.R.E. to line with G.S.O.1. Rear H.Q. left BOIRY ST MARTIN & arrived RANSART	
	4th		C.R.E. & adjt to ECOUST NOREUIL LAGNICOURT inspecting wells. Adjutant returned from leave. Field Corps near MORT HOMME.	
	5th		C.R.E. adjt & orderlies to new H.Q near MORT HOMME & to forward roads.	
HUMBERCAMP	6th		Adjt returned to RANSART. Divisional H.Q moved to HUMBERCAMP. 3 Field Corps moved to area N. of BIENVILLERS. C.R.E. & adjt to Hopkins bridge at ROSEL.	
"	7th		C.R.E. Coy Commander officers & N.C.O's to ROSEL to see HOPKINS bridge. Adjt & St Cook to 438th & 56th Fd Corps.	
"	8th		Enquiry on civilian killed by box car, driver exonerated. Field Corps training. Heavy bridging.	
"	9th		C.R.E. & Adjt to ROSEL LUCHEUX and C.E. VI Corps at ERVILLERS. Field Corps training.	
"	10th		C.R.E. & 529th Fd Coy. Adjutant & St Cook to 438th & 529th Corps. Rear'y bridging	
Triangle Copse Nr GOMIECOURT.	11th		3rd Divisional H.Q. moved to Triangle Copse near GOMIECOURT. 3 Field Corps RE. moved to area near AYETTE.	
"	12th		C.R.E. to 438th Fd Coy. Field Corps moved to area near MORT HOMME.	
"	13th		C.R.E. & adjt to Field Corps and to C.E. VI Corps. To tank demonstration in afternoon.	
"	14th		C.R.E. & St Cook to 2nd H.Q. 62nd Division. 56th Fd Coy moved to area near BEUGNY. Adjt office.	

Headqrs R.E. 3rd Division.

Month of SEPTEMBER 1918.

Army Form C. 2118.

Sheet 2.

WAR DIARY
or
INTELLIGENCE SUMMARY.
(Erase heading not required.)

Instructions regarding War Diaries and Intelligence Summaries are contained in F.S. Regs., Part II. and the Staff Manual respectively. Title pages will be prepared in manuscript.

Place	Date	Hour	Summary of Events and Information	Remarks and references to Appendices
Sunken road MORCHIES - BEUGNY	Sep 15th		C.R.E. & A.A.Q.M.G. to forward area by Canal. Divl. H.Q. moved to dugouts in sunken road between MORCHIES & BEUGNY with rear echelon in MARICOURT WOOD. Adjt to see rear echelon.	
"	16th		Field Coy Commanders arrived for conference at 9 a.m. C.R.E. to forward area. Adjt to rear echelon & Pioneers. Field Coys moved to area South of BEAUMETZ.	
"	17th		C.R.E. to forward area. Adjt to Corps & CRUCIFIX dump. To VAULX-VRAUCOURT dump & C.E. VI Corps. Coys on road work.	
"	18th		C.R.E. to forward area. Adjt to Field Coy horse lines. C.R.E. to conference at Divl. H.Q. Enemy attacked between repulsed. Lt. INGS 56th Fd Coy killed.	
"	19th		C.R.E. & O.C. 57th Fd Coy to YTRES R.E. dump re timber for proposed bridge, to CANAL in afternoon. Adjt to Pioneers, VAULX-VRAUCOURT dumps & C.E. VI Corps.	
"	20th		C.R.E. to forward area with C.E. VI Corps. Adjt to CRUCIFIX dump & C.E. VI Corps.	
"	21st		C.R.E. & G.S.O.1. to dugouts in HERMIES, spoil bank & advanced Divl. H.Q. being made by 436th Fd Coy. Adjt to 3 Field Coys who are working on roads.	
"	22nd		C.R.E. & Lt. Cook to CANAL & 9th Inf. Bde. Adjt to transport lines. C.R.E. & Pioneers & 56th repairing trestle bridge 529th on YORKSHIRE BANK road.	
"	23rd		C.R.E. to Corps & Guards Division. Adjt & Lt. Cook to VAULX dump.	
"	24th		Lt. Cook to forward area. C.R.E. & Pioneers. Adjt office.	
"	25th		C.R.E. G.S.O.1 & adjt to CANAL & HAVRINCOURT WOOD. Conference of Fd Coy Commanders at 4.30 p.m. re pending operations.	

Army Form C. 2118.
Sheet 3.

WAR DIARY
or
INTELLIGENCE SUMMARY
(Erase heading not required.)

Headquarters R.E. 2nd Division Month of SEPTEMBER 1918.

Place	Date	Hour	Summary of Events and Information	Remarks and references to Appendices
Sunken road MORCHIES ISOUGNY	Sep.26th		C.R.E & Ad. Cook to advanced Fwd H.Q. in HERMIES I.24.a.S.4. Rear echelon remained in Sunken road.	
	27th		Zero day. Bridge across CANAL DU NORD completed by 56th Fd Coy R.E. by 1-30am. 3rd Division captured all objectives. 438th Fd Coy making plank road on roof of Canal. 529th working on Yorkshire Bank road. C.R.E visited work. Adjt to forward H.Q. Zero hour 5.20am. Operation orders attached.	
	28th		C.R.E to Canal & Yorkshire Bank road. Adjt to forward H.Q. Pioneers working on roads through HAVRINCOURT to FLESQUIERES.	
	29th		C.R.E to FLESQUIERES. Adjt to forward H.Q. twice.	
	30th		C.R.E to line. Adjt to forward H.Q. Rear H.Q. R.E. moved from MORCHIES to HERMIES. C.R.E. bicycles to H.Q. south road of FLESQUIERES.	

S.G. Thompson
Capt. R.E.
for C.R.E. 3rd Division

4-10-18.

Headquarters R.E. 3rd Division

WAR DIARY
INTELLIGENCE SUMMARY
(Erase heading not required.)

Month of OCTOBER 1918.
Army Form C. 2118.
Sheet 1.

Place	Date	Hour	Summary of Events and Information	Remarks and references to Appendices
FLESQUIERS	Oct. 1st		Rear H.Q. R.E. moved from HERMIES to East of FLESQUIERS. 8th & 76th Inf Bdes captured RUMILLY. Pioneers on roads. Field Corps water supply. Id Corps moved to S. of FLESQUIERES	L.19.a
	Oct 2nd		C.R.E. & Lt. Cook to ESCAUT Canal & 76th Inf Bde. Adjt to Field Corps. 4 Pontoons & 2 trestles sent to C.R.E. 2nd Div.	
	3rd		C.R.E. & Adjt to rec Hopkins bridge over CANAL DU NORD, & to MARCOING & MASNIERES waterpoints	
	4th		C.R.E. & G.S.O.2 to MASNIERES. Adjt to select site near MARCOING for R.E. dumps & Pioneers	
	5th		C.R.E. & G.S.O.1 to forward area. Adjt to MARCOING, Pioneers & Fd Coys.	
	6th		Conference at D.H.Q. C.R.E. to Corps. Adjt to Coys. Guards Division accommodated near 3rd Div	
	7th		C.R.E. to Corps & Pioneers. Adjt to Lt Cook to BOURLON Wood. Coys resting & waterpoints	
	8th		Z day. Zero hour 4.30am O.C. 438th Fd Coy. 1st report received that 2nd objective LA TARGETTE road received 9.0am O.C. 438th Fd Coy called to ascertain situation. He was ordered to send up his section to work on water troughing at MARCOING. 9.45am C.R.E. & Adjt to 529th Fd Coy who were ordered to send party to waterpoint. C.R.E. to C.R.E. Guards Division re handing over. Pioneers on roads. C.R.E. & G.S.O.2 to fire to ascertain situation. Division handed over to Guards Division	
HERMIES	9th		H.Q. 3rd Division moved at 10.0 am to sunken road in HERMIES. 51st Fd Coy ordered to erect belts. 438th & 529th Fd Coys repairing bridges in MARCOING. Enemy settled on this front.	

Headquarters R.E. 3rd Division.

Month of OCTOBER, 1918.

Army Form C. 2118.
Sheet 2.

WAR DIARY
INTELLIGENCE SUMMARY

Place	Date	Hour	Summary of Events and Information	Remarks and references to Appendices
HERMIES	Oct 10th		C.R.E. & Adjt. to BAPAUME Quarry bridging dump. to Battle. on CANAL DU NORD & bridges in MARCOING & MASNIERES. Adjt. to C.E. VI Corps. C.R.E. to batts. again.	
"	11th		C.R.E. & Lt Cooke to inspect bridging in MARCOING & MASNIERES. Adjt to Corps.	
"	12th		C.R.E. & Adjt. to bridges in MARCOING & MASNIERES. Adjt. to FLESQUIERES.	
FLESQUIERES	13th		C.R.E. to MARCOING. H.Q. & Div. moved to FLESQUIERES. 56th Fd Coy moved to MARCOING	
"	14th		C.R.E. to bridges. Adjt & Lt Cooke to RUMILLY dump. Adjt to bridges & 56th Fd Coy.	
"	15th		C.R.E. to bridges. Adjt to Corps.	
"	16th		C.R.E. & Adjt to MASNIERES & MARCOING	
"	17th		C.R.E. to see C.E. VI Corps. Adjt to presente in Court Martial at 76th Inf Bde.	
"	18th		C.R.E. to 56th Fd Coy. Adjt to 438th & 529th Fd Coys.	
"	19th		C.R.E. & Adjt to C.R.E. 67th & Guards Divisions also to C.E. VI Corps 529th Fd Coy moved to CATTENIERES	
CATTENIERES	20th		Divl H.Q. moved to CATTENIERES. 56th Fd Coy to BEVILLERS. 438th Fd Coy to CATTENIERES. 529th Fd Coy to QUIEVY.	
"	21st		C.R.E. to ST PYTHON re advanced Divl. H.Q. Adjt to 56th & 438th Fd Coys. 438th Fd Coy to QUIEVY	
ST PYTHON & QUIEVY	22nd		C.R.E. & Lt Cooke to battle H.Q. in ST PYTHON. Rear H.Q. R.E. moved to QUIEVY. 56th Fd Coy from BEVILLERS to QUIEVY	
SOLESMES	23rd		Z day Zero hour 03.20. All first objectives gained. 438th & 529th Fd Coys made trestle bridges over River HARPIES. 56th Fd Coy put two trestle	

Headquarters R.E. 3rd Division.

Army Form C. 2118.

WAR DIARY
or
INTELLIGENCE SUMMARY.

Month of October 1918.

Sheet 5

Place	Date	Hour	Summary of Events and Information	Remarks and references to Appendices
SOLESMES	Oct 23rd		Bridges over SELLE River. C.R.E. to line to inspect work. & to ROMERIES in afternoon. Pioneers on roads. Div. H.Q. near H.Q.	
"	24th		Attack continued. Zero hour 0400. All objectives taken. 438th & 529th Fd.Coys moved to SOLESMES. 56th Fd.Coy moved to ROMERIES. C.R.E. to forward area to inspect work.	
"	25th		C.E. VI Corps called. C.R.E. to ROMERIES. Adjt. to ST VAAST R.E. dump. C.R.E. to forward areas. Adjt to 56th Fd.Coy, ESCARMAIN & VERTAIN. 438th Fd.Coy attached to 8th Inf. Bde in case enemy retires.	
"	26th		C.R.E. & Lt Cook to site of proposed bridge in ESCARMAIN. C.R.E. to PONT DE BUAT. Adjt. to select dump at ESCARMAIN & to R.E. dump at SOLESMES. 438th N. of BEAUDIGNIES.	
"	27th		C.R.E. & G.S.O.1. to forward area. Adjt & Lt Cook to bridge at ESCARMAIN being built by 56th Fd.Coy. 56th Fd.Coy moved to ESCARMAIN.	
"	28th		C.E. VI Corps called & went to forward area with C.R.E. Adjt to Corps.	
"	29th		C.R.E. to ESCARMAIN. Adjtn Lt Cook to ESCARMAIN. Division relieved by 2nd Division.	
"	30th		C.R.E. to forward area. Adjt to Corps. 56th & 438th Fd.Coys moved to SOLESMES.	
QUIEVY	31st		Div. H.Q. moved to QUIEVY. 56th Fd.Coy to CATTENIERES. 438th to BEVILLERS. 529th Fd.Coy working on roads.	

S.G. Thompson
Capt. & Adjt. R.E.
3-11-18. For C.R.E. 3rd Division.

SECRET

3rd. R.E. OPERATION ORDER No. 95.

Copy No. 10.

Ref. sheet 51a. S.E. 1/20,000.   22nd. October 1918.

(1) The Division is to resume the advance on 23rd. October.

(2) The 42nd. Division and after the first objective has been captured the N.Z. Division is advancing on the right. The 2nd. Division on the left.
If the IV Corps are not in a position to advance from the 2nd. objective at 12.12 hours, the VI Corps will not advance beyond this objective till the IV Corps is ready.

(3) The attack on the 3rd Division front will be carried out by the 76th. Inf. Bde. on the right and the 8th. Inf. Bde. on the left.
The 9th. Inf. Bde. will be in reserve.

(4) The objectives and inter-Division boundaries have been indicated to Field Company Commanders.
- 1st. objective ... RED.
- 2nd. objective ... GREEN.
- 3rd. objective ... DOTTED GREEN.
- Final objective ,,, BROWN.

(5) One Section from each Field Company will be allotted to Brigades as follows :-
- 1 Sec. 56th. Field Coy. to 9th. Inf. Bde.
- 1 Sec. 438th. Field Coy. to 8th. Inf. Bde.
- 1 Sec. 529th. Field Coy. to 76th. Inf. Bde.

O's. C. these Sections will report early today to the Brigade H.Q's. concerned for instructions as to rendezvous etc.   O's. C. each of these sections will detail a party of 5 or 6 men under a really good N.C.O. to carry out reconnaissance work. He will himself do as much reconnaissance as possible. The special duty of these sections is to assist in every way possible the advance of the Infantry and obtain early information of important Engineer work necessary.
Information is specially required as to obstacles and roads, and the information gained wil be sent to these H.Q's. as rapidly as possible.

(6) (a). On 22nd. October 76th and 8th. Inf. Bdes. will move to SOLESMES. Leading battalions will not arrive in SOLESMES before 16.00 hours. All battalions will be in SOLESMES by 21.00 hours.
(b). The battalions of the 62nd. Division will be moved from SOLESMES between the hours of 16.00 and 22.00.
(c). 9th. Inf. Bde. Group will move to QUIEVY at 18.00 hours on 22nd. October and will take over billets vacated by 76th. Bde. GRoup. (N.B. 529th. Field Coy. will not be moving from QUIEVY).

(7) The advance to objectives will start at following hours :-
- Advance to 1st. objective   04.20 hours.
- Do. 2nd. do.   08.40 do.
- Do. 3rd. do   12.12 do.
- Do. 4th. do.   60 minutes after arrival at 3rd.

(8) The advance to the last objective wil be carried out by the 9th. Inf. Bde. unless the enemy's opposition is very slight.

(9) A detachment of Tunnellers now attached to 62nd. Division will be *come under orders of CRE at Zero. They will* employed searching for mines and "booby traps". All R.E. Officers are, however, responsible for assisting in this work.

(10) O.C. 529th. Field Coy. is responsible for the erection of an artillery bridge or crossing over the River HARPIES in the 76th. Bde. area to the south of ROMERIES.

10/.

(10) cont. O.C. 438th Field Coy. is responsible for the erection of an Artillery bridge or crossing over the River HARPIES near the 8th. Bde area near the main road bridge W.21.d.3.9.

2nd. Division are responsible for the repair of main road bridge in VERTAIN.

As it will be light before the result of a reconnaissance can be obtained, it may be advisable to wait till the Infantry advancing to go through to the second objective cross the high ground east of SOLESMES under cover of a smoke screen before moving up trestle wagons.

Further information as to this will be issued to 438th and 529th Field Coys.

(11) 56th. Field . Coy will be responsible for the crossings over the River ST. GEORGES.

(12) The crossings first made will only be temporary to take Field Guns.

Later these will be replaced by crossings for heavier loads.

The following material is available and will be obtained if required and sent up.

Corrugated steel culverts 3' in diam.
18' Spans   20' R.S.J's,
20' Spans   22' R.S.J's.)
60' Spans   ) Very limited.
Timber   10" x 10"   9" x 9"   8" x 8"   and   6" x 6".

Reconnaissance of crossings should be made with special reference to the stores available and a definite opinion recorded as to the possibility of bridging gaps in one span or with a central pier.

Speed is of vital importance and stores are limited.

(13) The 20th. K.R.R.C. Pioneers will be responsible for the repair and improvement of forward roads.   First aid must first be administered to all important roads.

The main traffic route wil be SOLESMES - LE PIGEON BLANC - CHAPEL W.27.a.1.6. - ROMERIES - LE TROUSSE MINON - ESCARMIN.

Craters wil receive primary attention.   In making deviations careful reconnaissance for landmines must be made.

(14) 62nd. Division R.E.Dump is at QUIEVY C.24.b.0.5. and will be taken over by this Division after zero.

(15) Headquarters will be established as follows :-
Div. H.Q. QUIEVY (D.19.a.2.9.) at 12.00 hrs. 22nd.Oct.
Adv. Div. H.Q. ST. PYTHON (15.b.6.5.) at 16.00 hrs. 22nd.Oct.
8th.& 76th.Inf.Bdes from evening 22nd. SOLESMES (E.1.b.2.5.).
C.R.E's. H.Q. will be with Advanced Div. H.Q.
Adjutant R.E. will be at Div.H.Q. from which place stores should be indented for.

(16) ACKNOWLEDGE.

(Sd) R.P. Pakenham Walsh

Lieut-Col.R.E.
C.R.E., 3rd. Division.

Issued at 11.30 hours.

Copies to :- 1. 56th.Field Coy.R.E.
              2. 438th.Field Coy.R.E.
              3. 529th.Field Coy.R.E.
              4. 20th.K.R.R.C.
              5. 8th.Inf.Brigade.
              6. 9th.Inf.Brigade.
              7. 76th.Inf.Brigade.
              8. 3rd.Division "G".
              9. O.C.Tunnelling Detachment.
              10. File.

Headqrs. R.E. 3rd Division

Month of November 1918.

Army Form C. 2118.

WAR DIARY
INTELLIGENCE SUMMARY.
(Erase heading not required.)

Sheet 1.

Place	Date	Hour	Summary of Events and Information	Remarks and references to Appendices
QUIEVY	Nov 1st		C.R.E. to 529th Fd Coy. Adjt & Lt Cook to 3rd M.T. Coy. 529th Fd Coy working on roads.	
"	2nd		Conference of Field Coy Commanders re impending operations. 438th Fd Coy erecting baths at BEVILLERS.	
"	3rd		56th & 438th Fd Coys moved to SOLESMES. C.R.E. to forward area.	
"	4th		7 day. 62nd Division attached 3rd Divn. in support. C.R.E & Lt Cook to ESCARMAIN dump. Bridges that 56th & 529th Fd Coys were detailed to repair were intact.	
"	5th		C.R.E. to forward roads. Pioneers and Field Coys. 56th Fd Coy moved to ORSINVAL.	
RUESNES	6th		C.R.E's office moved to RUESNES. 529th Fd Coy moved to ORSINVAL. 438th Fd Coy to BELLEVUE Farm. C.R.E to inspect roads.	
"	7th		C.R.E. Adjt & Lt Cook to see work of Fd Coys & Pioneers who are all working on RAMPONEAU GOMMEGNIES main road. 56th Fd Coy fixing guard rails on bridge at RAMPONEAU	
"	8th		C.R.E Adjt & Lt Cook to FRASNOY re new sgrl. H.Q. C.R.E to roads. Adjt to 438th Fd Coy	
FRASNOY	9th		H.Q.R.E. & sgrl. H.Q. moved to FRASNOY.	
"	10th		Pioneers & Fd Coys working on roads. Adjt to Fd Corps.	
"	11th		H.Q.R.E. left at 06.50 ooun for MAUBEUGE. Recalled as Armistice is signed & hostilities cease at 11.00 hours. Adjt to 56th Fd Coy & 9th Suf. Bde re work on roads.	
"	12th		C.R.E. to roads. Adjt to Corps.	
"	13th		C.R.E & G.S.O.1 to LA LONGUEVILLE. Adjt & Lt Cook to Pioneers & 8th Inf. Bde.	
"	14th		C.R.E to Corps. Adjt to Pioneers	

Headqrs R.E. 3rd Division

Month of November 1918.

Army Form C. 2118.

Sheet 2.

WAR DIARY
INTELLIGENCE SUMMARY.
(Erase heading not required.)

Place	Date	Hour	Summary of Events and Information	Remarks and references to Appendices
FRASNOY	Nov. 15th		56th Fd Coy moved to LA LONGUEVILLE, 529th to SOUS-LE-BOIS.	
"	16th		C.R.E. to Corps.	
"	17th		C.R.E. Adjt & Lt Cook to 529th & 56th Fd Coys.	
SOUS-LE-BOIS	18th		Divl. H.Q. moved to SOUS-LE-BOIS.	
"	19th		C.R.E. to forward roads. Adjt & Lt Cook to lecture to 56th Fd Coy by Education Officer.	
COUSOLRE	20th		Divl. H.Q. moved to COUSOLRE. Fd Coys move under Brigade orders.	
"	21st		C.R.E. to forward roads. Lt Cook to 529th Fd Coy.	
"	22nd		C.R.E. & Adjt to BRUSSELS.	
"	23rd		C.R.E. & G.S.O.1 to forward roads. Adjt & Lt Cook to 529th Fd Coy & Pioneers.	
THUIN	24th		Divl. H.Q. moved to THUIN.	
LOVERVAL	25th		Divl. H.Q. moved to LOVERVAL. C.R.E. & G.S.O.1 to forward roads.	
"	26th		C.R.E. & Adjt to roads east of MEUSE.	
"	27th		Adjt & Office Lt. Cook to forward roads.	
BIOUL	28th		Divl. H.Q. moved to BIOUL.	
"	29th		Adjt to forward roads & EMPTINNE.	
EMPTINNE	30th		Divl. H.Q. moved to EMPTINNE.	

S.G Thompson Capt R.E.
Field 2-12-18. for C.R.E. 3rd Division

Headquarters, R.E. 3rd Division. WAR DIARY Month of December 1918.

Army Form C. 2118
Sheet 1.

INTELLIGENCE SUMMARY
(Erase heading not required.)

WM 53

Place	Date	Hour	Summary of Events and Information	Remarks and references to Appendices
EMPTINNE	Dec 1st		C.R.E. to 529th Feleny. Adjt to prosecute at F.G.C.M. at 9th Inf. Bde.	
	2nd		C.R.E. to 529th Feleny. Adjt office.	
	3rd		C.R.E. to forward roads. Adjt to CINEY.	
	4th		C.R.E. to forward roads. 3rd Corps moved with Brigade groups. Adjt to 3rd Cavalier.	
GRANDHAM	5th		Div. H.Q. moved to GRAND HAN.	
	6th		C.R.E. to forward roads.	
	7th		3rd Corps moved with Brigade.	
SALMCHATEAU	8th		Div. H.Q. moved to SALMCHATEAU C.R.E. to forward roads in Germany.	
	9th		C.R.E. + G.S.O.1 to forward roads. Adjt to C.E. VI Corps	
	10th		C.R.E. + G.S.O.1 to forward roads.	
	11th		C.R.E. + Adjt to see Division enter Germany + be inspected by Corps Commander. C.R.E. to 76th Inf. Bde to remain there for road reconnaissance.	
	12th		SALMCHATEAU.	
	13th			
LOSHEIM	14th		Div H.Q. moved to munition factory near LOSHEIM.	
	15th		LOSHEIM.	
EUSKIRCHEN	16th		Div H.Q. moved to EUSKIRCHEN. C.R.E. rejoined from 76th Inf. Bde.	
	17th		EUSKIRCHEN.	
	18th		EUSKIRCHEN.	

Headquarters R.E. 3rd Division

WAR DIARY Month of December 1918.

Army Form C. 2118.
S.C.C. 2.

INTELLIGENCE SUMMARY.
(Erase heading not required.)

Instructions regarding War Diaries and Intelligence Summaries are contained in F. S. Regs., Part II. and the Staff Manual respectively. Title pages will be prepared in manuscript.

Place	Date	Hour	Summary of Events and Information	Remarks and references to Appendices
DÜREN	Dec. 19th		Divl. H.Q. moved to DÜREN	
	20th		C.R.E. to conference at C.E. VI Corps. Adjt billetting 56th & 438th Fd Corps arrived at DÜREN.	
	21st		C.R.E. to Brigades.	
	22nd		C.R.E. to Brigades & C.E. VI Corps.	
	23rd to 31st		DÜREN. Requisitioning materials, arranging workshops etc. Demobilisation	

S.G. Thompson
Capt RE.
for C.R.E. 3rd Division

5-1-19.

Report on Engineer Work of
3rd Divnl: R.E. – July–Dec 1918.

(Rec: from R.E. Library 5th Dec 1934)

REPORT ON ENGINEER WORK OF 3rd DIVISIONAL R.E.,
PERIOD JULY to DECEMBER, 1918.
==

I joined the Division in July 1918, before which, I can give no account of Operations.

In July 1918, the Division were holding the LOCON Sector including the Defences of HINGES.

As the Forward Area of the Trench system in this Sector is liable to be absolutely waterlogged, the Defence consisted largely of reinforced mass concrete and block shelters, erected in houses which formed the bases of strong points.

Owing to the reduction in strength of Infantry Brigades, it was impossible for the Infantry to supply practically any working parties, except for their own Trench work.

Unskilled labour in connection with the concrete work, had therefore, largely to be obtained from the Pioneer Battalion, a most unsatisfactory arrangement and the dilution of R.E. Field Units with unskilled labour is once again strongly recommended. More Pillboxes were also being erected as O.P's and M.G. Emplacements but their value was not fully tested, as they were never hit.

The Division left this Sector early in August and trained first in the AUCHEL Area and later in the Area near LUCHEUX till 20th August, when it moved into close support to the 2nd Division.

On 21st August the Division moved through the 2nd Division on the first objective, near COURCELLES-LE-COMTE.

The R.E. Field Companies and Pioneers were retained in hand, but a reconnaissance Officer and party moved in Liaison with each Brigade Staff.

These Officers were given certain definite objectives, such as reconnaissance for water in villages and Road reconnaissance, but were instructed to report on all questions of Engineer importance.

The reconnaissance in these early days of the advance was sometimes extremely well done, but generally it was noticeable that Junior Officers had not sufficient training in general reconnaissance, and were liable to overclose adherence to definite objectives. This work certainly improved greatly as the advance continued.

Each Field Company was provided with about 100 Yards of light wire rope for exploiting wells, and this proved very valuable.

The chief work of both Pioneers and R.E's in these early stages, was the repair of roads, which were badly cratered, and the R.E. also recovered many wells and erected water troughs & storage tanks.

In this waterless area, where roads were bad, it was frequently found advisable to erect 10,000 Gallon canvas troughs as far forward as lorries could go, which were filled by water lorries from which Unit water carts could fill.

A Section of Tunnellers was attached to the Division for inspection for "Booby Traps". The Officers of this Section did invaluable work, but for this particular work the proportion of other ranks is too high, as an Officer must supervise such work.

Sep. 3rd — In the second phase of the battle i.e. in the fighting round ST. LEGER, ECOUST ST. MEIN and NOREUIL tank traps were encountered for the first time, and it became obvious then that R.E. Personnel in small parties must push up close to the fighting troops to locate and render harmless Tank traps which might have been missed by Tanks attacking, but which might catch the Tanks on the return journey.

This was experienced particularly later on near HAVRINCOURT where Second Lieut: COTTRELL, M.C., R.E., located and removed 64 Tank traps before the return of the Tanks or the advance of the Guns.

The state of the roads improved considerably after the first crater zone was passed, but much work was necessary at all times.

Sep. — From the engagements round the CANAL DU NORD and onwards, more essentially, R.E. work was encountered the crossing of the dry CANAL DU NORD necessitated primarily the fixing of a large number of ladders, and at one place the formation of a Ramp for the use of stretcher bearers.

Sep. 26th — On the night before the advance to MARCOING a bridge for Field Artillery was built by 56th Field Company, R.E., a special report on which has already been forwarded.

After the advance, a plank road was constructed on the Eastern Bank of the Canal, during the construction of a permanent bridge.

A Hamilton ropeway was

A Hamilton ropeway was found extremely useful in the carriage of material across the Canal to the centre of the road, and I consider for large bridging operations these ropeways would generally prove their use.

On the CANAL ST. QUENTIN between NOYELLES and MASNIERES a considerable amount of heavier bridging work was carried out and a large amount of Horse troughing erected.

A large part of the Pontoon Equipment was loaned to the 2nd Division who were not in a position to erect permanent bridges at first. This equipment was asked for in a great hurry and it seems a case for the retention of Pontoons with Divisions.

In the advance from the ST. QUENTIN CANAL to the RIVER SELLE at SOLESMES the Division were not engaged, and the R.E., and Pioneers were employed on road repair.

Oct. 23rd

In the advance from SOLESMES to beyond the LE QUESNOY-VALENCIENNES Railway a good deal of light and permanent bridging was carried out.

The enemy had carried out very complete demolitions of the bridges in this area as well as blowing some road craters.

In these operations the roads were to muddy for cyclists and the rapid transmission of reports became very difficult. Mounted orderlies proved the most efficient means of communication but the number of Riding Horses and available N.C.O's and Mounted Drivers considerably restricted the use of such Mounted Orderlies. Officers took time to realise that they should have their horses within close reach when on reconnaissance, and that often time was saved by waiting a bit, and then riding up when the situation was clear, and so having a means of rapid return.

On one occasion I rode up to see whether a bridge had been demolished or not, and by meeting an Officer returning from the bridge when I was myself not more than ten minutes ride from it, I got the information that the bridge was intact, and its approximate dimensions, and was able to ride back and transmit the message to the C.E., and the Staff sometime before the report arrived from the reconnaissance Officer whom I had sent out several hours before I had started myself, and whose Cyclist Orderlies had had to abandon their Cycles owing to the muddy road and walk.

During these latter stages, owing to the difficulties of Railway Transportation, the condition of the road became vital, and the Infantry of the Division, when out of the line, more than once turned out as many men as could be provided with tools to clear mud. A great deal can be done in a very short time on task work in this way without greatly fatiguing the troops.

The supply of road metal in this area was practically negligible and in one case near FRASNOY where the metal at each side of the pavé had worn down so that the edge of the pavé was breaking away, a satisfactory repair was made by laying a plank road six feet wide close up to the edge of the pavé, the material being obtained from a very large enemy dump of Mining timber in the vicinity.

With a little organisation, this was laid very quickly. Parties of 8 men were found most suitable, and these xxxxxxxxxx xxxxxxx worked at an average speed of nearly 1 foot per man per hour. A party of 8 doing about 20 yards per 8 hour day. This includes excavating and bedding in the "runners" and picketting the outer edge. Care needs to be taken to lay the decking level, ot slightly sloping _inwards_.

On 10th November the Division was ordered to move on 11th November to form the advance guard of the whole Third Army. It was arranged to send 2 Field Companies and the Pioneer Battalion with the Divisional Advance Guard, retaining 1 Field Company in hand for despatch to any special point. On the morning of 11th November the order was cancelled owing to the signing of the Armistice.

During the march to Germany the Field Companies marched with Brigade Groups and the Pioneer Battalion with the leading Group. As the 62nd Division at first and later the Canadian Corps were moving ahead of us, it was unlikely that any serious obstacle would be met with, and the arrangement proved

satisfactory

satisfactory. The leading Field Company had orders to remove all broken down German Transport which was in any way encroaching on the road.

Normally while on the march, little could be done by troops to improve the roads, but when during a halt, work was considered necessary on the roads having the Field Companies scattered through the Column ensured R.E. Supervision, wherever it was required.

In the latter portion of the march, I moved myself with the leading Brigade, and was able personally to reconnoitre the roads, and send back reports in good time. The necessity for the C.R.E., having a Car was here and time and gain exemplified. The importance of this work was considered so great, that although many of the Division cars had broken down, it was decided to detach this Car with me, even though "G" and "Q" had to share one themselves.

During the whole period under review every effort was made to inform Commanders direct of all Intelligence which might affect them, e.g. copies of reports on

    (1) Position and nature of water supply points
    (2) Roads
    (3) States of crossings over obstacles

etc, were sent direct to Infantry Brigades, GCRA besides to the Staff and C.E., and every effort was made to keep the Typewriter and Clerk well up during operations for this purpose. The Artillery particularly appreciated this help and it certainly seems to be a very important department of a C.R.E's duty in action.

To summarize, the following points were learned or emphasized

(1). R.E. Units need heavy dilution with un-skilled labour
(2) The Standard of Engineer Officers and their technical training requires to be kept high. It was found when Bridging work became more frequent some Officers' knowledge of calculations of stresses and strength of material was not by any means reliable. It is not possible to select Officers for their qualifications for work which may arise, and cases occurred where Section Officers started to build Artillery Bridges which were not satisfactorily calculated.
(3) The Training in reconnaissance work requires improvement. Reconnaissance can only be learned by continuous practice and training in a general way of the powers of observation. N.C.O's should be trained more fully in simple work of this nature.
(4) In semi-open warfare more than ever, the importance of holding the Technical troops in the hand of the C.R.E., was exemplified.
(5) Officers must use their horses, and Mounted Orderlies are frequently the most rapid means of communication.
(6) Arrangements for rapid dissemination of Engineer Intelligence should be made.
(7) It is very important for the C.E., of the Corps to give a policy, as regards roads, to be especially looked after, to C.R.E's and to co-ordinate their work. This, however, does not relieve C.R.E's of Divisions of the responsibility of early reconnaissance to decide which routes are in the best condition and which are most important to keep up. Frequently, it is impossible for C.E's to fix a line of responsibility of roads, between an attacking and a supporting Division, but if C.R.E's can be told approximately where their responsibilities cease, it enables them to select the most urgent work in their area. If the C.E., is unable to give this guide, C.R.E's must mutually agree on a line, the C.R.E., of the leading Division, having of necessity, the principal vote.
(8). Efficient protection must be arranged for the parapets of bridges from Lorries at night, by fixing bollards at the ends of the bridge and painting them white.

SPECIAL POINTS REGARDING EQUIPMENT:-

(9) In dry weather the Company bicycles would have proved invaluable and I do not consider they should be reduced.
(10) The R.E. Limber proved itself a very bad vehicle. The Limbered G.S. Wagon is better, but a good tip cart with a cape hood would be most useful all round, as so much of R.E. transport is required to cart stone, sand, etc.
The C.R.E. should have more transport both M.T. and horse at his disposal.
For the first month of these operations I had the use of a box car which was invaluable in getting up small stores to places

which lorries could not reach. Every C.R.E. should have a car and Box car directly at his disposal.

(11) One of my Companies was fortunate in having an R.E. G.S. Wagon as a Technical wagon and this vehicle has proved its superiority over the G.S. wagon in every way, mobility, light running and wear.

R. P. Pakenham-Walsh
Lieutenant-Colonel, R.E.,
Commanding Royal Engineer, 3rd Division.

2nd January, 1919.

APPENDIX.

The following figures show some of the work, exclusive of roads and water supply, carried out by 3rd Divisional R.E. during the period 21/8/18 to 11/11/18.

Heavy Bridges erected or partially rebuilt	4
Bridges for Field Artillery and Horse transport constructed	8
Footbridges	Several
Tank traps discovered and rendered inocuous	About 100
Charges removed from bridges	4

This is exclusive of the work of the attached Tunnellers of whose work I have no complete record, but they removed a very large number of Tank mines and demolition charges; nor does it include certain partially completed work taken over from, or handed over to other Divisions on relief.

WAR DIARY
or
INTELLIGENCE SUMMARY.
(Erase heading not required.)

Army Form C. 2118.

Headquarters R.E. 3rd Division. Month of JANUARY 1919. Sheet 1.

Instructions regarding War Diaries and Intelligence Summaries are contained in F. S. Regs., Part II. and the Staff Manual respectively. Title pages will be prepared in manuscript.

Place	Date	Hour	Summary of Events and Information	Remarks and references to Appendices
DÜREN	Jan 1st		Lot Coy'd making beds etc	
	3rd		C.R.E. went on leave.	
	22nd		C.R.E. returned from leave.	
			Lot Coys employed during the month on fitting up barracks at DÜREN erecting cookhouses, ablution benches, latrines, etc. Painting signs in villages.	
	2-2-19.			

S.G. Thompson
Capt R.E.
for C.R.E. 3rd Division

Headquarters, R.E. 3rd Division WAR DIARY or INTELLIGENCE SUMMARY.

Month of February, 1919. Army Form C. 2118.

Vol 33 Sheet

Place	Date	Hour	Summary of Events and Information	Remarks and references to Appendices
DUREN	6		Capt. S.G. THOMPSON R.E. and Lt. COOK left for England for demobilisation. Lt. CHAPMAN returned from leave. Capt A&E STHENSTONE R.E. took over duties of Adjutant.	
	8		Lt.Col. PAKENHAM-WALSH left for England for temporary duty on the Staff of the Staff War Office. Capt STHENSTONE took over duties of C.R.E. Lt. R. OWEN R.E., Lt. MUIRHEAD R.E. Newly commissioned officers from WOOLWICH joined for duty & were posted to S/Of & S/Of 2407 Coy. respectively.	
	22		5th Coy started move to COLOGNE under orders of 9th Inf. Bde. Capt STHENSTONE took over equipment etc. in COLOGNE Aerodrome Jelanowski.	
	24			
	28		529 Coy started for COLOGNE under orders of 76th Bde.	

A. Sthenstone
Capt R.E.
for C.R.E. 3rd Division

Headquarters RE 3rd Division WAR DIARY Month of March 1919 Army Form C. 2118.

Place	Date	Hour	Summary of Events and Information	Remarks and references to Appendices
COLOGNE	1.		CRE HQ moved in COLOGNE and came under orders of CRE upon CRE arrived in COLOGNE and established Headquarters in "Robert Blum Strasse.	
	2.		438 Coy RE moved from DUREN to KERPEN under orders of GWE	
	3.		437 Coy RE " " " KERPEN " COLOGNE	
	5.		Lt Col. PAKENHAM-WALSH RE returned from temporary duty at the War Office and took over duties of CRE from Capt SHENSTONE	
	15		The 3rd Division became the NORTHERN Division.	
			The work during this month was divided between the companies as follows	
			56th Coy RE 9 X Inf Bde, MGC and 76th Art Bde.	
			438 Coy RE 8 " " " 76th Art. Bde.	
			439 Coy RE 76 " " " 79th Art Bde	
			Work with artillery was mainly horse standings roofhouses.	
			The CRE workshops were taken over at 137 MARKWEG and Co-operated firms carpenters & labour varying from 23 to 26.	

A. Whinstone
Capt RE
for CRE 3rd Division

Headquarters RE Northern Division

Month of March 1919

Army Form C. 2118.

WAR DIARY
or
INTELLIGENCE SUMMARY.
(Erase heading not required.)

Instructions regarding War Diaries and Intelligence Summaries are contained in F. S. Regs., Part II. and the Staff Manual respectively. Title pages will be prepared in manuscript.

Place	Date	Hour	Summary of Events and Information	Remarks and references to Appendices
COLOGNE	15-22		Preliminary work for aerodrome at MANSDORF which is to be constructed by 179 Coy R.E.	
	22		Actual work on aerodrome started using about 150 P.O.W. by 7 A.M. 9/Capt L.A. GUTHRIE R.E. joined Headquarters to take over from Capt. SHENSTONE R.E.	
	25		Bt. Lt.Col. R.J. DONE R.E. joined to take over from Lt.Col. PAKENHAM WALSH	
	27		Lt.Col. DONE and Capt. GUTHRIE took over duties of CRE and Adjutant.	

A.G. Johnstone
Capt RE
for CRE Northern Division

Army Form C. 2118.

WAR DIARY
INTELLIGENCE SUMMARY
(Erase heading not required.)

Instructions regarding War Diaries and Intelligence Summaries are contained in F.S. Regs., Part II. and the Staff Manual respectively. Title Pages will be prepared in manuscript.

Month Dec

Place	Date	Hour	Summary of Events and Information	Remarks and references to Appendices
COLOGNE	27/3/19		(1) Lt. Col. R.J. DONE D.S.O. R.E. took over Command of Divl. R.E. Northern Div. Army of the Rhine- T/Lieut. A/Capt. H.R. GUTHRIE M.C. R.E. took on duties as A/Adjt. R.E.-	
			(2) Lt. Col. PAKENHAM-WALSH. R.E. left for PARIS. to join POLISH MISSION -	
			(3) Strength & disposition of Coys:- H.Q. R.E. 11. ROBERT BLUM-STR. LINDENTHAL. 2 Officers. 6 O.R. 56th Fd. Coy. R.E. 342 AACHENER. STR. BRAUNSFELD- O/c T/Lieut. A/Capt Major. C.J.M. YOUNG - STRENGTH- 5 Officers. 152 O.R. 65 animals. (to be reduced to cadre 'B'). 438th Fd. Coy. R.E. 569. AACHENER-STRASSE- O/c T/Lieut A/Major. E.L.MARTIN. M.C. R.E. STRENGTH. 8 Officers 181 O.R. 70 animals. 519th Fd. Coy. R.E. 21 CHRISTIAN GAD-STRASSE. BRAUNSFELD- O/c Lieut. A/Major H. HAITHEWAITE. R.E. STRENGTH- 6 Officers 171 O.R. 77 animals.	
			(4) Of above about 317. O.R. on awaiting Demobilization (including 65 O.R. retained in Cadre 'B' of 56th Fd. Coy. R.E.) and of the animals. 69 are of Z category.	
R.H.Q.	Sept 30th		G.O.C. inspected Field Coys. R.E. at R.E. Workshops MANNHEIM & say goodbye to 56th Fd. Coy. R.E.	

Army Form C. 2118.

WAR DIARY
INTELLIGENCE SUMMARY.
(Erase heading not required.)

Place	Date	Hour	Summary of Events and Information	Remarks and references to Appendices
COLOGNE	30.3.19		Following transposing of Officers in Field Coys entered.	
			56TH Fd Coy RE to 438TH Fd Cm RE.	
			T/Lieut A.W. CUNLIFFE. RE.	
			" " W.D.P. HUGHES. 12E.	
			56 Fd Cn RE. to 529th Fd Cn, RE.	
			T/Lieut A/Major C.J.T. YOUNG. RE.	
			T/Lieut. A.A. MADOX.	
			2/Lieut. O.L.R. OWEN.	
			HQ RE. to 56TH Fd Cy RE	Cross posting to take effect from 31/3/19.
			T/Capt A.G. SHENSTONE. RE	
			438TH Fd Cy RE. to 23rd Fd Cy, RE	
			T/Lieut. G.E. STEELEY RE	
			529TH Fd Cy Re to 56TH Fd Cy, RE	
			2/Lieut C.ST. CALDER RE. (T.F.)	
			7 O.R. 56TH to 438TH	
			25 O.R. " " 529TH "	
			2 O.R. " " H.Q. RE.	

WAR DIARY
or
~~INTELLIGENCE SUMMARY~~

(Erase heading not required.)

Army Form C. 2118.

Place	Date	Hour	Summary of Events and Information	Remarks and references to Appendices
COLOGNE	31/3/19		231st Fed An RE: arrived fm 40th Divn. Marching Strength. 5 Officers 106 OR 20 animals.	
		2108	HQ - 231st Fed A. 1A RASCHDORF STR. BRAUNSFELD. L.R. Guthrie. Capt & Adjt 231 Northern Divn RE Army of the RHINE -	

HEADQUARTERS, ROYAL ENGINEER.

NORTHERN DIVISION.

WAR DIARY — MONTH of APRIL 19

Army Form C. 2118.

WAR DIARY
INTELLIGENCE SUMMARY
(Erase heading not required.)

HQ RE NOV 770
6-7

Place	Date	Hour	Summary of Events and Information	Remarks and references to Appendices
COLOGNE	1/4/19		231st Fd Coy RE to relieve 56th Fd Coy RE & take over mess work as from 3rd April.	
"	3/4/19		T/Lieut A/Capt CJM Young RE transferred to 231 Fd Coy RE from 56th Fd Coy RE with effect from 31st Mar. 1919.	
"	5/4/19		438th Fd Coy RE moved from BRAUNSFELD to RIEHL — location FLORA GARTEN.	
"	6/4/19		231st Fd Coy RE moved into billets vacated by 438th.	
"	7/4/19		9 Reinforcements reported from 11th Div Fd Coy RE & posted to 438th Fd Coy RE.	
"	8/4/19		20 " " " " " 231st " "	
"	11/4/19		5 " " " " " 438 " "	
"	"		1 " " " " " " "	
"	"		13 " " " " " " "	
"	12/4/19		G.O.C. inspected 231st Fd Coy RE in STADT-WALD.	
"	13/4/19		24 Reinforcements reported from 222nd Fd Coy RE & posted to 529th Fd Coy RE.	
"	14/4/19		C/RE left for leave.	

WAR DIARY
INTELLIGENCE SUMMARY
(Erase heading not required.)

Army Form C. 2118.

Place	Date	Hour	Summary of Events and Information	Remarks and references to Appendices
LOB.	12/4/19		Major J.E. VILLA reported for duty & o/c 271 F.C.Cy. RE	
PSO	16/4/19		1 Lieut. T.E.F. TURNER left for duty with 4th Field Survey Battn.	
PMR	19/4/19		G.O.R.E & G.O.C. conference 14.30.	
PSO2	22/4/19		90 O-R fm 2nd Northern Brigade attached for duty & divided equally amongst Coys.	

L.R. Guthrie
Capt. & Adj. 1st RE
Northern Div.

War Diary for Month of
May 1914.

C.R.E. N^thn. Div:

WAR DIARY or INTELLIGENCE SUMMARY

Army Form C. 2118.

Place	Date	Hour	Summary of Events and Information	Remarks and references to Appendices
COLOGNE	5th		Practice parade for Div! Review near KLEINE-LACHEM.	
"	8th		Div! Review by HRH The Duke of Connaught. Representative parties of Div! Signal Coy. & Field Coys R.E. Paraded.	
			Strth.	
			Officers. 12.	
			O.R. 148.	
			Horses. 120.	
			Vehicles. 29.	
" Coy.				
"	17th		The whole under command of L'Col C.R.E.	
			Major A.F.Fawcett joined 529th Fuller Coy.	
" Coy.	24th		Northern Div. G.8874 "Instructions for Advance - No 1" received. Copy sent to each Field Coy.	
" Coy.	25th		Northern Div. A/326603/6 - Ordering Cadre of 56th Field Coy. R.E. to return for England on 2/6/19.	
" Coy.	27th		VI Corps Code Calls - list sent to each Coy.	
" Coy.	27th		Notes on Billeting Arrangements E. & N.E. of Cologne Bridge-Head. Sent to each Field Coy.	
" Coy.	29th		N.D. G.8874/6 amended march Table to Instructions No 1. - Circulated to each Coy.	
" Coy.	29th		Northern Div. "A" - Administrative Instructions for Advance. Copy sent to each Coy.	
" Coy.	29th		G.8874/9 - Amendment to March Table (G.8874/6). Circulated to each Coy.	
" Coy.	30th		G.8874/10 - received & cancelled same day.	
" Coy.	30th		G.8874/8 and 8874/11 received v copies sent to Field Coys.	
" Coy.	31st		British Army of Rhine - QA 3047/18 (Q.C.) Requisitions during Advance - received.	
			Appendix I to G.8874 of 24/5/19 received & circulated to Coys.	

L.R.Willie
Capt. R.E.
for C.R.E. Northern Div.

WAR DIARY
or
INTELLIGENCE SUMMARY.
(Erase heading not required.)

Army Form C. 2118.

Place	Date	Hour	Summary of Events and Information	Remarks and references to Appendices
Cologne	2nd June /17	p.m.	Capt. 56th Fld Coy RE- left for U.K. Capt. Shenstone. RE - Reference G.S.874/ dated 23rd May - orders received verbally that taken it J-3.	Appx 1.
"	"	"	231st Fld Coy which moved with a training camp at White City returned to their billets in BRAUNSFELD. tonight -	
"	"	"	Verbal order given by Commander to be prepared to move as a J-1.	
"	"	"	R.E. operation Order N°1 sent out - see appendix 1. (Appendices A.B.C+D to Ref Gm order)	
"	18	18.00	G.S.874/17 received	Appx 2.
"	"	19.30	Commander N° 1 Operation N°1 sent Copy	
"	19.		231st Field En. RE to KURTEN by M.T.	
"	"		Transport. BERG-GLADBACH-	
"	"		43rd Field En to WERMELSKIRCHEN. by M.T.	
"	"		Transport " TORRINGERT.	
"	"		529 Fld Coy. RE " BRUCK. motor Transport.	
"	20.		231st Fld Coy Transport to KURTEN.	
"	"		438 " " " DABRINGHAUSEN.	
"	"		529 " " " 2 miles SW LINDLAR.	
"	21		CRE + Adjt. horse all Coys	IMMEKEPPEL- Road

Army Form C. 2118.

WAR DIARY
or
INTELLIGENCE SUMMARY
(Erase heading not required.)

Instructions regarding War Diaries and Intelligence Summaries are contained in F. S. Regs. Part II. and the Staff Manual respectively. Title pages will be prepared in manuscript.

Place	Date	Hour	Summary of Events and Information	Remarks and references to Appendices
COLOGNE	28/6/19	18.15	CRE + Adjt moved to see all Grps.	
"	"		News received from Divn. HQ that Peace had been signed.	
	30/6/19		231st + 52nd Fld Coys dismounted returned to old billets in BRAUMSFELD - 438th dismounted remaining WERMELSKIRCHEN - Transport of all three Grps commenced journey to Cologne - staying for night.	

P C Hutton
Capt & Adjt R.E.
Northern Div.

Copy No. 11

SECRET.

ROYAL ENGINEERS, NORTHERN DIVISION. OPERATION ORDER NO. 1.

App 1.

Reference G.8874. Copies sent Coys. 26/5/1919.

(1). Companies will move as on amended March Table, Circulated to Coys, 27/5/1919. Under Order of Brigades as follows :-

      231st Field Company, R.E. 1st Northern Infantry Brigade.
      438th Field Company, R.E. 3rd   "   "   "
      529th Field Company, R.E. Northern Division Artillery.

(2) The 529th Field Company, R.E. will move by March Route complete with Transport.

Transport 231st Field Company, R.E. will move with 1st Northern Inf. Bde. Transport.

" 438th Field Company, R.E. will move with 3rd Northern Inf.Bde. Transport.

From "J" day onwards Transport of 438th Field Company, R.E. will move with 3rd Battn. M.G.Corps Group.

(3). 231 & 438th Field Companies will remain under Orders of G.O.C. Bdes., and 529th Field Company, R.E. under orders of C.R.A. Northern Division for movement and work until further Orders.

(4) <u>EXPLOSIVES.</u> In addition to Stores etc., already detailed to be carried with Dismounted Personnel - Demolition Stores including about 500 lbs of Gun Cotton will be carried by 231st and 438th Field Companies.

(5) 2 Cyclist Orderlies per Company, will report to C.R.E. in Marching Order at 08.30 hours on J - 1 day for duty.

(6) ACKNOWLEDGE. (Field Companies only.)

                                                    L.R. Guthrie
                                                    Lieut, Colonel, R.E.

Headquarters,
Northern Divn.
17/6/19.   C.R.E. NORTHERN Division.

Copies sent to :-

Northern Divn.G.	Copy No.1
" " 2.	" " 2.
1st Inf.Bde.	" " 3.
3rd Inf.Bde.	" " 4.
2nd Inf.Bde.	" " 5.
C.R.A.	" " 6.
A.D.M.S.	" " 7.
3rd Bat. M.G.C.	" " 8.
Nthn Div. Signals.	" " 9.
War Diary.	" " 10 & 11.
File.	" " 12.
438th Company, R.E.	" " 13.
231st " "	" " 14.
529th " "	" " 15.

ROYAL ENGINEERS NORTHERN DIVISION.

OPERATION ORDER NO. . APPENDIX "A".

1. Attention is called to "Admisintrative Instructions for advance". (Copies sent to Coys. 29/5/1919.)

2. Iron Rations will be withdrawn from Dump at 251st Field Coys, Q.M.Stores under Company arrangements.

3. Location of baggage and surplus Kit Stores together with lists of personnel left on guard, and Name of Unit by whom these men are to be rationed will be forwarded to this Office by 15.00 hours J-2 day. Copies will be handed to relieving Unit.

4. Barrack Stores - Requisitioned Tools or Stores etc, will be left in situ, handed over to relieving Unit and receipts obtained.

5. <u>Field Dressings.</u> Any deficiencies will be drawn from D.A.D.O.S. J - 3 day.

6. <u>Requisitions.</u> See attached copy of Army Instructions Appendix(B)

7. <u>Locations.</u> A list of Locations at various stages is attached. Appendix (C).

8. <u>Relieving Unit.</u> See Appendix (D)

                                      [signature] Capt RE

Headquarters,
Northern Divn.
17/6/1919.   for Lieut, Colonel, R.E.
                 C.R.E. Northern Division.

Copies to :-

     O.C. 251st Field Company, R.E. Copy No. 1.
     O.C. 438th Field Company, R.E.   "   "   2.
     O.C. 529th Field Company, R.E.   "   "   3.
     Wardiary.   "   "   4.
     "   "   "   5.
     File.   "   "   6.

Copy No. 6.

VI Corps.

British Army of the RHINE.
No. Q.A. 300/18 Q.C.

APPENDIX B

REQUISITIONS DURING THE ADVANCE.

1. G.R.O. 2704 as amended by G.R.O's 2751 and 2811 will hold good in the event of an advance, but the power to requisition,(G.R.O. 2704 Para.1.) will be extended to include :-

    S.M.T.Os, for Mechanical Transport, Stores and Services.

    D.A.D.O.S. for Ordnance Stores and Services.

2. Where in the opinion of the G.O.C. Division it is necessary to requisition in contravention of the above G.R.Os., authority is hereby given to G.O.C. Division to do so, but a report by wire is to be rendered to G.H.Q.

3. In the event of forrage not reaching the Troops, sanction is given for the requisitioning of fodder equivalent to the hay ration by the Supply Officers Concerned.

4. The above Orders are applicable only in and beyond the NEUTRAL ZONE.

                            Lt.Col.
                      for Major, General,
                            D.Q.M.G.

30th May 1919.   British Army of the RHINE.

Copies to :-

O.C. 231st Field Company, R.E.	Copy No.	1.
O.C. 438th Field Company, R.E.	" "	2.
O.C. 529th Field Company, R.E.	" "	3.
War Diary.	" "	4.
" "	" "	5.
File.	" "	6.

LOCATIONS OF D.H.Q. AND FIELD COMPANIES R.E.

APPENDIX "C".

J-1 Day.	231st Fd.Coy. R.E.	1st Nthn.Inf.Bde.Group.	to KURTEN.
"	438th " " "	3rd " " "	" WERMELSKIRCHEN.
"	529th " " "	N.Div. Arty.	" BRUCK.

TRANSPORT.

"	231st Fd.Coy. R.E.	1st Nthn.Inf.Bde. Transport Group:	BERG GLADBACH.
"	438th " " "	3rd " " " "	TURRINGERT.
"	529th " " "	N.Div.Arty.Transport Group.	BRUCK.

* *

J Day.	Advanced H.Q.		To. WERMELSKIRCHEN.
"	Rear Headquarters,		" SCHLEBUSCH.
"	231st Fd.Coy. R.E.	1st Inf.Bde.Group.	" ALTENA & LUDENSCHEID.
"	438th " " "	3rd " " "	" SCHWERTE & HAGEN.
"	529th " " "	Nthn. Div. Arty. Group.	" BIESFELD.

TRANSPORT.

"	231st Fd.Coy. R.E.	1st Nthn.Inf.Bde.Transport Group.	To.KURTEN.
"	438th " " "	3rd M.G.Corps Group.	" DABRINGHSN.
"	529th " " "	Nthn.Divn.Arty.Group.	" BIESFELD.

* *

J+1 day.	Advanced H.Q.		To.ISERLOHN.
"	Rear H.Q.		" WERMELSKIRCHEN.
"	231st Fd.Coy. R.E.	1st Inf.Bde. Group.	" MENDEN. & SCHWERTE.
"	438th Fd.Coy. R.E.	3rd " " "	" SOEST & WERL.
"	529th Fd.Coy. R.E.	Nthn.Divn.Arty. Group.	" WIPPERFURTH.

TRANSPORT.

"	231st Fd.Coy. R.E.	1st Nthn.Inf.Bde.Group.	" WIPPERFURTH.
"	438th Fd.Coy. R.E.	3rd M.G.C. "	" HUCKES WAGEN.
"	529th Fd.Coy. R.E.	Nthn.Divn. Arty. Group.	" WIPPERFURTH.

* *

J+2 day.	D.H.Q.		To. HALVER.
"	529th Fd.Coy, R.E.	Nthn.Divn.Arty.Group.	" S.E. of KIERSPE.

TRANSPORT.

"	231st Fd.Coy. R.E.	1st Inf.Bde.Transport Group.	To.South E. of KIERSPE.
"	438th Fd.Coy. R.E.	M&G.Corps " "	" OCKINGHSN & HALVER.
"	529th Fd.Coy. R.E.	Nthn.Divn.Arty. " "	" KIERSPE.

* *

J+3 day.	D.H.Q.		To. ALTENA.
"	529th Fd.Coy. R.E.	Nthn.Divn.Arty.Group.	" LUDENSCHEID.

TRANSPORT.

"	231st Fd.Coy. R.E.	1st Nthn.Inf.Bde Transport Grp.	To. LUDENSCHEID.
"	438th Fd.Coy. R.E.	M.G.Corps Transport Group.	To. ALTENA.
"	529th Fd.Coy. R.E.	Nthn.Divn. Arty. Transport Grp.	To. LUDENSCHEID.

* *

(2)

J+4 day.	D.H.Q.		To. ISERLOHN.
"	529th Fd.Coy. R.E. Nthn.Divn. Arty.Group.		" LEMATHE.

T R A N S P O R T.

"	231st Fd.Coy.R.E. 1st Nthn Inf.Bde. Transport Group		To. LEMATHE.
"	252th Fd.Coy.R.E. M.G.Corps, Transport Group.		" MENDEN.
"	529th Fd.Coy.R.E. Nthn.Divn. Arty. Group.		" LEMATHE.

* *

rejoin his Company, on the march.

Copy No. 5.

APPENDIX "D".

RELIEVING UNITS.

1. The 231st Field Coy, R.E. will be relieved by 226th Fd.Coy, R.E.
   "   438th   "   "   "   "   "   "   "   483rd   "   "   "
   "   529th   "   "   "   "   "   "   "   157th   "   "   "
   Advanced Parties should arrive on J-2 day and be shown Billets.

2. Companies will hand over details of work in progress, Stores &c to Relieving Units.

3. The O.i/c R.E. Workshops will be relieved by an Officer of the 226th Field Company, R.E. on J - 2 day and will hand over all Tools &c and obtain receipt. He will also hand over details of pay due &c for Civilian Workmen.
   O i/c R.E. Workshops will return to his Company on J-2 day.
   The Officer of 226th Field Company, R.E. will report at Headquarter 231st Field Company, R.E. and will be provided with a guide to R.E. Workshops.

4. Asst. Adjt will hand over to Adjt., LIGHT Division on J-1 and will rejoin his Company, on the March.

L.R.Guthrie
Capt RE
for Lieut. Colonel, R.E.

Headquarters,
Northern Divn.
17/8/1919.
C.R.E. NORTHERN Division.

Copies to :- 231st Field Company, R.E. Copy No. 1.
              438th Field Company, R.E.   "   " 2.
              529th Field Company, R.E.   "   " 3.
              War Diary.   "   " 4.
              "   "   "   " 5.
              FILE "   "   " 6.

Copy No. 5....   App.2

R.E. OPERATION ORDER NO. 1.

AMENDMENT, NO.1.

1.   J - 3 day was June 17th.
   Movements ~~Marches to~~ laid down for J - 2 day, and J - 1 day will be carried out, and all necessary steps taken to enable operations laid down for J day to be undertaken on the 20th.

   No action will however be taken on the 20th except as detailed below - nor will the present perimeter be crossed until definite Orders to that effect are issued by G.H.Q.

2.   The following movements will be carried out on the 20th inst. :-

   Northern Divn. Artillery Group to BIESFELD.
   1st Northern ~~Divn~~ Inf. Bde. Transport Group to KURTEN.
   Machine Gun Corps Group. to DABRINGHSN.

3.   Position on the 20th will therefore be as follows :-

   1st Nthn.Inf. Bde. Group. 231 Fd.Coy. R.E.& Transport. KURTEN.
   3rd   "   "   "   "   438   "   "   "   WERMELSKIRCHEN.
   3rd   "   "   "   Transport Group. 438 Fd.Coy.R.E.Transport.
                                                     DABRINGHSN.
   ~~3rd Nthn.Inf.Bde. Group.~~ M.G.C.Group.   DABRINGHSN.
   Nthn.Divn. Arty. 529 Fd.Coy.R.E. & Transport. BIESFELD.
   2nd Nthn.Inf.Bde. Group.   HILGEN & BURSCHEID.

4.   When the date for J Day is notified the advance will be resumed on general lines already laid down, but fresh March Details will be issued.

5. ACKNOWLEDGE.

                                                                        L.R. Luttin

Headquarters,   Captain, & Adjutant, R.E.
Northern Division.
17/6/1919.   for C.R.E. NORTHERN DIVISION.

Copy to :-
    O.C. 231st Field Company, R.E.   1.
    O.C. 438th Field Company, R.E.   2.
    O.C. 529th Field Company, R.E.   3.
    War Diary. Copy No. 4.5.
    File.   "   "   6.

Army Form C. 2118.

WAR DIARY
or
INTELLIGENCE SUMMARY
(Erase heading not required.)

Instructions regarding War Diaries and Intelligence Summaries are contained in F. S. Regs., Part II. and the Staff Manual respectively. Title pages will be prepared in manuscript.

Place	Date	Hour	Summary of Events and Information	Remarks and references to Appendices
Cologne A10	2nd July		Dismounted men of 231st Fd Coy RE proceeded to Training Camp WHITE CITY. COLOGNE. for training under their own officers.	
A08	3rd "		Observed as a holiday throughout Army of the RHINE to celebrate peace.	
A08	24th "		Lieut R.W. FITCH. 231st Fd Cy RE ⎫ hitherto compulsorily retained with Army " " A.P. WEIR. A38th " " " ⎬ of Occupation. were demobilised upon 2" " A.A. MADDY " " " " ⎪ this date. 2" " M.C. COWAN. 529 " " " ⎭	
A10	27th "		Dismounted branch 50q Fd Cy. RE proceed to MERHEIM - Furnished an escort for Army Horse Show.	
A08	28" "		Lt Col. R.J.Don. went on leave to U.K.	
			Major Martin. M.C. RE. a/c.R.E.	
A10	31st "		231st Fd Cy RE returned to billets in BRAUNSFELD. after Training.	D.F. Ruthie Capt. Adjt. Fd. Northern. Dr.

Army Form C. 2118.

WAR DIARY
or
INTELLIGENCE SUMMARY.
(Erase heading not required.)

AUGUST 1919.

Instructions regarding War Diaries and Intelligence Summaries are contained in F.S. Regs., Part II. and the Staff Manual respectively. Title pages will be prepared in manuscript.

Place	Date	Hour	Summary of Events and Information	Remarks and references to Appendices
COLOGNE	5th	0930	Practice Parade for Divl. Review.	
"	6th		Major Martin O/C RE reported sick.	
"	7th		Major E.T. VILLA. M.C. R.E assumes duty as O/C RE.	
"	12th		Practice parade & Corps Ceremonial Parade MERHEIM.	
"	15th		Major Martin returned from Hospital.	
"	16th		Practice parades for Review.	
"	17th		CRE returned from leave last evening.	
"	18th		VI Corps Review by Army Council.	

CRE. Col R. J. DONE. D.S.O. - RE
Major. DALLAS. M.C.   O/c Signal Coy.
" A.T. FAWCETT.   O/c Corps HQ Field Rs.
Capt. L.R. GUTHRIE.   Adjutant.
" HAITHEWAITE.   O/c Mounted Section.
Lieut BOWMAN } Field Coy
" BURT. }
" RORKE. } Signals.
120 O.R. 6 Vehicles Field Coy. 6 Vehicles Signals. on parade.

WAR DIARY
or
INTELLIGENCE SUMMARY.
(Erase heading not required.)

Army Form C. 2118.

Place	Date	Hour	Summary of Events and Information	Remarks and references to Appendices
Cologne	26/8/19		O/Capt. J.R GUTHRIE. RE. Adjutant - hands over to Lieut H.D. Macarthur. RE. 428th Field Coy. 529 Field Coy RE.	
	July 25/8/19		Lt. F.W Chapman R.E. - Stores officer - hands over to Lt. A.W. Cunliffe 231 Field Coy RE	
	29/8/19		Lt. a/capt CSM Young. 2nd in Command. 231 Field Coy RE. Repatriated to England for duty in Egypt	
	29/8/19		Lt. F.W. Chapman 529 Field Coy RE. ditto ditto	
	20/8/19		Lt J.B Evans 529 Field Coy R.E. proceeded to England to report	
			2 W.O. M. Phie Army A/910/94 (O.2)	
	14/8/19		Lt. T.L Brown 231 Field Coy RE	
			2 W.O.	

J.C. Macconochie
Lt. v. Adjt. RE. for
C.R.E. Northern Division
31/8/19

Army Form C. 2118.

WAR DIARY
or
INTELLIGENCE SUMMARY.
(Erase heading not required.)

Instructions regarding War Diaries and Intelligence Summaries are contained in F.S. Regs., Part II. and the Staff Manual respectively. Title pages will be prepared in manuscript.

SEPTEMBER 1919

Place	Date	Hour	Summary of Events and Information	Remarks and references to Appendices
COLOGNE	14/9/19		LT A/Major J.E. VILLA M.C. R.E. proceeded on special leave U.K.	
	16/9/19	10.00	C.R.E. attended a Divisional conference till 25/9/19	
	21/9/19		Capt. H. HAITHWAITE R.E. (529 Field Coy) Motor accident admitted to hospital COBLENTZ	
	22/9/19		A/Major E L MARTIN proceeded on leave to France (14 days) (438 Field Coy)	
	25/9/19		LT A/My J.E. VILLA returned from Special Leave to U.K. (231 Field Coy)	
	30/9/19		Capt. H. HAITHWAITE (529 Field Coy) rejoined unit from hospital Coblentz	
			During the month 2 officers & 111 ORs have been demobilized from Cologne from R.E.	

[signed] Capt V.D.J/c for C.R.E. N.D.

Army Form C. 2118.

WAR DIARY
or
INTELLIGENCE SUMMARY. RE. HQ Northern Division

(Erase heading not required.)

October

Instructions regarding War Diaries and Intelligence Summaries are contained in F. S. Regs., Part II. and the Staff Manual respectively. Title pages will be prepared in manuscript.

Place	Date	Hour	Summary of Events and Information	Remarks and references to Appendices
Ogugu	5/10/19		Maj. E.L. MARTIN MC RE OC 438 Field Coy Returned from leave & grant.	
—	13/10/19		Capt S.B. Brook joined 231 Field Coy as second in command, from 483 Field Coy.	
	19/10/19		Capt W.A. Evans left 438 Field Coy to join 219 Field Coy Independent Sub-area as second in command. 529 Field Coy	
	20/10/19		Lt. R.H. MUIRHEAD MC Lt. C.R. Richards ordered to report to War Office with Ship Ms. Army 592/57/(62) of 29/9/19. Lt. Richards obtained attached Summary dealt with affairs in Lalepia — Lt.C. Muirhead on leave UK 15/1/19 — 1/4/19.	
	2-3/10/19 27/10/19		Maj. J.E. VILLA MC OC 231 Field Coy proceeded to England for demobilization. RE HQ Northern Sub-Command disbandment as from this date Army 577/435/A.G.6. (M3. G 76/5) of 25/10/19	
	26/10/19		Capt. Brevet Maj. B.T. Wilson DSO RE took over command of 231 Field Coy RE having come from 438 Field Coy Ogugu Town.	
	27/10/19		Lt. E.A. Bellinger 438 Field Coy deft town.	
	28/10/19		438 & 529 Field Coy RE return to calate of 2.O.R.S. for & from Monorovia. Capt. R.T. Done DSO RE appointed CRE Monrovia Camp & Colour East Votato RE North Sub	

D. D. & L., London, E.C.
W.A.P.(26)—W4784 1300/F213. 350,000 s/15 5ch. 52 Forms/C.1119/16

www.ingramcontent.com/pod-product-compliance
Lightning Source LLC
Chambersburg PA
CBHW080820010526
44111CB00015B/2582